Catholic Mass
FOR
DUMMIES®

Catholic Mass

FOR

DUMMIES

by Rev. John Trigilio, Jr.,
Rev. Kenneth Brighenti,
Rev. Monsignor James Cafone

Nihil Obstat: Rev. Donald E. Blumenfeld, PhD, Censor Librorum
Imprimatur: Most Rev. John J. Myers, DD, JCD, Archbishop of Newark
January 19, 2011 — Newark, New Jersey

The Nihil Obstat and Imprimatur are official declarations that a book or pamphlet is free of doctrinal or moral error. No implication is contained therein that those who granted the Nihil Obstat and the Imprimatur agree with the contents, opinions, or statements expressed.

WILEY

Wiley Publishing, Inc.

Catholic Mass For Dummies®

Published by
Wiley Publishing, Inc.
111 River St.
Hoboken, NJ 07030-5774
www.wiley.com

Copyright © 2011 by Wiley Publishing, Inc., Indianapolis, Indiana

Published by Wiley Publishing, Inc., Indianapolis, Indiana

Published simultaneously in Canada

No part of this publication may be reproduced, stored in a retrieval system or transmitted in any form or
by any means, electronic, mechanical, photocopying, recording, scanning or otherwise, except as permitted under Sections 107 or 108 of the 1976 United States Copyright Act, without either the prior written
permission of the Publisher, or authorization through payment of the appropriate per-copy fee to the
Copyright Clearance Center, 222 Rosewood Drive, Danvers, MA 01923, (978) 750-8400, fax (978) 646-8600.
Requests to the Publisher for permission should be addressed to the Permissions Department, John Wiley
& Sons, Inc., 111 River Street, Hoboken, NJ 07030, (201) 748-6011, fax (201) 748-6008, or online at http://
www.wiley.com/go/permissions.

Trademarks: Wiley, the Wiley Publishing logo, For Dummies, the Dummies Man logo, A Reference for the
Rest of Us!, The Dummies Way, Dummies Daily, The Fun and Easy Way, Dummies.com, Making Everything
Easier, and related trade dress are trademarks or registered trademarks of John Wiley & Sons, Inc. and/or
its affiliates in the United States and other countries, and may not be used without written permission. All
other trademarks are the property of their respective owners. Wiley Publishing, Inc., is not associated with
any product or vendor mentioned in this book.

LIMIT OF LIABILITY/DISCLAIMER OF WARRANTY: THE PUBLISHER AND THE AUTHOR MAKE NO
REPRESENTATIONS OR WARRANTIES WITH RESPECT TO THE ACCURACY OR COMPLETENESS OF
THE CONTENTS OF THIS WORK AND SPECIFICALLY DISCLAIM ALL WARRANTIES, INCLUDING WITH-
OUT LIMITATION WARRANTIES OF FITNESS FOR A PARTICULAR PURPOSE. NO WARRANTY MAY BE
CREATED OR EXTENDED BY SALES OR PROMOTIONAL MATERIALS. THE ADVICE AND STRATEGIES
CONTAINED HEREIN MAY NOT BE SUITABLE FOR EVERY SITUATION. THIS WORK IS SOLD WITH THE
UNDERSTANDING THAT THE PUBLISHER IS NOT ENGAGED IN RENDERING LEGAL, ACCOUNTING, OR
OTHER PROFESSIONAL SERVICES. IF PROFESSIONAL ASSISTANCE IS REQUIRED, THE SERVICES OF A
COMPETENT PROFESSIONAL PERSON SHOULD BE SOUGHT. NEITHER THE PUBLISHER NOR THE
AUTHOR SHALL BE LIABLE FOR DAMAGES ARISING HEREFROM. THE FACT THAT AN ORGANIZA-
TION OR WEBSITE IS REFERRED TO IN THIS WORK AS A CITATION AND/OR A POTENTIAL SOURCE
OF FURTHER INFORMATION DOES NOT MEAN THAT THE AUTHOR OR THE PUBLISHER ENDORSES
THE INFORMATION THE ORGANIZATION OR WEBSITE MAY PROVIDE OR RECOMMENDATIONS IT
MAY MAKE. FURTHER, READERS SHOULD BE AWARE THAT INTERNET WEBSITES LISTED IN THIS
WORK MAY HAVE CHANGED OR DISAPPEARED BETWEEN WHEN THIS WORK WAS WRITTEN AND
WHEN IT IS READ.

Excerpts from the English translation of The Roman Missal © 2010, International Commission on English in
Liturgy Corporation (ICEL); excerpts from the English translation of Rites of Baptism for Children © 1969,
ICEL; excerpts from the English translation of Rite of Marriage © 1969, ICEL; excerpts from the English
translation of Rite of Confirmation (Second Edition) © 1975, ICEL; excerpts from the English translation of
Pastoral Care of the Sick; Rites Anointing and Viaticum © 1982, ICEL; excerpts from the English translation
of Order of Christian Funerals © 1985, ICEL. All rights reserved.

For general information on our other products and services, please contact our Customer Care Department
within the U.S. at 877-762-2974, outside the U.S. at 317-572-3993, or fax 317-572-4002.

For technical support, please visit www.wiley.com/techsupport.

Wiley also publishes its books in a variety of electronic formats. Some content that appears in print may
not be available in electronic books.

Library of Congress Control Number: 2010943065

ISBN: 978-0-470-76786-3

Manufactured in the United States of America

10 9 8 7 6 5 4 3 2

WILEY

About the Authors

Rev. John Trigilio, Jr., PhD, ThD: A native of Erie, Pennsylvania, Father Trigilio serves as the pastor of Our Lady of Good Counsel (Marysville, Pennsylvania) and St. Bernadette Catholic Churches (Duncannon, Pennsylvania). He is the president of the Confraternity of Catholic Clergy and executive editor of its quarterly journal, *Sapientia* magazine. Father Trigilio cohosted several weekly TV series on the Eternal Word Television Network (EWTN): *Web of Faith, Council of Faith, Crash Course in Catholicism,* and *Crash Course in Pope John Paul II.* He also serves as a theological consultant and online spiritual advisor for EWTN. He is a Cooperator in Opus Dei, was listed in *Who's Who in America* and *Who's Who in Religion,* and is a member of the Fellowship of Catholic Scholars. He was ordained a priest for the Diocese of Harrisburg (Pennsylvania) in 1988.

Rev. Kenneth Brighenti, PhD: A native of New Britain, Connecticut, Father Brighenti is the Director of Pastoral Field Education and an assistant professor at Mount Saint Mary University and Seminary (Emmitsburg, Maryland). He is the managing editor of *Sapientia* magazine and a member of the Board of Directors for the Confraternity of Catholic Clergy, and he cohosted three weekly TV series on Eternal Word Television Network (EWTN). Father Brighenti also served as a U.S. Naval Reserve Chaplain for ten years and was ordained a priest for the Diocese of Metuchen (New Jersey) in 1988. He and Father Trigilio coauthored *Catholicism For Dummies* (2003), *The Everything Bible Book* (2004), *Women in the Bible For Dummies* (2005), *John Paul II For Dummies* (2006), and *Saints For Dummies* (2010), and he authored *Marriage as Covenant* (2009). Fathers Brighenti and Trigilio are also Knights of Columbus and members of the Order Sons of Italy of America (OSIA) and the National Italian American Foundation (NIAF).

Rev. Msgr. James Cafone, STD: A native of Belleville, New Jersey, Msgr. Cafone serves as tenured assistant professor in the Religion Department of Seton Hall University, South Orange, New Jersey. He is the vice-chair of its Board of Trustees and a member of the Board of Regents and the Committee on Mission and Identity. He teaches full-time at the university and serves as minister to the 47 members of the Priest Community at Seton Hall. He also serves as chaplain to the Alumni Board of the university. Monsignor wrote the foreword to *John Paul II For Dummies* (2006), written by Frs. Brighenti, Toborowsky, and Trigilio.

Dedication

This book is dedicated . . .

In honor of the Blessed Virgin Mary, under the title Our Lady of the Blessed Sacrament, whose maternal intercession and guidance helped us throughout the research, writing, and editing of this project.

In honor of St. Joseph, Spouse of the Virgin Mary, Head of the Holy Family, and Patron of Universal Church, for his paternal protection on our ourselves, our families, and our friends.

In honor of St. Thomas Aquinas, OP, whose love of the Holy Eucharist inspired us throughout our seminary formation and continuing into our priesthood.

In memory of Pope Pius XII, who initiated the reform and restoration of many aspects of Divine Worship in the Sacred Liturgy.

To the members of the Confraternity of Catholic Clergy, a national association of priests and deacons, which seeks to foster ongoing spiritual, theological, and pastoral formation of the ordained in a fraternal environment so as to be better prepared and equipped to serve the needs of the souls entrusted to our care.

To the priests and deacons, seminarians, and faculty of Mount St. Mary Seminary, Emmitsburg, Maryland, for their dedication to forming competent, orthodox, pastoral, and reverent men to serve Holy Mother Church and the People of God.

A very special note of admiration and gratitude goes to his Holiness, Pope Benedict XVI and to his Master of Ceremonies, Msgr. Guido Marini, for their efforts and example to offer true, fitting, and reverent worship of God through the Holy Sacrifice of the Mass. As priests who celebrate the Mass daily, we are edified and encouraged by Pope Benedict's love and appreciation of the Sacred Eucharistic Liturgy, which is the source and summit of the Catholic faith.

Authors' Acknowledgments

Monsignor Cafone and Fathers Brighenti and Trigilio would like to express their deep appreciation and gratitude to the following persons:

Archbishop John J. Myers, JCD, DD (Newark); Archbishop Edwin F. O'Brien, STD, DD (Baltimore); Bishop Michael P. McFadden, DD (Harrisburg); Bishop Paul G. Bootkoski, DD (Metuchen); Msgr. Steven Rohlfs; Fr. Robert J. Levis, PhD; Cordelia Cafone (mother); Percy and Norma Brighenti (parents); Elizabeth Trigilio (mother); Priscilla Brighenti Collin (sister); Mark Trigilio (brother); Lou and Sandy Falconeri (friends); Drs. Keith and Christina Burkhart (friends); Thomas and Bridgette McKenna; Michael Drake; Dr. Elizabeth Frauenhoffer; and Dr. Helen Hull Hitchcock.

And special mention to Mother Angelica of the Poor Clare Nuns in Hanceville, AL, and foundress of EWTN (Eternal Word Television Network), as well as to all the sisters at Our Lady of the Angels, Monastery; Sister Servants of the Eternal Word at Casa Maria Retreat House, Irondale, AL; Discalced Carmelite Nuns, Erie, PA; Cloistered Dominican Nuns of the Perpetual Rosary, Lititz, PA; Pontifical Institute of the Religious Teachers Filippini (Maestre Pie Filippini), Morristown, NJ.

Publisher's Acknowledgments

We're proud of this book; please send us your comments through our Dummies online registration form located at http://dummies.custhelp.com. For other comments, please "contact our Customer Care Department within the U.S. at 877-762-2974, outside the U.S. at 317-572-3993, or fax 317-572-4002.

Some of the people who helped bring this book to market include the following:

Acquisitions, Editorial, and Media Development

Senior Project Editor: Tim Gallan

Acquisitions Editor: Tracy Boggier

Copy Editor: Caitlin Copple

Technical Editor: Rev. Patrick Beidelman

Assistant Editor: David Lutton

Editorial Manager: Michelle Hacker

Editorial Assistants: Jennette ElNaggar, Rachelle S. Amick

Art Coordinator: Alicia B. South

Cover Photo: ©Emerka / Dreamstime.com

Cartoons: Rich Tennant (www.the5thwave.com)

Composition Services

Project Coordinator: Nikki Gee

Layout and Graphics: Claudia Bell, Carl Byers

Proofreaders: Rebecca Denoncour, Betty Kish

Indexer: Dakota Indexing

Publishing and Editorial for Consumer Dummies

    Diane Graves Steele, Vice President and Publisher, Consumer Dummies

    Kristin Ferguson-Wagstaffe, Product Development Director, Consumer Dummies

    Ensley Eikenburg, Associate Publisher, Travel

    Kelly Regan, Editorial Director, Travel

Publishing for Technology Dummies

    Andy Cummings, Vice President and Publisher, Dummies Technology/General User

Composition Services

    Debbie Stailey, Director of Composition Services

Contents at a Glance

Table of Contents

Chapter 8: Extending the Mass: Liturgy of the Hours and Eucharistic Devotions 133

Chapter 9: Eastern Catholic Divine Liturgy. 143

Introduction

• •

*T*he very heart and soul of Catholic Christianity is the Holy Mass, yet it's also one of the most mysterious and often misunderstood rituals of human history. Going back 2,000 years, this religious ceremony is considered the most sacred and precious of all rites by Catholics around the world. For the believer, it's a direct pipeline to God's divine grace. Catholicism teaches its members that the Mass is a reenactment of both the Last Supper, when Jesus gathered on Holy Thursday with his Apostles the night before he died, and Jesus's crucifixion, when he died on Good Friday at Calvary.

Because Catholicism is practiced all over the world, Mass is said in many languages. It also takes a variety of forms based on tradition and custom. The two main classifications of Catholic worship are East (also called *Oriental*) and West (also sometimes called *Roman* or *Latin*). This division goes back to the days of the ancient Roman Empire, which was divided in half between east and west.

The skeletons of these two forms are the same, but the skin is different. The Latin Mass (celebrated in the Western Church) and the Greek Divine Liturgy (celebrated by the Eastern Church) are the same in that both are centered on the celebration of the Word — reading of Sacred Scripture, the Bible — and the celebration of the Eucharist — praying over the bread and wine by the priest with the words Jesus spoke at the Last Supper.

Lex orandi, lex credendi is an ancient axiom that translates to "the law of prayer is the law of belief." In other words, to understand what Catholicism is about, to appreciate its moral and doctrinal teachings, the best source to go to is the heart and soul of Catholic prayer. The Holy Mass is the highest prayer of the Church and it incorporates all doctrine and dogma as well as Catholic spirituality and piety. Understanding the Mass is understanding Catholicism.

About This Book

This book isn't just for Catholics to better understand the Mass; it's for all Christians, Jews, Muslims, and people of any other religion, as well as for those with no religious affiliation whatsoever. It's intended for anyone who has an interest in the Mass with all its various differences within the Catholic tradition. Whether you regularly attend Mass or have never set foot in a Catholic church, this book will give you insight into the practices, history, and significance of Catholic Mass.

The old, more traditional Extraordinary form of the Roman Rite is explained, as is the newer and recently retranslated Ordinary form. More subtle differences between Masses are examined, too, like the unique rituals and prayers performed at a Catholic funeral Mass as opposed to a regular Sunday parish Mass. Confirmation, Ordination, and wedding (Nuptial) Masses are explained, as are more rare celebrations such as Canonization, Beatification, and Coronation.

Mass has existed for two millennia, but plenty of changes have taken place during that time. For instance, Mass was allowed to be spoken only in Latin until the Second Vatican Council (1962–1965) made adaptations to the Roman Rite. Since 1970, most Catholics have been familiar with the vernacular Mass (Mass said in their native tongue). The Byzantine and other Eastern Catholic traditions retained the ancient practice of having the priest face east, but the Western Church now allows the priest to face the congregation. Another change for Western Catholics took place under Pope John Paul II (1978–2005) and continues under Pope Benedict XVI (2005–), both of whom opened up access to the Extraordinary form of the Roman Rite (previously called the Tridentine Latin Mass). Until 1988, it was rare to find public celebrations of the old Mass, because only elderly priests who were ordained before Vatican II, that is, before 1962, were allowed to say it. The new Mass, Ordinary form, became normative in 1970. Pope John Paul II broadened the usage of the Extraordinary form, and Pope Benedict XVI made it accessible to any priest in 2007.

Whereas the Ordinary form (New Mass, Novus Ordo, or Mass of Paul VI) was a result of the Second Vatican Council, the Extraordinary form dates to the Council of Trent in the 16th century. The former can be and is usually celebrated in the vernacular tongue of the local area while the latter is only and always celebrated in Latin.

The changes taking place the First Sunday of Advent (November 27, 2011), are not as major as those following Vatican II. These corrections are to the English translation from the Latin. They restore some reverence and conform to the accurate authentic text as well as make the English coincide with the other modern language translations.

This book looks at the old and the new; the changes and the unchanging facets of Mass. It covers the Latin and English Masses and peers into the new translations that will become the official norm in the Western Church. It also examines the richness of culture, tradition, music, and art in the Church, as well as offering an explanation of the various duties and assignments performed during the ceremonies and rituals of Mass.

Some cosmetic changes took place a few years ago concerning gestures, such as when to stand at the Preparation of the Gifts. Now the changes are mostly to vocabulary, making more accurate and faithful translations from Latin to English.

Conventions Used in This Book

The Catholic Church uses certain terms, and we use many of those conventions throughout this book. Following are a few of the most commonly used terms:

- ✔ **Holy Mass** refers to sacred worship in the Western (Roman) Catholic Church, and **Divine Liturgy** refers to sacred worship in the Eastern or Byzantine Catholic Church.

- ✔ **Sacred Scripture** is the same as the Bible.

- ✔ The supreme head of the Catholic Church is the **pope,** who is simultaneously the **Bishop of Rome.**

- ✔ The phrase **Real Presence** refers to the Catholic belief that the bread and wine of Communion have been really, truly, and substantially changed into the Body and Blood of Christ while retaining the outward appearances of bread and wine.

- ✔ **Holy Communion** and **Holy Eucharist** both refer to the consecrated bread and wine that Catholics believe become the real Body and Blood of Christ. The former (Communion) is used to describe the Holy Eucharist as it is being given to the faithful to eat and drink during the Holy Mass or Divine Liturgy. The latter (Eucharist) is used to describe either the Mass itself or when the Holy Eucharist is reserved in the tabernacle (so the priest can bring it to the sick and dying and so that the faithful can come before it to give worship to the Real Presence), and it is also referred to as the **Blessed Sacrament.**

The "Eastern Church" also requires some clarification. The Byzantine Rite is composed of several Eastern Catholic Churches that are autonomous and self-governing (yet they are in full communion with Rome and accept the primacy and infallibility of the pope) while acknowledging the authority of the pope. Other Eastern Rites, however, like the Alexandrian, Antiochian, Armenian, and Chaldean, are different. Hence, when something in this book applies to all these Churches, *Eastern* or *Eastern Catholic* is used. If it is something unique to one particular Church, like the Byzantine Ruthenians, then that's specified. The major branches originate in the ancient patriarchates of Rome, Antioch, Alexandria, and Constantinople. Jerusalem was always a patriarchate but did not author its own liturgical tradition like the other four did. Even after the Schism in 1054 when the Greek Orthodox split from union with Rome, the Eastern Catholic traditions continued.

To help you navigate through this book, we use the following conventions:

✔ We use this symbol ✠ to indicate that you make the sign of the cross.

✔ **Boldface** font is used for key words and phrases.

✔ We use *italics* for emphasis and to highlight new words or terms that we define in parentheses.

✔ We use monofont for Web addresses and e-mail addresses. Note that some Web addresses may break across two lines of text. If that happens, rest assured that we haven't put any extra characters (such as hyphens) to indicate the break. So when using one of these Web addresses, just type in exactly what you see in this book, pretending the line break didn't exist.

What You're Not to Read

This book is a reference book, so you don't have to read everything. Sidebars, which are text enclosed in shaded gray boxes, give you information that's interesting to know but not necessarily critical to your understanding of the chapter or section topic. You can skip them if you're pressed for time and still get the most important information.

Foolish Assumptions

In writing this book we made some assumptions about you, the reader. If any of the following descriptions fit you, then this book is for you:

✔ You're Catholic and want to know more about the origins of your form of worship or at least discover the diverse traditions and customs.

✔ Whether or not you've been to Holy Mass or Divine Liturgy, you want to know what makes it so special to Catholics and why.

✔ You aren't Catholic, but you are intrigued by the Christian symbols, rituals, and ceremonies that literally define the faith of Catholicism as a religion.

✔ You have no religious affiliation whatsoever, but you have respect for the heritage of other cultures and faith.

✔ You're curious about what Catholics do every weekend when they go to Mass.

How This Book Is Organized

This book comes in five parts consisting of 16 chapters, but you can start anywhere you like without having to worry if you didn't read the previous chapter(s). Each part and chapter can stand on its own. In some places, we refer you to other parts of the book to find out more information on certain topics so you can get a better understanding of what we're discussing.

Part 1: The Lord Be with You: Welcome to Mass

This section of the book deals with the origin and foundations of the Mass, from Jewish roots found in the Passover Seder meal to the rituals in the Temple of Jerusalem and culminating in the Last Supper of Jesus with his twelve Apostles in the upper room.

Part 11: Forms of Catholic Worship

This section concerns the differences between East and West and Ordinary and Extraordinary forms of Catholic worship. We look at the variety of words and gestures found within the one substantial essence of Sacred Liturgy.

Part 111: Tools of the Trade

This part is about the physical items used for the Mass, for instance, the books, garments, and other paraphernalia. What the priest and deacon wear, what texts are said, and what artifacts are used for worship are all described and explained.

Part 1V: The Part of Tens

A characteristic of all *For Dummies* books, the Part of Tens gives you lists and brief overviews of ten important features; in this case, ten fascinating things about the Catholic Mass. Here we look at ten famous sites of miracles where Mass is celebrated as well as comments on the Mass from ten saints and beatified persons.

Icons Used in This Book

In this book, we use little pictures, called *icons,* to highlight important information.

This icon flags helpful tips, tidbits, and secrets that may give you an upper hand in understanding the Mass.

This icon flags text that contains important concepts that you shouldn't forget.

We use this icon to highlight interesting contextual or historical information.

Where to Go from Here

If you want to start with a basic overview of the Mass, you can start right now with Chapter 1. If you want to dig into more detail about the Roman Rite, skip right on to Chapter 5. Or if you want to find out about some particular topic, go immediately to the table of contents or index to find just the bit of information you're looking for.

If you want even more information on the Catholic Church, we wrote a book called *Catholicism For Dummies* that covers everything from sacraments and worship, including the Mass, to doctrines and dogmas, to morality and ethics, to hierarchy and canon law. We also recommend *The Lamb's Supper: The Mass as Heaven on Earth* by Scott Hahn; *Worthy Is the Lamb: The Biblical Roots of the Mass* by Thomas Nash; and *The Mass Explained* by Msgr. James Moroney.

You can watch the daily Mass and even read the daily Scripture passages on www.ewtn.com, where the Sacred Liturgy is broadcast via Internet. (It's also available via satellite, cable, and shortwave.) The United States Conference of Catholic Bishops also have a Web site for Bible readings at Mass at www.usccb.org/nab.

Part I

The Lord Be with You: Welcome to Mass

The 5th Wave   By Rich Tennant

"When did we stop saying 'amen' and start giving the 'wave?'"

In this part . . .

*W*e discuss the origin and foundations of the Mass, from Jewish roots found in the Passover Seder meal to the rituals in the Temple of Jerusalem, culminating in the Last Supper of Jesus with his 12 Apostles in the upper room.

Chapter 1

Understanding the Mass

• •

• •

*W*hat Catholic Christians believe and how they worship are integrally connected. Those beliefs are efficiently expressed in the worship service known as the Holy Mass, also sometimes called Divine Liturgy and Sacred Worship. In this chapter we look at how the keystone of Catholic doctrine is celebrated in Mass around the world.

Introducing the Catholic Mass

Catholicism is a Christian religion. It professes the belief that Jesus Christ is the Son of God and the Second Person of the Holy Trinity, and therefore we are to worship him with the same adoration given to God.

With its roots in Judaism, Catholicism shares many steadfast beliefs and traditions with that religion; most prominently, the belief in one God (monotheism) and the use of sacred texts divinely inspired by God. Both faiths perform certain rituals, such as praying, giving blessings, reading the texts from God, and offering some sort of sacrificial offering. In ancient times an animal was sacrificed as a symbolic rite for the purification of sins.

Christian worship, and Catholic Mass in particular, is rooted in both word and ritual. Its followers consider Mass to be the ritual reenactment of the Last Supper and the unbloody reenactment of the Sacrifice of Calvary when Jesus died on the cross.

The Mass is the heart and soul of Catholic worship and belief. It is rooted in the Bible, and this sacred text is read aloud during Mass. The Church has foundations in both parts of the Bible, the Old Testament (the Hebrew Scriptures) and the New Testament. Both testaments show the enormous value of ritual sacrifice as signs of *covenant.* The Old Testament is the covenant between God and his Chosen People, the Jews; the New Testament is the covenant between God and the whole human race, which is at the core of Catholicism.

The Hebrew word for covenant is *berit,* in Greek it is *diatheke,* and in Latin it is *testamentum.* All three biblical and ancient translations refer to a sacred oath and agreement, much more permanent, personal, and profound than a mere legal contract. Covenants are not temporary and cannot be dissolved. Covenants can be broken insofar as one party may neglect to fulfill its obligations, but even that neglect doesn't destroy the relationship it created. Catholicism believes in and celebrates in Mass the covenant between God and his faithful followers.

Honoring God every week on a special day is very important to Catholics. Jews have observed the Sabbath day, Saturday, since the time of Moses and the giving of the Ten Commandments, but Christians worship on Sundays. The Church didn't change the Sabbath from Saturday to Sunday, as some people claim; rather, it considers itself bound by the New Law of the New Testament, not the Old Law of the Old Testament, so the day of worship became the day of Resurrection, which was Sunday.

Christian Churches, including the Catholic Church, remember the Last Supper on Holy Thursday when Jesus celebrated the Passover (the annual Jewish sacred feast) with his Apostles. Bread and wine are used during the Mass, and the words Christ spoke at that event are repeated by the ordained priest: "this is my body" (over the bread) and "this is my blood" (over the wine).

What Mass Means to Catholics

Latin, or Western, Catholics are familiar with the word *Mass,* from the Latin word *missa,* which is said by the priest or deacon at the end of the liturgy. *Ite missa est* has been inaccurately translated over the years as "Go, the Mass is ended." Literally, however, it should read "Go, [the congregation] is sent." In other words, the command is to go, because the people are now sent *(missa est)* into the world.

These last words of the Mass, *missa est,* were used to describe the entire sacred liturgy that is the heart and soul of Catholic divine worship. Why the last and not the first words? Well, every Catholic prayer and sacrament begins with the same words: *in the name of the Father, and of the Son and of the Holy Spirit.* Each sacrament and prayer have different endings. Latin is also a language where the verb and/or the most important word of the sentence appears at the end and not the beginning.

A Communion service is not the same as a Mass. Only a priest or bishop can celebrate Mass, but any deacon or designated lay-person (called an *extraordinary minister of Holy Communion*) may preside at the distribution of Holy Communion outside Mass. A Communion service has Scripture readings, meditation, prayers, the Our Father (Lord's Prayer), and concludes with Holy Communion. These services are common in places where no priest is available for weekly Mass but the faithful are in need of the sacraments.

Holy Mass, on the other hand, is more than the giving of Holy Communion. It is foremost a sacrifice (of Jesus to his heavenly Father) and then a sacrament (a source of divine grace) and sacred banquet (spiritual food for the soul). The Sacred Liturgy is the worship of God, so the focus is on the Lord and not on mankind.

In Catholicism, Holy Communion (also called the Holy Eucharist) is not only believed to be the Body, Blood, Soul, and Divinity of Christ, but also the intimate union of God and believer. Simultaneously, it is also the union of all the members who partake of the same Body and Blood of Christ. The analogy used by St. Paul is that the Church is like a human body with many parts but is one whole, unified being. Each part is distinct but connected to the whole.

People often refer to the Mass using other terms. Here are a few examples:

- ✔ **Breaking of Bread:** The *breaking of bread* is the first reference to the unique form of Christian worship rooted in the Last Supper, commemorating the moment Jesus took the loaf of bread, broke it into pieces, and handed it to the apostles.

- ✔ **Liturgy:** *Celebrating the liturgy,* a phrase common in Apostolic times, is what Latin or Western Catholics call the Holy Mass. Liturgy is a public service or ministry, and the *Divine Liturgy* was the public worship of God. Catholicism used the term *liturgy* to refer to the Mass and the other sacraments as well as the Divine Office or Breviary (also known as the Liturgy of the Hours).

✔ **Lord's Supper:** The *Lord's Supper* was a term coined by St. Paul in his first epistle to the Corinthians (11:20) to describe the sacred event. He chastises the Corinthians, however, for misbehaving at these gatherings, admonishing them that the sacred liturgy is not the place to get drunk, have arguments, or spread false teachings. (Imagine going a Mass where that happened!)

✔ **Sacrifice, Offering,** or **Oblation:** *Sacrifice, offering,* or *oblation* were other common terms during the time of the Apostles and Fathers of the Church to describe the main offering of Jesus the Son of God the Father to save mankind from sin. Christian priests, particularly Catholic and Orthodox, offer the sacrifice of the Son to the Father because they act in the name and in the person of Jesus Christ by virtue of their ordination.

✔ **Gathering** or **Synaxis:** Sometimes the words *gathering* or *assembly* are used to describe the congregating of people, but the many secular and nonreligious uses of the words make them not unique to worship. The Greek usage, however, is predominantly religious and sacred, hence *synaxis* is used to refer to the Divine Liturgy and also to Vespers, Matins, Lauds, and for commemorating several saints in one service.

✔ **Eucharist:** The word *Eucharist,* meaning *thanksgiving,* can be traced to the ancient church. It was used by Justin Martyr in the second century as a means of describing the attitude of thankfulness the faithful must present when participating in the divine worship of God. Christians then adopted the word, and the Sacrament of Holy Eucharist refers not only to the Holy Communion but to the worship service in which it occurs.

Different Catholics, Different Masses

The substance of the Mass is the same everywhere in the world. Sacred Scripture is read, prayers are offered, and the Last Supper is commemorated. Wheat bread and grape wine are used, and only ordained priests or bishops perform the celebration of Mass, the holiest ceremony and service in the Catholic religion.

The word *catholic,* however, comes from the Greek word *katholikos,* meaning *universal.* "Unity among diversity" is the definition St. Thomas Aquinas (a 13th-century Catholic theologian) gave for beauty, and it is the description he gives to the Church. While Catholicism professes unity of doctrine (teachings), discipline (law), and divine worship (sacraments), the Church still has a lot of diversity. The language of worship ranges from ancient Greek and Latin to modern-day English, Spanish, Italian, Polish, Vietnamese, Korean, and so on.

The Church's liturgical division between East and West pre-dates the division of the Roman Empire in the fourth century. Christianity began in Jerusalem then spread to Antioch (Syria) and Alexandria (Egypt) and finally found its way to Rome. This is how Constantine's mother, St. Helena, embraced the Christian religion. While no specific date is evident, over time the Christian communities in the East (at Antioch, Alexandria, and Constantinople) had profound influence over liturgical practice.

The Church's liturgical division led to the development of different rites. A *rite* is a tradition of how the seven sacraments are celebrated. In other words, rites are ways in which sacred liturgy is said and done. According to Canon 28 of the Code of Canon Law for the Eastern and Oriental Churches, a rite is "the liturgical, theological, spiritual and disciplinary patrimony, culture and circumstances of history of a distinct people."

The Catholic Church has four major liturgical rites: Western (also called Latin) and three Eastern branches: Antiochian, Alexandrian, and Byzantine. Within the four rites, numerous ritual churches are associated within Catholic Christianity. A ritual church is a group of Christian faithful united by a hierarchy and, especially among the Eastern (sometimes called Oriental) Catholics, with its own patriarch or metropolitan.

Western Rite

Some small liturgical traditions exist in the Western, or Latin, Church, from religious orders like the Dominicans to new converts from the Protestant Anglican Church. But the most predominant form by far is the Roman Rite, which originated in Rome, the diocese of the pope. The Roman Rite takes two forms: Ordinary and Extraordinary.

Celebrating Mass regularly in the Ordinary form

Mass in the Ordinary form is celebrated according to the *Missale Romanum* of 1970, promulgated by Pope Paul VI, currently in its third edition (2002). The vernacular editions of this Missal, as well as the rites of the other sacraments, are translated from the Latin typical editions revised after the Second Vatican Council. As its name suggests, the Ordinary form is the typical and most common form of the Mass celebrated in the Western Catholic Church.

Preserving the traditional Mass as the Extraordinary form

The Extraordinary form of the Mass is celebrated according to the *Missale Romanum* of 1962, promulgated by Blessed Pope John XXIII. It is sometimes inaccurately referred to as the Tridentine Mass (after the Council of Trent from the 16th century) or the

TLM (Traditional Latin Mass), but technically it is different. Pope Benedict XVI clarified that the Extraordinary form was never abolished and has remained valid and allowable at all times since the Second Vatican Council established the Ordinary Mass. Any priest is allowed to celebrate the Extraordinary form of the Mass without special permission from his bishop.

The Extraordinary form is exhibited in different ways:

- ✔ **Anglican Use:** Since the 1980s, the Holy See (the pope) has granted some former Anglican and Episcopal clergy converting with their parishes the right to celebrate the sacramental rites according to the Book of Common Prayer.

- ✔ **Mozarabic:** The rite of the Iberian Peninsula (Spain and Portugal) dates from the sixth century. Beginning in the 11th century it was generally replaced by the Roman Rite, although it has remained the Rite of the Cathedral of the Archdiocese of Toledo, Spain, and six parishes that sought permission to adhere to it. Its celebration today is generally semiprivate.

- ✔ **Ambrosian:** The Rite of the Archdiocese of Milan, Italy, consolidated by St. Ambrose, continues to be celebrated in Milan, though not by all parishes.

- ✔ **Bragan:** The Rite of the Archdiocese of Braga, the Primatial See of Portugal, dates from the 12th century or earlier. It is occasionally used in the United States and Brazil but is very rare.

- ✔ **Carmelite:** The Rite of the Order of Carmel was founded by St. Berthold around 1154.

- ✔ **Carthusian:** The Rite of the Carthusian Order was founded by St. Bruno in 1084.

- ✔ **Dominican:** The Rite of the Order of Friars Preacher (OP) was founded by St. Dominic in 1215.

Eastern Rite

The Eastern Rite is made up of the Churches that developed in Constantinople, Alexandria, and Antioch and all the Rites that stem from those patriarchates. The East-West Schism of 1040 separated many of the Eastern Churches, subsequently called *Orthodox,* from the Western Church and Rome. The Eastern Catholic Church of today is comprised of the formerly Orthodox Churches that later reunited with Rome and the other Churches in the Eastern part of the world that didn't separate in the schism.

The largest number of Eastern Catholics practice the Byzantine Rite. This rite developed in Constantinople, which was established by Emperor Constantine as the second capital city of the Roman Empire in the fourth century AD. (The name *Byzantine* comes from the city's original name, which was also given to the whole region.) But many other Eastern Catholics use rites that stem from the Churches of Antioch and Alexandria. In this section we explore some of the smaller rites within the Eastern Church as well as the Byzantine.

Antiochian family of liturgical rites

The Church of Antioch in Syria was founded by St. Peter, and its liturgy is attributed to St. James and the Church of Jerusalem. This branch of liturgical churches is primarily divided by Eastern or Western Syriac language (dialect of Aramaic) usage, and then each of those branches is further subdivided by language and tradition.

Following are the rites categorized as West Syriac:

- **Maronite:** Under the jurisdiction of the Maronite Patriarch of Antioch, this Church never separated from Rome. Three million Maronites in Lebanon (the place of origin), Cyprus, Egypt, Syria, Israel, Canada, the United States, Mexico, Brazil, Argentina, and Australia are members of the Maronite Church. The liturgical language is Aramaic.

- **Syriac:** Under the jurisdiction of the Syriac Patriarch of Antioch, the Syriac Orthodox Church reunited with Rome in 1781 from the Monophysite heresy. About 110,000 Syriac Catholics live in Syria, Lebanon, Iraq, Egypt, Canada, and the United States. They use the Liturgy of St. James.

- **Malankarese:** Under the jurisdiction of the Major Archbishop of the Syro-Malankara Catholic Church, this Church was started in the south of India by St. Thomas, using the West Syriac liturgy. The Church reunited with Rome in 1930. Liturgical languages are West Syriac and Malayalam. India and North America are home to 350,000 Malankarese Catholics.

The following rites fall under the umbrella of East Syriac:

- **Chaldean:** Under the jurisdiction of the Katholicos Patriarch of Babylon in Baghdad, Babylonian (Chaldeon) Catholics returned to Rome in 1692 from the Nestorian heresy. Liturgical languages are Syriac and Arabic. There are 310,000 Chaldean Catholics in Iraq, Iran, Syria, Lebanon, Egypt, Turkey, and the United States.

- **Syro-Malabarese:** Under the jurisdiction of the Major Archbishop of Kerala for the Syro-Malabar Catholic Church, this church was started in southern India using the East Syriac liturgy. It never severed ties to Rome and has 3.5 million members worldwide, mostly in India.

Alexandrian family of liturgical rites

The Church of Alexandria in Egypt was one of the original centers of Christianity; like Rome and Antioch, it had a large Jewish population that was very open and amenable to early Christian evangelization. Its liturgy is attributed to St. Mark the Evangelist and shows the later influence of the Byzantine Liturgy in addition to its unique elements.

- ✔ **Coptic:** This Church was started by Egyptian Catholics who were separated from the pope but returned to communion with Rome in 1741. The Patriarch of Alexandria leads the 200,000 faithful of this rite, who are spread throughout Egypt and the Near East. The liturgical languages are Coptic (Egyptian) and Arabic.

- ✔ **Ethiopian/Abyssinian:** Comprised of Ethiopian Coptic Christians who returned to Rome in 1846. The liturgical language is Ge'ez. The 200,000 faithful are found in Ethiopia, Eritrea, Somalia, and Jerusalem.

Armenian liturgical rite

The Armenian Apostolic Church formally broke from Rome in the fifth century, and despite the early efforts of some Armenian bishops to reestablish unity with Rome, unity wasn't established until the Crusades in the 15th century. That reunion was short-lived, though, and only in 1742 was full communion achieved when Pope Benedict XIV formally established the Armenian Catholic Church.

Considered either its own rite or an older version of the Byzantine (see the following section), the exact form of the Armenian Rite is not used by any other Byzantine Rite. It is composed of Catholics from the first people to convert as a nation, the Armenians (northeast of Turkey), and who returned to Rome at the time of the Crusades. Under the jurisdiction of the Patriarch of Cilicia of the Armenians in Lebanon, the 350,000 Armenian Catholics are found in Armenia, Syria, Iran, Iraq, Lebanon, Turkey, Egypt, Greece, Ukraine, France, Romania, the U.S., and Argentina. The liturgical language is classical Armenian. Most Armenians are Orthodox, not in union with Rome.

Byzantine family of liturgical rites

Although all Byzantine Catholics are Eastern Catholic, not all Eastern Catholics are Byzantine. Many Roman or Latin Rite Catholics erroneously identify all Eastern Catholic Churches as "Byzantine," when in reality the term is specifically used to identify mainly those formerly Eastern Orthodox communities that independently reestablished union with Rome in the 17th and 18th centuries. Orthodox (non-Catholic) Churches use some of the doctrine of the Catholic Church:

- ✔ *Oriental* Orthodox Churches refer to those traditions that only accept the first three Ecumenical Councils (Nicea in 325, I Constantinople in 381, and Ephesus in 431).

> ✔ *Eastern* Orthodox Churches refer to those traditions that embrace those three councils and the four that followed (Chalcedon 451, II Constantinople 553, III Constantinople 681, II Nicea 787), thus making the first seven councils their source of doctrinal authority.

Both the Oriental Orthodox and the Eastern Orthodox Churches are separated from Rome and exist as independent religions. However, Eastern Catholic Churches, including the Byzantine Rite, are in full communion with the Bishop of Rome (also known as the pope) while retaining their own autonomy in terms of local jurisdiction.

Changes to the Mass Over the Years

The Eastern Liturgical Rites have not had significant changes over the past few centuries. The Roman Rite, however, has gone through a few modifications of significance.

No matter what changes take place, the substance of the Mass has remained the same from the time of the Last Supper. What Jesus used (wheat bread and grape wine) and what he said over them ("this is my body . . . this is my blood") have been repeated in the Mass by an ordained minister for two millennia.

The early days

The first changes took place when the language of the Sacred Liturgy went from Aramaic (the dialect of Hebrew spoken by Christ and his Apostles) to Greek (the proper and eloquent tongue of the educated) and finally to Latin (the common and official language of the Roman Empire). After Christianity spread throughout the Empire, those parts that spoke Greek (the Eastern Empire) used Greek for the Sacred Liturgy, and those parts that spoke Latin (the Western Empire) used Latin for public worship.

At that time, the Romance languages, like French, Spanish, Portuguese, and Italian, and the Germanic tongues, like German and English, were just starting to be formulated with rules of grammar and syntax. Latin and Greek, however, were ancient languages that had vast vocabularies and had been around long enough to have set rules and defined meanings. In that time, if you were literate, you could read and write in Latin and/or Greek. The other European languages weren't developed enough to use at any scholarly or liturgical level.

After 300 years of illegality and persecution by the Roman Empire, Christianity was legalized in AD 313 by the Edict of Milan, issued by Emperor Constantine. Five centuries later, when Charles the Great was crowned Holy Roman Emperor by the pope on Christmas Day in AD 800, he sought to solidify Christendom in the West under one faith and one sword. The Roman Rite became the predominant liturgical way of worshipping God just as the Byzantine did for much of the Eastern Empire.

The Middle Ages and Renaissance

When Martin Luther and the Protestant Reformation appeared in the 16th century, the vernacular was more sophisticated and formalized. Some people were concerned, however, that because of all the new languages then spoken, mistranslations of Sacred Scripture and liturgical texts used for Divine Worship could easily happen. For the sake of uniformity and accuracy, liturgical and biblical language remained the fixed and structured Latin in the West and Greek in the East.

The use of Latin, therefore, was not intended to make the Bible's contents difficult for people to understand, but rather to keep the structure and form in a uniform language. Latin ensured accuracy, formality, and, most of all, universality in a religion that used the very word *(catholic* means *universal)* as one of its names.

When the Protestant Church openly embraced vernacular language, the Catholic response was to even more vigilantly maintain the use of Latin in the Western Church. This difference helped Catholicism maintain a unique identity distinct from Protestant Christianity and from Eastern Orthodoxy (which separated from Rome in 1054).

Adapting in the 20th century

The modern world of the 1960s saw another change in the celebration of the Mass as a result of the Second Vatican Council (1962–1965), also called Vatican II. After two world wars, depression, and globalization, the Catholic bishops of the world were called by Pope John XXIII to see how the Church could adapt its methods while retaining its content.

Pope Pius XII had done tremendous work during the post–World War II era to develop more external participation by the faithful at the Mass. Vatican II suggested some use of the vernacular and offered the option of the priest facing the people while he celebrated Mass. Until then, the priest and the people both faced the same direction — either geographical east or liturgical east (facing the tabernacle). The orientation toward the east was ancient, historical, biblical, theological, and liturgical. Christ rose at the break of day. The sun rises in the east every morning. And eastward orientation was seen as an orientation toward the Lord. But during the aftermath of the Second Vatican Council, a push was made by some liturgists to have the celebrant face the people. The Missal never mandated the change in position, but because of the spreading use of free-standing altars that accommodate facing the people, the practice merely disappeared on its own.

Three generations of Catholics have known only the *Novus Ordo* of Pope Paul VI (1970), which is now called the Ordinary form of the Roman Rite. The old traditional Latin Mass (TLM, also sometimes called Tridentine Mass and now classified as the Extraordinary form) was given more opportunity for use by Pope John Paul II in 1988. Finally, Pope Benedict XVI issued his own *motu proprio, Summorum Pontificum,* granting universal authorization for any priest of the Latin Rite to celebrate the Extraordinary form and urging him to do so whenever requested by his parishioners. Previously, priests had to secure permission from their own bishops.

Getting the Most Out of Mass

Catholics are obligated by church law to attend Mass each and every Sunday (or Saturday evening) and holy day of obligation. And not only are they required to be physically present, but they are also expected to participate fully, actively, and consciously. When someone says "I don't get anything out of the Mass," the priest or deacon responds that "it is not what you or I *get out of* Mass that counts, rather, it is what we ourselves *give to* the Mass." Being there in the church is one component, and the other is offering up yourself to God. Spending time each weekend in the House of God is a sign of love for God.

The job of the priest and his crew

When a priest celebrates Mass without a congregation, he is united with all the believers around the world (called the Pilgrim Church or the Church Militant) as well as with all the saints in heaven (called the Church Triumphant) and all the faithful departed, deceased souls in purgatory (called the Church Suffering). The priest-celebrant prays for and with the Universal as well as local Church.

Acolytes and/or lectors are men installed in these offices by the local bishop who are in the process of formation to later be ordained deacons or priests. The lector reads the Scripture readings of the Mass (except the Gospel), and the acolyte assists the deacon during Mass and can help distribute Holy Communion (only in the Ordinary form of the Roman Rite, however).

Laymen and laywomen — that is, the non-ordained and non-religious (meaning not monks or nuns) common folk — can also help in the Ordinary form as readers and as extraordinary ministers of Holy Communion in those dioceses where the local bishop authorizes them to do so. Most parishioners who attend Mass, however, do not have any liturgical office. Nevertheless, their participation is still real and valid.

The role of the congregation

The clergy in the sanctuary have specific things to do and say, but so does the congregation in the pews. The Ordinary form requires the whole congregation to sit, stand, and kneel at specified times. They are required to make the proper responses to the priest or deacon, sing hymns, and say aloud prayers and creeds.

Participation doesn't mean everybody does or says the same thing. In parts of the Mass, the congregation and the celebrant jointly pray together (for the Gloria, Creed, Sanctus, Our Father, and Agnus Dei), and other parts are reserved for one or the other. For example, the priest says, "the Lord be with you," and the people respond, "and with your spirit."

Body gestures and positions are the same for the entire congregation. Everyone kneels during the Consecration while the priest stands at the altar and says the Eucharistic Prayer (which is reserved for the priest alone). The harmony of combining the separate actions and words of the people and the celebrant is like the different sections of a symphony orchestra coming together to make a song.

The highest form of external participation by the faithful is the physical reception of Holy Communion at Mass. Holy Communion is available only to people in full communion (meaning that they accept all Catholic doctrine-teachings, discipline-laws and worship-sacraments and in fact are members of the Catholic Church). They must also be properly disposed, which means they are validly married or single, have fasted for one hour, and are in the state of grace (free from mortal sin).

Internally, people participate by listening and meditating on what is happening. Making a deliberate and conscious intention to give glory and praise to God is internal participation at the Sacred Liturgy. Spiritually uniting with the Sacrifice on the Altar is internal participation. Asking Jesus to come into your heart and soul, especially when you are unable to receive physical Holy Communion, is called making a Spiritual Communion.

Chapter 2

The Foundations of Mass

In This Chapter

▶ Finding the Church's foundations in the Bible

▶ Taking instruction from the Old and New Testaments

A ll three of the Abrahamic religions — Judaism, Christianity, and Islam — have sacred writings that their followers believe were inspired and revealed by God. All three monotheistic (belief in one god) religions encourage their fold to privately read these holy texts but also to participate in public worship where these same words are proclaimed aloud. While all three share a common heritage, Catholic Christianity especially focuses its Divine Worship on the sacred covenants, sacred rituals, and holy sacrifices found in the sacred texts.

In this chapter, we explore the Biblical foundations and writings, or Scripture. Worship within the Catholic Christian Church is very biblical, rooted in both the Hebrew Scriptures of the Old Testament and the Christian New Testament. Readings from the Bible are said aloud during worship, and the ordained minister preaches on the inspired text.

Old Testament: Roots of Judaism

Knowing the past, how and why things came to be, leads to a deeper understanding of the present, which can ultimately point to where things are going. Exploring the roots of Catholicism in the Jewish texts give the faithful a foundation on which to base their beliefs and thoughts about what happened long ago, what is happening now, and what will happen in the years to come.

Genesis and the creation story

If you want to gain a better understanding of the Catholic Mass, you're best off starting at the beginning. Biblically speaking, that's the Book of Genesis, or the book of *beginnings,* which is the first book in the Bible. Scholars believe that the people of Israel told this story of beginnings to their children and to each other for many years before it was ever recorded in writing.

Genesis tells the story of God creating the universe and everything in it. It describes the making of the sun, moon, stars, and earth, with its dry land, oceans, and streams. It teaches about the creation of animals, and says that God made humans in his own image (Genesis 1:26).

By giving humans this certain resemblance to himself, God enabled humans to be his friends. And although human beings were made in much the same way as all of God's creation — from the earth — God gave them one thing that made them special and godlike: free will.

God provided that unique friendship to the first humans he created, Adam and Eve. He made a special garden, Eden, in which they could live in peace and have an abundance of food and shelter. And though they had free will, the one caveat to their peaceful living was that they stay away from the tree in the middle of the garden.

An evil voice came to Adam and Eve in the body of a serpent and convinced them to pick the fruit from the tree and eat it. By giving in to the temptation, the two demonstrated their lack of gratitude to God for all he had given them. They were cast out of the garden and forced to live their lives, as were all of their descendants, with Original Sin — thoughts of greed and lust and other impurities would always be present.

In a story of redemption, the Old Testament tells of God's anger at the humans he created. He was prepared to drown them all in a great flood, but relented a bit and told his friend Noah to build a great ark and fill it with good people and pairings of animals (Genesis 8:20). Those survivors then repopulated the earth.

Beyond the story of creation, the Old Testament tells the stories of the relationship between God and his people and of his love for them despite their unfaithfulness to him. The Old Testament highlights God's refusal to abandon the humans he created. And it doesn't highlight just the ways God's people disappointed him; there are many stories of God's followers offering sacrifice to their Lord in a showing of true love and faith.

Pope Benedict XVI wrote that love is both possessive and obla-
tive (sacrificial). In other words, true love involves both need to
be with and the willingness to sacrifice for the one you love. As
described in numerous Old Testament stories, God expected his
children to make sacrifices to him in appreciation and gratitude
for his love and friendship. While the people were the recipients
of God's generosity, mercy and forgiveness, they also were to give
back worship and adoration, but of him alone. God did not tolerate
any idolatry or false worship of other deities.

Sacrifice of Abel

According to the Book of Genesis, Adam and Eve had two sons,
Cain and Abel. Both sons offered sacrifice to God, but Abel's gift
of the best of his livestock was pure and spotless, and Cain's gift
of inferior, inedible produce was cheap and irreverent. When the
offerings were burned, the smoke from Abel's sacrifice rose right
up to heaven and the smoke of Cain's inferior offerings blew back
into his own face. Cain was so infuriated by the rebuke that he
killed Abel out of pure envy. Abel's sacrifice, however, is a model
of the proper kind of sacrifice a child of God should always perform.

Sacrifice of Abraham

Later in Genesis you meet Abraham and his wife Sarah, who were
old and childless. Their faithfulness to the Lord was rewarded with
a son, Isaac, who was to be with them the rest of their days.

God called Abraham to enter a covenant, or sacred agreement,
that they would love each other. As part of this covenant, God
asked Abraham to prove his love by sacrificing his only son, Isaac.
Abraham loved his son dearly, but his love for God was stronger,
and Abraham showed that he was willing to obey God and sacrifice
his only son. God spared Isaac and entered into another sacred
covenant with Abraham promising that he would make Abraham's
descendants "as numerous as the stars in the heavens and the sands
on the shore of the sea" (Genesis 22:17). In fact, as noted earlier in
this chapter, all three monotheistic religions (Judaism, Christianity
and Islam) consider themselves spiritual children of Abraham.

Sacrifice of Melchizedek

Abraham met the mysterious priest Melchizedek as he was
returning from a victorious battle. Melchizedek, king of Salem,
is described in both the Old and New Testaments as a "priest of
God Most High" (Genesis 14:18, Hebrews 7:1–28). At this meeting
Melchizedek offered a sacrifice (priestly act) of bread and wine as

an expression of praise and gratitude to God. Melchizedek was not a Hebrew priest and not a member of a priestly family (dynastic according to the tribe of Levi and the lineage of Aaron), but he gave Abraham a priestly blessing. Melchizedek's priesthood was recognized by the Scriptures and became part of the priestly inheritance of the Old Testament, foreshadowing the eternal priesthood of Jesus Christ. Both have a priesthood which is not hereditary but unique to their person. Both offered bread and wine. Both were kings (Melchizedek, King of Salem; Jesus, King of Kings).

The memory of the Old Testament's long procession of priestly sacrifices ultimately were fulfilled and pointed to the sacrifice that would be offered by Jesus on the cross and by the long line of Christian priests who would come after him.

Passover (Seder) meal

The Passover, or Seder, meal is a symbolic ritual that pays homage to the freeing of the Hebrew people by Moses under the Lord's direction.

Joseph, one of the two youngest of Jacob's 12 sons, was sold into slavery by his older brothers and sent to Egypt. He was used by God as a trusted counselor and advisor to the pharaoh and eventually became Governor of Egypt and moved his family out of the desert.

The dynasty of the pharaohs who ruled Egypt at that time was overthrown, and a new line of kings took the throne. The new rulers enslaved the Hebrews, including the Twelve Tribes of Israel.

Hundreds of years later, Moses was appointed by God to deliver his Chosen People into freedom and deliver them to the Promised Land. Moses knew all too well that danger accompanied the pharaoh's anxiety: The pharaoh had ordered the execution of the infant Moses and all firstborn Hebrew males to slow the procreation of the Hebrew people. Moses's mother saved him by putting him in a bassinet and floating him down the Nile River, where he was found by the pharaoh's daughter and raised as her own.

He grew into adulthood in the court of the pharaoh, only to be exiled when his Hebrew roots were discovered.

The Lord came to Moses in the form of a burning bush and instructed him to return to Egypt and "let my people go" (Exodus 5:1). Ten plagues were cast upon the people in Egypt, the last of which was to be death of the firstborns in each home. The night before this final plague, however, Moses told the Hebrew people to sacrifice a lamb and sprinkle its blood on the doorpost, identifying the home as one the Angel of Death must "pass over."

Faithful Jews still celebrate the Passover with a Seder meal, in which unleavened bread (to symbolize the Hebrews' hasty departure from Egypt) and grape wine are used just as in the time of Moses. That same meal was celebrated by Jesus and his Apostles the night before his Crucifixion and Death.

Sacrifice by Levite priests in the Temple

Levi was a son of Jacob and great-grandfather to Moses, Aaron, and Miriam. His descendants became the tribe of Levi, or Levites.

The Tribe of Levi was the Priestly tribe, which meant that all Levite males were expected to learn ritual worship as prescribed by God and recorded in the *Torah* (the Hebrew word for *law* and the first five books of the Bible).

Sacrifice is an integral part of the Levite's history. In the early years, Levite priests offered up animal sacrifices in the wilderness to honor God. The deaths of these animals would be considered a symbolic act later when the Messiah offered himself as a sacrifice to atone for the sins of the world.

Centuries later, when the Israelites became a civil entity and kingdom, the son of King David built a temple to house the Ark of the Covenant (the special receptacle or tabernacle that housed the stone tablets on which God wrote the Ten Commandments). This Temple of Solomon was also the place where the high priest would celebrate the sacrifice of the lamb for Passover and where the services for Yom Kippur (Day of Atonement) took place.

The Levitical Priesthood performed ritual worship on the Sabbath and all Jewish holy days as mandated by Mosaic Law. They continued the tradition of blood sacrifice in the Temple of Jerusalem, accepting offerings of sheep, oxen, and doves as an expression of gratitude and praise to God. The priests would slaughter the sacrificial animal and allow its blood to run down the altar as a sign of atonement for sin. The smoke then rose heavenward as the animal was cooked over the fire, and then the people would eat the animal as a sign of their covenanted relationship with the Lord.

The physical Temple of Jerusalem would one day be destroyed by the Romans in AD 70. Jesus, however, spoke of the temple of his body: "Destroy this temple and in three days I shall raise it up" (John 2:19). Later, after his Death and Resurrection, the Christian Church sees herself as the living temple on earth. The baptized (men and women of faith) are the living stones which make up the temple of God.

Coming to him as to a living stone, rejected indeed by men, but chosen by God and precious, you also, as living stones, are being built up a spiritual house, a holy priesthood, to offer up spiritual sacrifices acceptable to God through Jesus Christ. (1 Peter 2:4–5)

Biblical covenants

The Bible is filled with covenants made between God and his people. God made a covenant with Noah after the flood, promising that the waters of the sea would never again drown the whole earth. Later, God made a covenant with Abraham, promising him that his descendants would be as numerous as the stars in the heavens and the sand on the shore of the sea. After that, through Moses, God made what is called the Old Covenant, or Mosaic Covenant. This was God's definitive covenant with his chosen people, but what exactly did this mean?

The Old Covenant was a sacred promise and permanent contract that God made with the Jewish people through Moses on Mount Sinai. It was a mutual pact or treaty: I will be your God if you will be my people.

But in the Old Testament writings of the prophet Jeremiah, God promises a *New Covenant,* which would not be written on stone, but rather on the people's hearts (Jeremiah 31:31–34). Jesus offers this New Covenant to his Apostles at the Last Supper. This new covenant is discussed in the New Testament, the second part of the Bible, which teaches about the fulfillment of the Old Covenant in the person of Jesus and of a new covenant between God and all his people, Jew and Gentile alike (that is, the whole human race).

New Testament: Origin of Christianity

Long before the coming of Christ, which is told of in the New Testament, God made promises of a glorious future for the Chosen People. The Book of Jeremiah in the Old Testament offers prophetic glimpses of an eternal kingdom that God would create with the coming of the Messiah. Many examples of these hope-filled expectations can be found in the messianic prophecies scattered throughout the Old Testament, especially in the prophetic books.

By the time Jesus was born into the world, however, many of these messianic prophecies had been given false interpretations by some of the religious leaders of his day. Their country was occupied by Roman armies, and many viewed the Messiah (the Anointed One)

as a political and military leader whose mission would be to save the people of Israel from foreign oppression at the hands of the Roman forces.

As is clear in the New Testament, Jesus is a very different kind of Messiah. This part of the Bible contains many of the stories and teachings that Catholicism is based on. The foundation of the relationship between God and people changes from the Old to New Testament in ways that significantly affect the Church's beliefs.

Making a new covenant at the Last Supper

The Last Supper was a significant event in Jesus' time, and its remembrance remains a sacred part of the Catholic Mass today. The events of the Last Supper explain how Jesus represents the New Covenant, the definitive relationship between God and people.

Jesus sat at the table with his Apostles and celebrated the Jewish Passover meal just before being arrested and taken away by soldiers. The words spoken by Jesus at this Last Supper are found in the Gospels of Matthew, Mark, and Luke and serve as the basic foundation for the Christian Eucharistic Liturgy. Jesus gave his Apostles bread and wine, telling them: "This is my body which is given for you. . . . This cup which is poured out for you is the new covenant in my blood."

Jesus describes the giving of his Body and Blood as the new and eternal covenant because it symbolizes the start of a new relationship between God and his people. The suffering that Christ would endure on the cross is God's way of expressing that his love for humanity has no limit; in the Passion and Death of Jesus, God has gone as far as he can go. After the Crucifixion of Christ, there is nothing else God can do to convince people that he loves them; that he longs to forgive all their sins; that he has an unconditional and infinite desire to share his divine life with them.

Jesus makes a New Covenant because he wants people to know that he is no longer bound to the Old Testament way of doing things. His New Covenant with all the people of the earth will no longer depend upon the people's faithfulness to God. God's faithfulness to his people is what will bind them to him — God will faithfully love them, whether or not they are faithful to him (Romans).

 Nevertheless, in the New Covenant, an element of reciprocity remains. In fact, this aspect of reciprocity is a very important part of the messianic message and Jesus articulates it clearly and carefully in many passages of the New Testament. The parable of the

Good Samaritan is a powerful expression of the reciprocity that Jesus teaches: "Go and do likewise," he says. "Love one another as I have loved you. . . . My heavenly Father will treat you in exactly the same way that you treat your neighbor. The measure you measure out to others will be measured back to you." The heart and soul of Christ's moral and ethical teaching can be summed up in his words to the disciples: "Whatsoever you do to the least person, you did to me."

Seeing how the New Covenant changes things

The New Covenant offered by Jesus differs from the Old Covenant in two specific ways.

Under the Old Covenant, to stay in God's good graces, God's people were expected to perform rituals and sacrifices and obey the Ten Commandments as given to Moses. With the New Covenant, however, God's people are no longer under penalty of law. Instead, they're given the chance to receive salvation as a free gift as part of the Lord's true sacrifice, that of his Son dying on the cross.

Another important difference between the Old and New Covenants is that the New Covenant is not offered for only one group of people, but for all humanity. God's Son, the Second Person of the Trinity, took on a human nature and was born of a woman (Virgin Mary). He died for all men and women, Jew and gentile (non-Jew) alike.

The Old Covenant between God and the Hebrews was rooted in the promise "I will be your God and you will be my people." The New Covenant did not dissolve or cancel out the first one; instead, it is considered by Christians to be the fulfillment of the Old Covenant — "For God so loved the world that he gave his only Son" (John 3:16).

The Old Covenant was remembered and celebrated with the slaughter of an innocent lamb whose blood was poured out, which saved the Chosen People from death. Likewise, the New Covenant is sealed in the blood of the Lamb of God (the name John the Baptist calls Jesus while baptizing him in the River Jordan), which was shed on the wood of the cross on Good Friday.

Remembering the covenant and the Last Supper

In the telling of the Last Supper in the Gospel of Luke (22:19), Jesus adds the sentence that instructs his followers to: "Do this in remembrance of me." In other words, celebrate the Lord's Supper as a sacred ritual, again and again. The ancient Christians did this every Sunday, and when the state finally legalized the religion, every day (when possible, of course).

Bread and wine are used during Mass, just as they were at the Last Supper. The words of Jesus — "this is my body" and "this is my blood" — have been meticulously preserved and repeated over bread and wine all over the world for more than 2,000 years. The Mass always includes these *exact words* spoken at the Last Supper (usually translated into whatever language the Mass is spoken in). The words are included regardless of whether Mass is celebrated in a basilica, cathedral, or local parish church; or whether by a pope, bishop, or priest.

Discovering the Real Presence

The first words of John's Gospel are a conscious attempt to parallel the opening of the Book of Genesis: "In the beginning. . . ." Genesis tells the story of the physical creation of man and earth, whereas John's Gospel speaks of God's spiritual creation that occurs with the coming of Jesus the Messiah. John the Baptist (a different John) points at Jesus and tells the people, "Behold the Lamb of God who takes away the sins of the world." John (the writer of the Gospel) makes a special effort to compare Jesus to the paschal lamb by making it clear that not a bone of his was broken: the same requirement for the lambs offered by the Israelites in their Passover meals (John 19:36).

Although John's narration of Jesus's words to his Apostles at the Last Supper is much longer than that of any other Gospel and doesn't specifically contain the words of Consecration ("this is my body; this is my blood"), Scripture scholars tell us that the entire sixth chapter of the Gospel of John is Eucharistic in nature and intent.

The sixth chapter of John's Gospel provides the strong foundation for the Catholic belief in the *Real* Presence of Christ in the Eucharist. When Jesus tells the people that he will give them his Body and Blood as food and drink, many listeners find this hard to believe: "How can this man give us his flesh to eat?" (John 6:52). But Jesus does not back down from his words, telling them: "Truly, truly, I say to you, unless you eat the flesh of the Son of man and drink his blood, you have no life in you" (John 6:53). Catholics believe that Jesus meant exactly what he said, so when they receive Holy Communion, they have faith that they are truly receiving the Body and Blood of Jesus.

According to Scripture scholars, the sixth chapter of the Gospel of John provides even more preparation for the gift of the Eucharist that Jesus will give to his followers. After multiplying the loaves and fishes to feed the people, he assures them that he is the bread of life, sent by God the Father. "I am the living bread which came down from heaven; if anyone eats of this bread, he will live forever; and the bread that I will give for the life of the world is my flesh" (John 6:51). When his followers argue among themselves, asking how Jesus can give them his flesh to eat, he responds in a passage that beautifully describes the gift of the Eucharist: ". . . he who eats my flesh and drinks my blood has eternal life, and I will raise him up at the last day. For my flesh is food indeed and my blood is drink indeed" (John 6:53–55). He goes on to say, "This is the bread which came down from heaven, not such as the fathers who ate and died; he who eats this bread will live forever" (John 6:58).

Other New Testament foundations

The Epistle to the Hebrews compares the bloody sacrifice of Jesus on the cross to the blood sacrifices in the Temple of Jerusalem and refers very directly to the Blood of Christ cleansing and sanctify-ing those defiled by sin (Hebrews 9:13–14). Paul's First Letter to the Corinthians contains the words of consecration (the words Jesus spoke at the Last Supper over the bread and wine: *this is my body . . . this is my blood*) as well as many other references to the Eucharist (I Corinthians 10:16, 10:17, 11:20, 11:27, 11:28, and more).

In the Book of Revelations, the Bible's last book, the name given to Jesus by John the Baptist is brought to its fulfillment. Jesus is again referred to as *the lamb* (at Passover, a lamb had to be slain in sacri-fice. Then the night before he died on the cross, Jesus became the lamb who would be sacrificed on the wood of the cross), indicat-ing that the sacrifice of his Body and Blood on the cross becomes the fulfillment of the Old Covenant Passover meal. The marvelous description of heaven's eternal liturgy of praise and gratitude to God is referred to as *the supper of the lamb* and the *marriage supper of the lamb* (Revelations 19:7–9). The image of Jesus as the *lamb of god* not only appears in the mouth of John the Baptist.

Chapter 3

The Liturgical Year

The idea of marking significant events during the year isn't exclusive to Christianity. From pagan times, people observed a calendar that was usually centered on the agricultural cycle: Spring meant planting and new birth among the animals, summer symbolized growth, fall represented the harvest, and winter stood for dormancy, not just for the animal kingdom but the plant kingdom as well.

Christianity also has its own seasonal *liturgical* calendar. Just as the pagan calendar observed holidays according to nature's cycle of life, the Christian calendar celebrates holy days according to historical biblical events.

Judaism plays a significant role in the Christian liturgical calendar. The Christian observance of Easter originally took place during the Jewish feast of Passover; Christians believe Holy Thursday is when Christ instituted the Sacraments of Holy Eucharist and Holy Orders, one day before his Passion and Crucifixion. Three days later was his Resurrection.

The Church liturgical year has two cycles, the Temporal and the Sanctoral. The Temporal (from Latin *tempus,* meaning *time* or *season*) cycle focuses on the life of Christ, from Birth to Death, Resurrection to Ascension. The entire paschal mystery (Passion, Death, and Resurrection) is ceremonially celebrated in the divine worship given each Sunday and holy day of the year during the Temporal cycle. The Sanctoral (from Latin *sanctus,* meaning *saint*) cycle focuses on the various holy men and women of faith who the Church endorses as saints. These heroes of the Catholic religion are normally celebrated on the day of their death, which is considered their heavenly birthday. While the Sanctoral cycle follows the days of the Gregorian calendar (the normal January to December calendar), the Temporal cycle follows the seasons of the year, beginning in winter with Advent and Christmas, going through spring with Lent and Easter, continuing through summer (Ordinary Time), and ending in fall with the Feast of Christ the King.

Worshipping through the Temporal Cycle

The liturgical year is a year of grace. Christians view it as an opportunity to enter into the Sacred Mysteries of redemption and receive God's life. This prospect unfolds itself throughout the year through the different aspects of salvation from the beginning of Christ's life — the Advent and Christmas season — to the earthly end — the Lent and Easter season. The months in between mark Ordinary Time and the celebration of the saints.

The liturgy not only recalls the sacred events of our salvation from history, but also makes them alive in the annual celebration of the Temporal cycle. After the Roman Empire fell and Europe was overrun by the barbarian invaders, the Dark Ages ensued, and many common folk were unable to read and write. They were taught, however, not by books, but by the Sacred Liturgy. The Temporal cycle of the liturgical year taught the faithful about the Birth, Death, Resurrection, and Ascension of Jesus, year after year. Just as we have the same four seasons year after year, we have the Birth of Christ every winter and the Resurrection of Christ every spring. Although Christmas is a fixed date, Easter changes every year based on the equinox and full moon in the lunar cycle.

Preparing for Christ Our Light: Advent and Christmas

The season of Christmas and the four weeks of preparation, known as Advent, begin the new liturgical year of grace and the Temporal cycle. This new year is marked by the changing lectionary cycle, or cycle of readings. Sundays are divided into three lectionary volumes, and weekdays are divided into two volumes. The First Sunday of Advent means a change of volumes for both Sundays and weekdays.

Christmas developed as a liturgical celebration of the birthday of the Savior. The word itself means *Christ's Mass,* the Mass in honor of the Birth of Jesus Christ. Christians wanted to celebrate and commemorate the Birth of Christ, but no one knew the exact date. Emperors and kings and other powerful people had their birthdays remembered because of public celebrations. Ordinary folks, like a son of a carpenter in Nazareth, would not have had his birthday marked down on any calendar. Only after his Death, Resurrection, and Ascension did the followers of Jesus want to honor his Birth (since they already were celebrating the day he died).

Many theories concern the date of the Savior's Birth in Bethlehem. Some scholars believe it occurred in the spring because the shepherds and their animals were outside at night, and even in the Mediterranean the nights are chilly during spring and summer and quite cold in December.

Although the pagan Romans celebrated the feast of the sun at the winter solstice, St. Augustine (who lived in the fourth century AD) wrote that Christians also used that time of year to honor the birthday of their beloved founder. The reason was based on the symbolism of daylight. The shortest day of the year occurs in December, and by December 25 (Christmas), the amount of daylight begins to increase in the Northern hemisphere. Conversely, the longest day of the year occurs in June, so that by June 24 the amount of daylight begins to slowly decrease day by day until the shortest day arrives and the opposite takes place.

According to St. Augustine, two passages in the Bible relate to the shortest and the longest days of the year.

- ✔ In John 3:30, "I must decrease while he must increase" was spoken by St. John the Baptist in reference to his cousin, Jesus Christ the Lord.
- ✔ Jesus said "I am the Light of the world" in John 9:5.

So the Church celebrates the birthday of John the Baptist on June 24 (when sunlight is beginning to decrease) and the birthday of Jesus on December 25 (when sunlight is beginning to increase).

Advent

The four-week season of Advent helps prepare Christians for the Solemnity of Christmas. *Advent* comes from the Latin and means *arrival,* a fitting word because the season is in preparation for the arrival of Christ. The season is broken up into the various weeks of preparation: the Sundays are First, Second, Third (Gaudete Sunday), and Fourth, beginning on the Feast of the Apostle Andrew on November 30 and ending on December 24, the Vigil of Christmas. Each season in the liturgical calendar is symbolized by a specific color, and for Advent, the liturgical color is purple.

Advent focuses on the historical arrival of Jesus over two millennia ago and also symbolizes the Second Coming of Christ that will take place at the end of world. Advent is a season characterized by preparation, reflection, hope, and anticipation. Spiritual reflections are taken from key people noted in Scripture: Isaiah the prophet; John the Baptist; Elizabeth and Zechariah, the parents of John; and Joseph.

The Solemnity of the Immaculate Conception of Mary is during the Advent season, on December 8. The feast is a celebration of the Divine Plan, which provides that Mary was preserved from Original Sin while in the womb of Ann, her mother. Nine months later, the birthday of Mary is celebrated on September 8.

Following are other Advent season feasts, which each have their own unique customs and traditions that add to the festivity of the season:

- ✔ December 6: St. Nicholas Day (the origin of Santa Claus)

- ✔ December 12: Our Lady of Guadalupe, patroness of the Americas

- ✔ December 13: St. Lucy, virgin and martyr, and patron saint of eye maladies

Changes to the Mass and additional prayers

The Gloria praise hymn, originally a Christmas hymn, is not sung during Advent's preparation season. Unlike during Lent, which is more penitential, the Alleluia still can be sung during the liturgy in Advent in the Ordinary Rite, but is omitted in the Extraordinary form of the Roman Rite. Flowers may adorn the altar during this season, and often greenery is brought into the church.

A special novena known as the Christmas Novena is prayed during this season as a tool of preparation. The novena asks God to grant request in the honor of the Birth of his Son at Christmas. It is a pious custom that revolves around the family, as many of the customs of Advent and Christmas do.

Christmas Novena

Hail, and blessed be the hour and moment
At which the Son of God was born
Of a more pure Virgin
At a stable at midnight in Bethlehem
In the piercing cold
At that hour vouchsafe, I beseech thee,
To hear my prayers and grant my desires [mention request]
Through Jesus Christ and his most Blessed Mother. Amen.

The Advent wreath

The Advent wreath has become a very popular sacramental in the Universal Church. Three of the candles are purple, symbolizing the preparation and anticipation of the season. The fourth candle is rose and is lit on Gaudete Sunday. Before electricity, candles were the source of light in the church, so lighting these candles during the darkest time of year gave a great expression of Christ, the light of the world.

The following prayer is used on the First Sunday of Advent. The subsequent candles are lit in silence on the following Sundays until Christmas Eve.

> **Prayer of Blessing of the Advent Wreath**
>
> O God, by whose word all things are sanctified,
> Pour forth thy blessing upon this wreath
> Grant that we who use it may prepare our hearts
> For the coming of Christ and
> May receive from thee abundant graces.
> Through Christ our Lord. Amen.

Christmas

The season of Christmas begins at the evening liturgy of Christmas Eve and lasts until the Feast of the Epiphany. In Europe, Epiphany falls on January 6, which coincides with the traditional count of the 12th day of Christmas. By special permission in many dioceses, including those in the United States, this solemnity has been transferred to the Sunday nearest January 6. However, the Christmas season actually extends to the Feast of the Baptism of the Lord, which is observed the Sunday after Epiphany.

Christmas is the celebration of the Birth of the Light of the World, Jesus Christ, when the long promised Messiah of the Old Testament materialized. For Catholics in the Northern Hemisphere, it is the darkest and coldest time of the year. Though the actual date of the Lord's Birth is not known, December 25 became the set date; for Orthodox Christians who observe the Julian calendar, however, Christ's Birth is celebrated on January 6.

Four special Masses are assigned for Christmas, each with its own prayers, and readings: the Vigil Mass, Mass at Midnight, Mass at Dawn, and Mass during the Day. Any one of these Masses fulfills the Catholic obligation to attend Mass on the holy day.

Traditionally, the Mass at Midnight is the most special, with much pomp and ceremony exhibited. Usually a long procession takes place with a figurine of the Baby Jesus placed in a crèche (nativity set) in the crib, which is blessed with the Prayer of Blessing:

Prayer of Blessing

God of every nation and people, from the very beginning of creation
You have made manifest your love:
When our need for a Savior was great
You sent your Son to be born of the Virgin Mary.
To our lives he brings joy and peace, justice, mercy, and love.
Lord bless all who look upon this manger;
May it remind us of the humble Birth of Jesus,
And raise up our thoughts to him, who is God-with-us and Savior of all,
And who lives and reigns for ever and ever. Amen.

The formal Proclamation of the Birth of Christ is also recited at the Midnight Mass. The text, which comes from the Roman Martyrology, situates the Birth of Christ within the context of salvation history. It begins with the creation of the world and culminates with the Birth of the Savior during the Roman Empire. Note the connection with human history (Caesar Augustus, Greek Olympiad) and biblical events to help situate the Birth of Christ.

The Proclamation

In the 5,199th year
of the creation of the world
from the time when God in the beginning
created the heavens and the earth;
the 2,957th year after the flood;
the 2,015th year from the birth of Abraham;
the 1,510th year from Moses
and the going forth of the people of Israel from Egypt;
the 1,032nd year from David's being anointed king;
in the 65th week according to the prophecy of Daniel;
in the 194th Olympiad;
the 752nd year from the foundation of the city of Rome;
the 42nd year of the reign of Octavian Augustus;
the whole world being at peace,
in the sixth age of the world,
Jesus Christ the eternal God and Son of the eternal Father,
desiring to sanctify the world by his most merciful coming,
being conceived by the Holy Spirit,
and nine months having passed since his conception,
was born in Bethlehem of Judea of the Virgin Mary,
being made flesh
the nativity of our Lord Jesus Christ according to the flesh.

Christmas symbols

Many Christmas symbols that seem to have a secular appearance have religious significance, as well. The Christmas tree, which originated in Germany, developed from medieval religious plays. One such play was about the mystery of Paradise and the expulsion of the first parents, and the Garden of Eden was presented as an evergreen tree. The plays always ended on a hopeful note promising the Messiah, and this was portrayed by Christmas candles on the tree that reflect the deep mystery of Christ the Light of the world.

Other symbols of Christmas are holly, Christmas roses, and poinsettia. Holly berries symbolize Christ's blood and the holly represents the crown of thorns, which prefigures the Passion of Christ. The Christmas rose is a symbol of Jesus, who is the Rose of Sharon, and his Mother, the Mystical Rose. Poinsettia flowers are indigenous to Mexico, and the Mexicans have always seen the red leaves of this plant in relationship to the deep love for Jesus.

After Christmas: The celebration continues

Christmas Day doesn't end the Christmas season. The following feasts are celebrated after December 25:

- The **Octave of Christmas** starts December 26 with the Feast of St. Stephen, which commemorates the first martyr for Christ.

- December 27 is the **Feast of St. John the Beloved Disciple** and one of the four Gospel writers, known as Evangelists.

- December 28 is the **Commemoration of the Holy Innocents**, the babies that Herod had destroyed in Bethlehem in pursuit of killing the Christ child. Today they are patron saints of the aborted child and the pro-life movement.

- **Holy Family Sunday** is observed on the Sunday following Christmas. The liturgy remembers Jesus, Mary, and Joseph as the patrons of Christian families.

- January 1, in the secular sphere, marks the passing of the year. In the liturgical calendar it is the **Celebration of Mary as the Mother of God.**

- The **Feast of the Epiphany** in Rome and many European countries is observed on January 6, the 12th day of Christmas. In countries where Catholicism is not the state religion, the Epiphany is transferred to the Sunday after the Feast of Mary the Mother of God, January 1. Therefore, instead of being an immovable feast it changes from year to year.

  Epiphany means *manifestations*. It is the day that celebrates the arrival of the Three Wise Men or Three Kings, known as the Magi, who are called Caspar, Melchior, and Balthazar. The manifestation of the Savior to the Magi is significant, because it's when God makes his appearance known to the world. The Magi brought gifts of gold, frankincense, and myrrh, which represent the threefold role of the Messiah: King, Prophet, and Priest. The magnificent cathedral in Cologne, Germany, is believed to hold the relics of the Magi.

✔ The **Solemnity of the Baptism of the Lord**, celebrated after the Epiphany, is the last major feast of the Christmas season. It commemorates the Baptism of Jesus in the Jordan River by John the Baptist and signals the next season of the Church. On this day, the Holy Father celebrates the Sacrament of Baptism in which he baptizes a select few in the Sistine Chapel.

Celebrating Christ Our Life: Lent, Holy Week, and Easter

Easter, the celebration of the Passion, Death, and Resurrection of the Lord, is the high point of the liturgical year. Lent, the 40-day period before Easter, is a time of preparation that includes increased prayer, penitence, almsgiving, and self-denial.

Churches themselves seem to undergo a sort of decorative fast as well. The absence of flowers and ornate decorations and the use of purple offer a certain austerity for the season of penance. The Gloria and Alleluia usually sung at Mass and the Liturgy of the Hours are omitted for Lent, and ostentatious displays of music are also skipped.

Closer to Holy Week — the week before Easter, beginning with Palm Sunday — the statuary and crucifixes are covered as a reminder that parishioners are readying themselves for something much more important, the world to come, and that things of this world are transient. This season has also been known as the "Great Retreat," which commemorates the 40-day fast and retreat the Lord made before his passion.

Lent is a time to receive many graces by God. The faithful grow closer to the Lord through self denial (prayer, fasting, and almsgiving) and other Lenten disciplines. Examples include the Stations or Way of the Cross (usually celebrated in parish churches on Friday nights during Lent); praying the rosary, especially as a family in the home; having a poor man's meal of soup and bread one day a week; and giving up a favorite food, alcoholic beverages, movie theaters, dances, and so on.

In the Extraordinary form of the Roman Rite, the three weeks prior to Ash Wednesday contain a series of specially named Sundays in preparation for Lent: Septuagesima (seventh), Sexagesima (sixth), and Quinquagesima (fifth). It was considered a time of preparation for the season of Lent that culminated on Carnival, the day before Lent actually commenced. In the Ordinary form of the Roman Rite this time of preparation has been dropped and replaced simply by the season of Ordinary Time.

Lent

In the Western Church (Latin Rite), Lent begins with the imposition (marking on the forehead) of ashes on Ash Wednesday, which takes place 46 days before Lent. Sundays aren't technically included in the 40 days of Lent as they are considered "Little Easters."

For Byzantine Catholics, Lent does not begin on Ash Wednesday but on Clean Monday, two days prior to Ash Wednesday. On the two preceding Sundays, Byzantines observed Cheesefare Sunday and Meatfare Sunday; the customary practice was to abstain from dairy products during Lent from Cheesefare Sunday to Easter, and from meat products from Meatfare Sunday to Easter. In addition to fasting, abstinence, prayer, confession, and almsgiving are common in the Byzantine Church.

Lent concludes with Easter, which occurs on a different Sunday from year to year.

The date of Easter is determined according to a lunar calendar; it is the first Sunday after the full moon after the spring equinox, believed to be the actual date of the Jewish feast of Passover. The Last Supper (Holy Thursday) happened during Passover.

The Fourth Sunday of Lent is known as *Laetare* Sunday. This is considered the halfway point of Lent. It gets its name from the opening lines of the antiphon of the Mass, "Laetare Jerusalem," meaning "Rejoice, O Jerusalem." Like Gaudete Sunday, the color of the vestments, antependium, chalice veil and burse, and tabernacle veil is rose. Rose symbolizes joy and hope in the midst of penance. Flowers are permitted on this Sunday, and exuberant music pieces are performed.

Some of the Sundays during Lent have been reconfigured. In the Extraordinary form of the Roman Rite, the Sunday before Palm Sunday is known as Passion Sunday, and it is on this day that the Passion is read and the statues in the church are veiled. In the Ordinary form of the Roman Rite, which most parishes follow, the reading of the Passion has been transferred to Palm Sunday (and no Passion Sunday is celebrated).

The following three major feasts may fall during Lent:

- ✔ February 22: The Chair of St. Peter
- ✔ March 19: Solemnity of St. Joseph
- ✔ March 25: The Annunciation of the Blessed Virgin Mary

Each of these feasts can be celebrated with solemnity unless they fall during Holy Week, which takes precedence over any other celebration. St. Joseph and Annunciation can be observed before or after Holy Week depending upon their proximity to it.

Ash Wednesday

On Ash Wednesday, ashes are placed on the foreheads of the faithful during the liturgy and are put in the sign of the cross, the symbol of salvation. The traditional prayer of imposition, from Genesis 3:19, is recited:

> Remember, O man, that you are dust, and unto dust you shall return.

Ashes are traditionally made from old palms from Palm Sunday of the previous year. Burnt, sifted, and blessed ashes become a sacramental and synonymous with the day. They're a symbol of penance and serve to remind the faithful that they have embarked on a 40-day religious journey of prayer, fasting, and almsgiving. All these things are done not only to improve the religious character of the person, but to prepare the soul for heaven in general.

Fasting and abstinence during Lent

Fasting has many meanings. When the doctor tells the patient to fast the night before a procedure, that means to eat and drink *nothing.* Some people have interpreted religious fasting as eating nothing at all or as only having bread and water once or twice during the day. But typically the modern Church defines fasting as the eating of two small meals along with one regular, full meal. The small meals if combined would not to equal the one normal meal.

Today the Catholic Church only demands that the faithful between ages of 18 and 59 fast a minimum of two days — Ash Wednesday and Good Friday. In previous eras, the entire season of Lent was a time of fasting (except on Sundays to honor the day of Resurrection). Some Eastern Catholics and Eastern Orthodox maintain the older tradition of fasting most if not all of Lent.

Along with fasting, another discipline of Lent is abstinence. Catholics are required to abstain from eating meat on Ash Wednesday and all Fridays of Lent. Meat is defined as the flesh of warm-blooded animals. This rule binds Catholics aged 14 and older.

Catholics should abstain from meat on *all* Fridays throughout the year. However, in his Apostolic Constitution *Paenitemini* of 1966, Pope Paul VI allowed the faithful to substitute another form of penance in place of abstaining from meat on Fridays outside of Lent.

The Stations of the Cross

The Stations (or Way) of the Cross are prayed publicly in church during Lent, usually on Wednesdays and Fridays. The celebrant is usually vested in a cassock, surplice, stole, and possibly a cope. The colors for the Stations are usually purple, red, or black.

Two acolytes typically accompany the celebrant, holding lit candles and a crucifer, as the celebrant walks through the church and the stations. The traditional hymn, "Stabat Mater" ("Sorrowful Mother"), is sung between each Station.

Holy Week

The Sixth Sunday of Lent is traditionally known as Palm or Passion Sunday, and it marks the beginning of Holy Week. The liturgy takes a dramatic turn and focuses more on the Passion of Christ and the immediate preparation for the Holy Triduum and Easter. Statues and crosses are still veiled on this day, although it is an optional custom. Once they're veiled, the statuary remains this way until the Vigil of Easter. The only statuary never veiled during the Lenten season are the Stations of the Cross.

In the Ordinary form of the Roman Rite, the Passion is read in a dialogue fashion, and a procession takes place at the beginning of Mass with newly blessed palm fronds. Palms are a commemoration of the triumphant entry of Jesus into Jerusalem directly before his Passion. The Byzantine Church substitutes pussy willow branches for the palms because they were more accessible in their native countries than palms.

Holy Week ends with the Easter Triduum, consisting of Holy Thursday, on which the Mass of the Lord's Supper is celebrated, Good Friday, on which the Passion of Our Lord is remembered, and Holy Saturday, on which the vigil of the Lord's resurrection held. This is the heart of the liturgical year and technically the end of the 40 days of Lent.

The Chrism Mass

The Chrism Mass, in which the sacred oils used in some of the Sacraments are blessed, occurs during Holy Week. Priests renew their commitment and surround the bishop during this Mass, as well. Traditionally, this Mass took place on the morning of Holy Thursday, but it's now most commonly observed on Holy Monday due to the distance many pastors must drive to the cathedral and their busy parish schedules during Holy Week.

Following are the three oils to be blessed:

- ✔ Oil of catechumen, used in the Sacrament of Baptism

- ✔ Oil of the infirmed, used in the Anointing of the Sick

- ✔ Chrism oil, used in the Sacraments of Baptism, Confirmation, and Holy Orders and to consecrate a church or altar

Enough oil must be blessed for every parish or religious institution in the diocese. It is a symbol of unity that the bishop blesses the oil and then disperses it amongst his parishes in the diocese.

In preparation of this Mass, parish oil stocks are usually collected and the remaining oil is burned. After being cleaned out, the parishes are ready to receive fresh stock of blessed oil. Each parish brings the new oils back to their churches, and usually they are solemnly presented at the evening Mass of the Lord's Supper on Holy Thursday. They are stored in an *ambry,* a special box, which is usually visible to the congregation.

Holy Wednesday

Holy Wednesday, sometimes called Spy Wednesday for Judas's paid betrayal of the Lord, is marked by the reading of Tenebrae. *Tenebrae,* the Latin word for *shadows,* is a set of readings from Psalms and the Book of Lamentations. The Tenebrae candle, a 15-candle candelabra, is lit. After each major section of the readings, two candles are extinguished, until the middle candle, the Christ candle, is all that remains. The Christ candle is then taken away from the sanctuary by a server, and a large crashing sound is made. The crashing sound is in remembrance of the earthquake that took place upon the Death of the Savior on Good Friday. Then the still-lit candle is brought back into church as a sign of hope in the Resurrection.

Holy Thursday

On Holy Thursday, the central part of the Mass of the Lord's Supper is the remembrance of the two Sacraments Christ instituted at the Last Supper — Eucharist and the Mass, and the Priesthood, the way Mass is perpetuated throughout the centuries. The sanctuary, although it can have some decorations and flowers, still remains simple. The color of vestments can be white or gold. The three oils blessed at the Chrism Mass are announced and brought into the church and placed in the ambry. The Gloria is sung and bells are rung, and from this point until the Easter Vigil the organ and bells remain silent. Liturgy of the Word begins and the Gospel is proclaimed. The homily focuses on the Institution of the Blessed Sacrament and the Holy Sacrifice of the Mass that was instituted at the Last Supper.

The traditional washing of the feet takes place after the homily, commemorating Jesus' washing his Apostles' feet at the Last Supper. It is a symbol of humility and service, both qualities to emulate in the priesthood.

The Mass continues in the usual fashion until the last prayer. In a section of the church or even a chapel, a temporary altar with a tabernacle is created. Suitable decoration of flowers and candles is arranged. The Blessed Sacrament that was prepared at this Mass and enough for the following day's service is carried throughout the church by a priest in vestments and with humeral veil. A traditional hymn called the "Pange Lingua," composed by St. Thomas Aquinas, is sung. Then the Blessed Sacrament is placed in the repository (a temporary tabernacle to hold the Holy Eucharist, consecrated hosts), and after proper incensation (ritual burning of incense in a brass container held by chains), there is time for private adoration.

Normally, the sanctuary is stripped bare of any of its refinements before the final prayer. The main tabernacle doors are left open. The sanctuary lamp is extinguished. Holy water fonts are emptied. These gestures symbolize the great Passion of the Lord and his Sacred Death. After midnight, if the repository is in the main church, it's usually dismantled and the Blessed Sacrament is placed in a secure area with a sole candle lit to note the Real Presence.

Good Friday

Good Friday commemorates the Passion of our Lord on the cross, and the vestments are red. This service usually takes place at 3 p.m., the hour at which Christ died, but for pastoral reasons the ceremony can take place in the evening. In addition, the Stations of the Cross can be prayed publicly before or after the service. Between noon and 3 p.m., the Church traditionally preaches and meditates on the Seven Last Words uttered by Christ on the Cross. Not literally only seven words, the Seven Last Words, or Sayings, of Jesus are:

1. Father forgive them, for they know not what they do.

2. Today you will be with me in paradise.

3. Behold your son; behold your mother.

4. My God, my God, why have you forsaken me?

5. I thirst.

6. It is finished.

7. Father, into your hands I commit my Spirit.

The Passion of the Lord, the Good Friday Service, is not a Mass. In fact, Good Friday is the only day of the year in which Mass cannot be celebrated. The service is divided into three parts:

1. The Liturgy of the Word is given, including the dialogue of the Passion, followed by a homily and chanting of the General Intercessions.

2. Veneration of the cross is done solemnly. The celebrant, flanked by candles, brings a veiled crucifix into the church and stops three times, each time chanting, "This is the wood of the cross on which hung the Savior of the World," and revealing a bit of the cross. When he reaches the sanctuary he venerates the whole crucifix.

3. The final part of the liturgy is Holy Communion. The altar is dressed with a simple cloth, upon which the candles from the procession of the crucifix are placed. A corporal, purificator, ablution cup, and sacramentary are all placed on the altar and the Blessed Sacrament is brought into the sanctuary. Our Father is prayed and Communion is distributed, and after the closing prayer all depart in silence. The simplicity of the liturgy expresses the deep-hearted sorrow every Christian has in reflecting that it is their sins that have crucified the Lord.

Easter Vigil

The Easter Vigil is by far the oldest and most respected of all the Church's liturgies. The church is decorated for Easter with candles, flowers, a white tabernacle veil, white antependium (full frontal altar cloth), and white vestments, but the church usually has all its lights off, and the congregation waits in anticipation in darkness. They are all given candles that will be lit during the liturgy.

The Easter Vigil has many components. First is the Service of Light. In the entrance of the church or in another suitable place where the faithful can gather, a fire is prepared, lit, and blessed. The Easter or paschal candle, usually 6 to 9 feet tall, is prepared for its blessing. It is a symbol of the Risen Jesus.

The candle is lit and the procession into the dark church commences. When inside the church, the candle is lowered three times and the people light their little vigil candles from the Easter candle.

The second part of the liturgy is the Easter Proclamation. The deacon or priest makes the proclamation in darkness except for the paschal candle and vigil candles that are lit. The chanted Easter Proclamation is a review of the history of our salvation culminating in Christ.

The third section of the liturgy is the Liturgy of the Word. Seven readings and psalms from the Old Testament, ranging from the Book of Genesis to the Book of the Prophet Ezekiel, can be done. At a minimum, readings 1, 3, 5, and 7 must be used, but the priest may choose to add readings 2, 4, and 6. After the last psalm, the choir and congregation sing the Gloria again, the church bells are rung, the lights are turned on, the candles used at Mass are lit from the Easter candle, and if the church has a statue of the Risen Christ, it is unveiled. Afterward is a reading from the New Testament, followed by the solemn chanting of the Alleluia, which was omitted during Lent, and a homily.

The fourth part is the celebration of the Sacraments of Baptism and Confirmation of people who are joining the Catholic Church. To prepare for these Sacraments, the Litany of Saints is sung, the priest blesses water as holy water, the candidates pledge their renunciation of sin and profession of faith, and then the actual Baptism takes place. Following the Sacrament of Baptism, the congregation gives a general renewal of the renunciation of sin and profession of faith. The priest then blesses all the people with the Easter water.

If any candidates have already been baptized in non-Catholic churches, before the celebration of the Sacrament of Confirmation they make their formal reception into Full Communion with the Church. The Confirmation concludes the celebration of Baptism and Confirmation. Mass continues as usual, but at the conclusion of Mass a double Alleluia is sung by the celebrant and congregation.

After the Easter Vigil, the Easter season has begun. For the entire Easter season the paschal candle remains in a prominent place, usually near the pulpit, and is lit for every liturgy. White is the color used for the season.

Easter

Easter is the primary solemnity of the Church. It is first celebrated in a special Octave; that is, a liturgical period of eight days. Each day of the Octave ranks the same as Easter Sunday — the highest level. Any saints' feast days that fall in the Octave are not commemorated at that time. Whitsunday, which is also known as Divine Mercy Sunday, ends the Octave, and the Easter season continues until Ascension Thursday. This feast falls 40 days after Easter and commemorates the Ascension of the Lord into heaven. In some dioceses this feast is celebrated on the Seventh Sunday of Easter. After the Octave, the paschal candle is moved to the area of the baptismal font and used only for the Sacraments of Baptism and Confirmation and Mass of Christian Burial.

Pentecost, 50 days after Easter, finishes this season, and it commemorates the descent of the Holy Spirit upon the Apostles and the Blessed Virgin Mary in the Upper Room. Pentecost is considered the birthday of the Church. The vestment color of red represents the fire of faith that the Holy Spirit imparts.

Pentecost is an appropriate day for adult celebration of the Sacrament of Confirmation, because the first Confirmations took place at Pentecost. The diocesan bishop typically visits the local parish during the calendar year to confirm boys and girls (anywhere from 2nd to 8th grades to high-school age), and he also likes to have all the adults of the diocese who need to be confirmed do so with him at the cathedral.

The Pentecost liturgy ends with the double Alleluia at the dismissal, and the Easter season ends. This service also usually ends *mystagogy,* the period of postinstruction for adults who received the Sacraments of Initiation at the Easter Vigil.

Filling in the Gaps with Ordinary Time

Ordinary Time is the period when the Church celebrates the mystery of Christ in all its aspects. Also called *ferial days* and *time throughout the year,* it is the part of the liturgical calendar between the major seasons. It follows Christmas and ends at Ash Wednesday, and then resumes after the Solemnity of Pentecost and concludes at the First Sunday of Advent. In the calendar of the Extraordinary form of the Roman Rite, Ordinary Time is called *the season after Epiphany* and *the season after Pentecost.* It is the longest liturgical season of the Church and can last up to 34 weeks of the year. The normal color for this season is green, the color of hope.

Following are some special feasts observed on Sundays in Ordinary Time.

> ✔ **Solemnity of the Blessed Trinity** is the Sunday directly after Pentecost. This feast focuses on the theological fact of the One God in Three Divine Persons. In the liturgy of the Blessed Trinity the special preface, prayers, and Scripture readings try

to unfold this deep and most important element of doctrine in what it means to be a Christian.

✔ *Corpus Christi* **(Body of Christ) Sunday** follows the Solemnity of the Blessed Trinity. It was established in the 13th century to mark a Eucharistic miracle that took place in Bolsena, Italy. Today it is technically known as the Solemnity of the Most Holy Body and Blood of Christ, but most people still remember and refer to the older Latin designation of Corpus Christi.

✔ **Solemnity of Christ the King** is celebrated on the last Sunday of the liturgical year, which falls the week before the First Sunday of Advent. It was established by Pope Pius XI in 1925 to counteract the effects of nationalism and secularism. The feast highlights the culmination of all the Church's doctrines and beliefs in the Second Person of the Blessed Trinity, Jesus Christ. It also makes Catholics aware that they are made for the Kingdom of Heaven and not for this earth.

Coming not long after the Christmas season, the **Feast of the Presentation of the Lord** on February 2 is formally known as the **Purification of the Blessed Virgin Mary**. It commemorates the Jewish tradition of the presentation of firstborn male children in the Temple in Jerusalem 40 days after their birth by their mothers, who in turn received a blessing. Before the Second Vatican Council, this day marked the end of Christmas instead of the Baptism of the Lord, but now it falls in Ordinary Time. This day is also called *Candlemas Day* because it was also the day the candles to be used in Divine worship in the church were blessed.

On February 3, some of the candles that were used on the preceding day are used for the commemoration of St. Blaise. On **St. Blaise Day**, after Mass the priest holds two candles in a crisscross fashion under the chin of the faithful and makes a special blessing for deliverance of any maladies of the throat or other illnesses:

St. Blaise Prayer

Through the intercession of St. Blaise, bishop and martyr
May God deliver you free from every ailment of the throat
And from every other illness.
In the name of the Father and of the Son
And of the Holy Spirit, amen.

The following solemnities or feasts are celebrated instead of the regular liturgy when they fall on a Sunday in Ordinary Time:

✔ February 2: Solemnity of Presentation of the Lord

✔ June 24: Solemnity of the Birth of St. John the Baptist

✔ June 29: Solemnity of SS. Peter and Paul

- ✔ August 6: Feast of the Transfiguration of Christ
- ✔ August 15: Solemnity of the Assumption of the Blessed Virgin Mary into Heaven
- ✔ September 14: Exaltation of the Holy Cross
- ✔ November 1: Solemnity of All Saints
- ✔ November 2: Commemoration of All Souls
- ✔ November 9: Dedication of the Basilica of St. John Lateran (in honor of both St. John the Baptist and St. John the Evangelist)

In addition, the Feast of the Sacred Heart of Jesus falls 19 days after Pentecost on a Friday. This feast day is a culmination of devotion to the Sacred Humanity of the Lord that began in the 12th century. St. Margaret Mary Alacoque, a cloister Visitation Nun in France, received private revelations of the Sacred Heart of Jesus, raising interest in holding a Feast of the Lord under this specific title, and in the 19th century Pope Pius IX instituted this feast day. In the 20th century Pope Pius XII elevated it liturgically to the highest rank of importance, without attaching an obligation to attend Mass.

Honoring Saints in the Sanctoral Cycle

The *Sanctoral cycle,* or Proper of the Saints, is the listing of the feast days of the saints commemorated in the Church, according to the Roman Missal. The feast days are given in sequence, from January through December.

Catholics worship God alone and only *venerate,* or honor, the saints. The theological distinction is as follows:

- ✔ *Latria* is worshipping God exclusively.
- ✔ *Dulia* is honoring the saints.
- ✔ *Hyperdulia* is highest honor given to the Virgin Mary.

In no way does the Catholics' love and respect for the saints supersede or even rival their love and adoration of God.

Feasts of the Virgin Mary

Mary is the premier saint because of her attributes, all of which are related to the fact that she is *Theotokos:* the Mother of God. She is mother in the sense that she gave the Jesus, the Second Person of the Blessed Trinity, his Sacred Humanity. Mary is celebrated for her part in the Incarnation, making flesh from the word of God.

The angel Gabriel announced to Mary that she was pregnant with Jesus, the Son of God (celebrated March 25 with the Feast of the Annunciation). Jesus is the Divine Person, but he has two natures, Divine and Human. In the sense that you cannot split the Divine Person, Mary is the Mother of God (celebrated January 1). As the Mother of God, she could not have been under the contagion of sin, even Original Sin, because God prepared a perfect receptacle to give humanity to the Redeemer (the fact of which is celebrated as the Immaculate Conception, December 1). If she did not have Original Sin, she therefore did not have to suffer the consequences (celebrated as Dormition or Assumption of Mary, August 15). And as Christ is our King, then Mary is Queen Mother (and is honored on the day of the Queenship of Mary, August 22).

Following are other feasts of Mary:

- ✔ January 8: Our Lady of Prompt Succor
- ✔ February 11: Our Lady of Lourdes
- ✔ May 13: Our Lady of Fatima
- ✔ May 24: Our Lady Help of Christians
- ✔ May 31: Visitation of Our Lady
- ✔ June 27: Our Lady of Perpetual Help
- ✔ July 16: Our Lady of Mount Carmel
- ✔ September 8: The Nativity of Mary
- ✔ September 12: The Most Holy Name of Mary
- ✔ September 15: Our Lady of Sorrows
- ✔ October 7: Our Lady of the Most Holy Rosary
- ✔ October 8: Our Lady of Good Remedy
- ✔ November 21: Presentation of Our Lady
- ✔ December 12: Our Lady of Guadalupe

Feasts of the saints

The saints are celebrated according their distinction in life. The Litany of Saints distinguishes angels, patriarchs, prophets, apostles, evangelists, martyrs, bishops, confessors, priests, monks, hermits, virgins, and widows. Pope John Paul II highlighted another class of saints, holy men and women who are secular but attained holiness according to their state in life.

Devotion to the saints was developed in early Christian times during the severe persecution by the Roman Empire and the many martyrs. Early Christians would visit martyrs' tombs and often celebrate Mass there, bringing the faithful closer to the saint. Many people would pray to God that they receive the same strength exhibited by these martyrs.

The names of the saints were collected into a list called the *Roman Martyrology*. In the 16th century, Pope Gregory XIII published the first edition of this list with his reform of the calendar, the Gregorian calendar. The current edition, published in 2001, contains over 7,000 officially canonized saints, beatified and blessed, and the current liturgical calendar of saints takes its form from this list.

Not every country celebrates every saint. Local saints of a certain geographical area may only appear on the local Episcopal Conference Calendar. However, some saints have universal appeal.

The saints are seen as bringing us closer to God by what they said and did and their prayers for the faithful. Christian men and women have distinguished themselves in their dedication and service to Christ and his Church in their lives, some to the point of shedding their blood (martyrs). When Catholics venerate a saint, they are acknowledging and proclaiming the victorious grace of Christ at work in the holy person's life.

Chapter 4

Meet the Players: Liturgical Ministers

· ·

· ·

*J*ust as the Mass can be broken down into its various elements, those ministers offering the Mass, too, play different roles within the hierarchy of the Church. Of course you have the celebrant, who presides at the Mass. But other folks take part as well, including acolytes and non-ordained lay ministers. This chapter covers the functions of these different roles.

According to the Second Vatican Council, all the baptized faithful are required to participate in the Sacred and Divine Liturgy fully, actively, and consciously. The level and type of participation, however, is distinctly different for the ordained ministerial priesthood and for the common priesthood of the baptized. The *clergy* (ordained ministers: bishops, priests, and deacons) participate through the sacrament of Holy Orders at the altar, and the *lay faithful* (parishioners; common folk) participate through the sacrament of Baptism in the pews of the congregation. Non-ordained lay ministers also play a distinct role. This chapter covers the functions of all these different roles.

Identifying the Celebrants

The ordained celebrant participates in Mass in a very public, obvious, and official capacity. The *celebrant* is the clergyman (usually a priest but could also be a bishop) who offers the Mass. He represents the institutional and hierarchical Church founded by the Savior and entrusted to St. Peter and the Apostles. The celebrant's participation in the Mass is very prescribed, and his location in the sanctuary, visible vestments, words, actions, gestures, and posture are all part of his mode of participation.

Bishop

The principal celebrant at Mass is the bishop of the diocese, who is the chief teacher of the faith, shepherd of the faithful, and dispenser of the Sacraments. The General Instruction of the Roman Missal, known as GIRM, states in paragraphs 91 and 92,

> *The Eucharistic celebration is an action of Christ and the Church, namely, the holy people united and ordered under the Bishop . . . every legitimate celebration of the Eucharist is directed by the bishop, either in person or through priests who are his helpers.*

The episcopacy ("bishophood") contains the fullness of the priesthood — bishop, priest, and deacon. In the celebration of the Mass, the unity of the diocese is best expressed when the bishop gathers around the altar with his priests and deacon. As main celebrant, he emphasizes his role as the chief pastor of the diocese.

In the Ordinary form of the Roman Rite, bishops celebrate three types of Masses: Solemn, Medium, and Simple form.

✔ **Solemn form** is also known as Pontifical High Mass and is primarily celebrated at the bishop's cathedral in the diocese. Most Catholics are familiar with Solemn form if they attend Mass at the cathedral for the Chrism Mass, Holy Thursday, anniversary of the diocese, or the patronal feast of the cathedral. Solemn form can also be celebrated in a parish church when the bishop visits it to celebrate the anniversary of the parish or confer the Sacrament of Confirmation. In the Solemn form, the bishop wears a cassock, amice, alb, cincture dalmatic, stole, chasuble, pectoral cross, skull cap, ring, and miter and carries a crozier.

✔ **Medium form** is often celebrated by the bishop when he makes a pastoral visit to one of the parishes, chapels, or shrines within his diocese. In the Medium form, he wears everything mentioned above except the dalmatic.

✔ **Simple form** is celebrated on weekdays with no special celebration. In the Simple form, the bishop wears the same vestments as in the Solemn except that he omits the dalmatic, and the use of the miter and crosier are optional. The bishop isn't always the main celebrant at the Simple form of Mass; a priest may serve as celebrant on such occasions as the funeral of a parent of a priest or a significant anniversary of the priest. When not the main celebrant, the bishop wears choir dress, skullcap, and biretta. (At services outside of Mass with only one main celebrant, a bishop also wears choir dress.)

Priest

The General Instruction on the Roman Missal delineates the duties of the Priest. Number 93 states,

> *A priest also, who possess within the Church the power of Holy Orders to offer sacrifice in person of Christ stands for this reason at the head of the faithful people . . . presides over their prayer, proclaims the message of salvation to them, associates the people with himself in the offering of sacrifice through Christ in the Holy Spirit to God the Father.*

Through his priestly ordination, the priest has the power to offer the Sacrifice of the Mass, preach, bless, baptize, and anoint the sick. Although the priest, through the Sacrament of Holy Orders, has the power to forgive sins in the Sacrament of Penance, witness marriages, and confer the Sacrament of Penance, the bishop of the diocese must delegate or give the faculties to exercise these powers to the priest.

In the absence of the bishop, the priest dispenses the Sacraments. The priest celebrates Solemn or Simple Mass; Solemn Mass often takes place on solemnities, the patronal feast of the parish, and Sundays during the liturgical year. The principal Mass on Sunday is typically a Solemn Mass. Simple Masses often occur during the week and at the nonprincipal Masses on Sundays. Simple masses may include music but often exclude incense. They also often exclude processions, though at Sunday Masses processional and recessional processions are customary. Priests may wear a black cassock but must wear an alb, cincture, stole, and chasuble for all Holy Masses.

Deacon

Deacons function as ordained ministers and typically assist the priest at Mass. The name *deacon* comes from the Greek *diakonos,* meaning *minister* or *servant.* Paragraph 94 of the General Instruction of the Roman says,

> *At Mass the deacon has his own part in proclaiming the Gospel, in preaching God's word from time to time, in announcing the intentions of the Prayer of the Faithful, in ministering to the priest, in preparing the altar and serving the celebration of the Sacrifice, in distributing the Eucharist to the faithful, especially under the species of wine, and sometimes in giving directions regarding the peoples' gestures and posture.*

During the Mass, the celebrant is flanked by the deacons; the Deacon of the Word stands and sits to the left of the celebrant and the Deacon of the Eucharist stands and sits to the right. When only one deacon is present, he stands and sits to the celebrant's right. In addition to functioning at Mass, deacons can also baptize, witness marriages, bury the dead, and celebrate Evening Prayer.

Deacons may wear a cassock but must wear an alb and cincture and then place a stole over the top. Typically on Sundays and solemn feast days, deacons also wear a dalmatic over the alb and stole just as the priest and bishop wear the chasuble over their alb and stole.

The Non-Ordained Ministers

Clergy (ordained ministers) may be assisted in Sacred Worship by *non-ordained ministers,* certain lay parishioners and consecrated religious (monks, nuns, sisters, brothers, and so on). Some ministries, or roles, are part of the formation and process of becoming a deacon or priest. Other ministries are called *extraordinary* in that they function whenever ordinary ministers are not available to do the job. Men studying in the seminary or formation program leading toward Holy Orders (diaconate or priesthood) are admitted to ministries such as lector and acolyte (formerly known as minor orders) as part of their preliminary education.

Acolyte

The word *acolyte* comes from Greek and means *attendant* or *helper.* The acolyte's duty, as described in the General Instruction of the Roman Missal, is "to serve at the altar and assist the priest and deacon." At Mass, acolytes light altar candles, carry candles in procession, assist deacons and priests at the Mass, bring the wine and water to the altar at the offertory, ring bells during the consecration, help in distribution of Holy Communion by placing a paten under recipients' chin or hands, and wash the celebrant's fingers in purifying vessels after Holy Communion. A *formally instituted* acolyte (meaning a seminarian authorized by his bishop to help distribute Holy Communion) can also distribute Holy Communion as an extraordinary minister of Holy Communion.

Because Holy Orders (the roles of bishop, priest, and deacon) are reserved for baptized males, the *installed ministries* or *minor orders* of acolyte and lector are also only for men. In the present Code of Canon Law, the ministry of acolyte is open to all laymen (nonclergy male members of the congregation). In the reform of the liturgy after the Second Vatican Council, the pope intended to extend the role of acolyte beyond seminarians who are preparing for priesthood.

Although the office of acolyte is reserved for men, the function is not. In the Ordinary form of the Roman Rite, women with the consent of the local bishop and parish pastor may function as *readers* (similar to lectors) and as *altar servers* (similar to acolytes).

The proper vesture for an acolyte is cassock and surplice or an alb-like robe.

The Extraordinary form and the Eastern Catholic Church still retain the minor order of subdeacon, which ranks above acolyte, but in the Ordinary form of the Latin Rite, that office was taken over by the installed acolyte. Subdeacons in the Eastern Orthodox and Extraordinary form of the Latin Rite assist the deacon as the deacon in turn assists the celebrant. Subdeacons prepare by pouring the wine into the chalice, carrying the chalice with wine to the altar, and reading the Epistles before the people.

Extraordinary ministers of Holy Communion

Extraordinary ministers of Holy Communion are not instituted by the bishop; rather they have been given temporary permission from the bishop to distribute Holy Communion. At Mass they help the bishop, priest, and deacon (the ordinary ministers of Holy Communion) to distribute the Blessed Sacrament. The extraordinary ministers of Holy Communion also customarily transport the Eucharist to sick and shut-in members of the congregation, especially on Sundays.

The term *extraordinary* has a literal definition here; it refers to exceptional occasions when an ordinary minister of Holy Communion is unavailable. All members of the ordained clergy — bishops, priests and deacons — are considered ordinary ministers of Holy Communion and normally perform all the tasks of the extraordinary ministers. Religious men and women and laity can be authorized by the local bishop to be extraordinary ministers of Holy Communion.

To be eligible to become an extraordinary minister of Holy Communion, a layperson must have received all the Sacraments of Initiation (Baptism, Confirmation, and Holy Eucharist). Extraordinary ministers are trained and authorized by the bishop.

Vesting for an extraordinary Eucharistic minister is Sunday dress clothes. Some dioceses permit extraordinary Eucharistic ministers to wear albs. However, normally albs are reserved for the ordinary ministers.

Lector

The General Instruction of Roman Missal defines the lector as a congregant who is instituted to proclaim the readings from Sacred Scripture, with the exception of the Gospel. The lector may also announce the intentions for the Prayer of the Faithful and, in the absence of a psalmist, proclaim the psalm between the readings. The proper place for a lector to do Scripture readings at Mass is the ambo or pulpit, and he normally reads the General Intercessions at the lectern. When a deacon isn't present, the lector may carry the Book of the Gospels in procession.

Like acolytes, lectors are also formally installed ministers, and therefore the positions can be filled only by men from the lay congregation. Being a lector is also one of the steps toward entering the Holy Orders.

Reader

Laymen and laywomen may function as *readers* if an instituted lector is not present. Their duties are the same as lectors', and they are trained to read Scripture clearly and audibly. Like extraordinary Eucharistic ministers, commissioned readers must have received all the Sacraments of Initiation and, if married, have a valid marriage. Bishops authorize lay readers to function in the diocese for a period of one to three years. From time to time, priests may appoint a reader to read at a certain Mass without a formal commissioning.

Psalmist/cantor

The General Instruction for Roman Missal outlines the position of *psalmist,* or *cantor,* a layperson who sings the psalm in between the Old and New Testament readings. The cantor aids the congregation in singing. The cantor often works in conjunction with the choir. Psalmists can wear choir robes or Sunday dress.

Organist/music director

The *organist* can be the parish music director or someone else. The organist and/or music director must not only be well versed in music, but also have a working knowledge of Catholic liturgy and the liturgical calendar. In addition, the organist/music director is integral with the choir and works very closely with the clergy to plan the music to be sung at the liturgy. The organist can wear a cassock and a special sleeveless surplice to play the organ and conduct the choir, or may wear Sunday dress clothes.

Choir

The *choir* augments the singing of the congregation during Mass. The choir should never serve as a substitute for the congregation's singing, although at times the choir may sing pieces separate from the congregation. Members of the choir often wear choir robes or Sunday dress clothes.

Commentator

Not to be confused with the cantor, psalmist, or lector, the *commentator* provides the congregation with brief explanations and commentaries. Normally, the commentator speaks from the lectern where the cantor leads music. Commentators are not mandatory but are used at important celebrations for the sole purpose of introducing the particular celebration. They are appropriately employed at Solemn Pontifical Masses, dedications of churches, anniversaries of parishes, celebrations of priestly or religious vocations, and state functions in which Mass is being celebrated, as in the case in papal visits.

Altar servers

Most Catholics are generally familiar with the people who serve at Mass, the *altar servers*. They assist the celebrant at Mass and serve in place of instituted acolytes. They can have the following roles:

- **Thurifer:** A thurifer carries the censer to be used at Mass and also leads processions while gently swinging it so that billows of incense ascend to God. In addition, the thurifer can incense at the consecration of the Mass.

- **Crucifer:** The crucifer, the cross-bearer, carries the processional cross situated atop a long staff. He is employed anytime a procession takes place. When a thurifer is not present, he leads the procession.

- **Book bearer:** The book bearer holds the missal at Mass for the celebrant.

- **Episcopal attendants:** At celebrations when the bishop is present, two altar servers are employed to hold the miter and crosier during the ceremony. The server wears a special garment, the vimp, over his cassock and surplice in order not to soil the sacred vestures.

- **Servers:** Servers aid the celebrant at the altar.

None of these types of server is an instituted ministry, and as with extraordinary Eucharistic ministers and readers, laymen and laywomen can function as altar servers. Normally, altar servers wear a cassock and surplice. However, in some parishes, white albs are used.

Ushers

The General Instruction for the Roman Missal mentions ushers' role of preserving orderliness at Holy Mass:

> *Ushers take up the collection in the church. Those who, in some places, meet the faithful at the church entrance, lead them to appropriate places and direct processions.*

In addition to collecting the offertory giving of the faithful, ushers can distribute the bulletins after Mass, aid congregants who have physical disabilities, help direct the ordinary or extraordinary minister of the Eucharist to distribute Holy Communion, especially to disabled people, and serve as a reference for people attending the Mass.

Ushers often are the first people you meet when arriving at Mass. They can be very useful in disseminating valuable information. In special processions, ushers control the crowd and promote orderliness in the sacred march. In many parishes, ushers wear a uniform jacket with the parish coat-of-arms on the breast pocket so that the congregants can easily identify them.

Master of ceremonies

At Solemn Masses, a *master of ceremonies* is often used. He acts as a director of the flow of the liturgy.

Ordinary Catholics often come into contact with a master of ceremonies when the bishop comes to their parish for a specific celebration, such as conferring the Sacrament of Confirmation. The master of ceremonies can also be employed for solemn celebrations in which the bishop isn't present, such as the Easter Triduum.

Whether a priest, deacon, or layman, the master of ceremonies is well versed in the norms of the liturgy. He works closely with all the key players of the liturgy — the main celebrant, the musicians, and the servers. In complicated ceremonies in which many variables arise, especially when a bishop is the main celebrant, the master of ceremonies has to have a fine sense of judgment, well-organized thoughts, and, most of all, good coordination in order for the liturgy to proceed smoothly.

The master of ceremonies typically leads the rehearsals of servers and musicians. During the liturgy, he must be able to look ahead at the pending action in order to be prepared and on time with the elements and servers. The proper dress for master of ceremonies is usually a cassock and surplice. If the master of ceremonies is a priest or deacon, he wears a stole during Holy Communion.

Sacristan

The *sacristan* is very important to the liturgy. The General Instruction for the Roman Missal describes the sacristan as one "who carefully arranges the liturgical books, the vestments, and other things necessary in the celebration of Mass." He provides an invaluable service to the priest by setting up the Missal, placing on the credence table the chalice, ciboria, and cruets, making sure the church is opened and either the heat or air conditioning is turned on, and handling anything else that must be taken care of prior to the start of Mass.

A sacristan also takes charge of the care of the vestments and vessels of the church. This person makes sure the sacred linens, altar cloths, albs, and vestments are cleaned and plentiful; he makes sure that chalices, ciboria, and candlesticks are polished; and that flowers and other devotional items are in good condition and in their correct places.

Ministers in the Extraordinary Form of the Roman Mass

As you may expect, the functions of some of the ministers in the Extraordinary form of the Roman Mass are slightly different from those in the Ordinary form of the Mass. In addition, another type of minister, called a subdeacon, plays a role in the Mass.

Acolytes

In the Extraordinary form of the Roman Mass, acolytes function as they do in the Roman Rite. They are exclusively male and wear a cassock and surplice.

In the Eastern Catholic Church, acolytes serve in a similar fashion with some differences. They can carry liturgical fans, which are decorated with icons, prepare the hot water to be added to the chalice, and arrange the *antidoron* — unconsecrated bread that is distributed to the faithful after the Divine Liturgies and feast days.

Lectors

In the Extraordinary form of the Roman Rite and Eastern Churches, lectors are among the four minor orders in which a cleric is ordained. The lectors in these cases function like lectors of the Ordinary Rite. Because they belong to the minor orders, only males are to be admitted to this step. As in the case of the Ordinary Rite, lectors read the liturgical passages of Sacred Scripture.

Subdeacon

The role of *subdeacon* is one that has been omitted from the Ordinary Latin form (and the duties have been taken over by the acolyte), but it remains in use in the Extraordinary form of the Roman Rite and Byzantine Rite.

In Solemn High Masses, subdeacons sing the Epistle, hold the Book of the Gospels while the deacon proclaims it, and then carry the Book back when the deacon is finished. The subdeacon assists the priest and deacon in setting the altar. A subdeacon wears a cassock, amice, cincture, maniple, alb, and tunic, but no stole. He also wears a humeral veil while holding the paten from the Offertory to the recitation of the Our Father.

In the Byzantine Rite, the subdeacon's role is primarily that of servant to the bishop. During liturgies without the bishop present, he serves as the highest ranking minor clergy serving the liturgy. Normally he coordinates and leads the serving team. Subdeacons wear a sticharion, which functions like an alb in the Roman Rite, and the color corresponds to the liturgical season. In addition, the orarion is tied around his waist. This vestment distinguishes the priest, deacon, and subdeacon.

Deacon

In the Extraordinary form of the Roman Rite, deacons wear a cassock, amice, alb, cincture, maniple, stole, and dalmatic. The function of the deacon is similar to that in the Ordinary form of the Roman Rite, but it has some minor additions. In the Eastern Church, the deacon reads the Gospel, assists in distributing Holy Communion, incenses the icons and people, leads the litanies, calls people to prayer, and has a role in the dialogue of the Eucharistic Prayer. Like the subdeacon, he wears a sticharion and orarion. However, he also wears epimanikia, or cuffs.

Part II
Forms of Catholic Worship

"I'm not sure, but I think he just tweeted the homily."

In this part . . .

We explain the differences between East and West and Ordinary and Extraordinary forms of Catholic worship. And we look at the variety of words and gestures found within the one substantial essence of sacred liturgy.

Chapter 5

Ordinary Form of the Mass

· ·

In This Chapter

▶ Beginning the Mass with introductory rites

▶ Reading and speaking the Word of God in the Liturgy of the Word

▶ Preparing and serving communion in the Liturgy of the Eucharist

· ·

The Ordinary form of the Mass is just as its name implies — it's the normal or standard form of Mass with which most Catholics are generally familiar. It differs from the Extraordinary form and Tridentine Mass (sometimes called the Traditional Latin Mass), which developed during the time of Charlemagne in the 9th century and was made normative in the 16th century by the Council of Trent.

This chapter walks you through the Ordinary form of the Mass from the opening procession to the closing hymn.

We denote the most recent changes to the English translation of the Mass in **boldface** type.

Introductory Rites

The first part of the Ordinary Mass is the introductory rites. Mass typically starts with a procession from the back of the church, near the front door, down the middle aisle and into the sanctuary. During weekday Masses, particularly those with just a few congregants in attendance, the priest, deacon, and any servers may just enter the sanctuary from the sacristy.

An entrance hymn is sung during Sunday and Saturday evening Mass. When the procession and hymn are omitted, the Introit or Entrance Antiphon may be recited.

The Extraordinary form of the Roman Rite has the celebrant begin Mass by praying at the foot of the altar. The *Novus Ordo* Mass of Paul VI, now called the Ordinary form, eliminated those prayers and starts Mass with the priest making the sign of the cross and introducing the Mass from the altar or chair.

Greeting

The Mass formally begins when the priest blesses himself. He says, "In the name of the Father, and of the Son, and of the Holy Spirit" while tracing a cross over his torso: He places his right hand first on his forehead and then moves it down to his breast; then he moves his hand across to his far left and then to his far right. (This act is symbolized in this book by ✠.) The people make the same gesture and respond, "Amen."

Next, the celebrant can say simply "the Lord be with you" (taken from Ruth 2:4) or he may use a more elaborate address taken from St. Paul: "the grace of our Lord Jesus Christ, and the love of God, and the **communion** of the Holy Spirit be with you all." The one change here in the new version of the Mass is the replacement of the word *fellowship* with the more accurate word, *communion* (*communicatio* in Latin). Although similar in meaning, the word *communion* has much more theological impact. *Fellowship* expresses a fraternal relationship, whereas *communion* goes further to express an organic and necessary connection that transcends body and soul.

The big change to this greeting occurs in the people's response to the priest's invitation, "**the Lord be** with you." Previously, the congregation said "and also with you." Now the people give the literal translation of the Latin text *et cum spiritu tuo,* "**and with your spirit.**" This phrase is biblical; we see it in Galatians 6:18 and 2 Timothy 4:22 when St. Paul addresses a community of believers.

"And also with you" became too colloquial and pedestrian. It was like someone saying "yeah, you, too," which isn't appropriate, because the spirit of the priest or bishop who celebrates the Holy Mass is changed when he is ordained. He is made an *alter Christus* (another Christ) so he can celebrate the sacraments *in persona Christi* (in the person of Christ). (That is why the first-person singular pronoun is used at the consecration of the bread and wine: "this is *my* body . . . this is *my* blood" as the ordained minister speaks in the name and in the person of Christ himself by virtue of Holy Orders.) Now, by saying "and with your spirit," the congregation affirms the doctrine that the priest and bishop are ordained to represent Christ whenever the Sacred Worship is given to God.

When the bishop is the main celebrant at Mass, he begins with "Peace be with you," as found in John 20:26. However, a priest is only allowed to say "the Lord be with you." This is a subtle way the Sacred Liturgy identifies the distinction between the bishop and the priest (who represents the local bishop at every parish celebration of the Holy Mass).

The unalterable importance of the altar

The altar is not only the place where the Holy Sacrifice of the Mass is offered, it also represents and symbolizes Christ himself. At the beginning of Mass, the altar is always reverenced by the clergy who are concelebrating by bowing before it and kissing it before going to their respective places. Before the introductory rites start, the main celebrant, escorted by one or two deacons, may incense the altar in a very dignified and elegant movement around it. The altar is also reverenced with a kiss at the end of Mass.

All immovable altars must have altar stones, slabs of stone about the size of a netbook computer. The altar stone is placed on a full size altar (made of marble or wood). Under the stone are relics of one or more of the ancient martyrs. Even though the altar is covered with linens during Mass, the bread and wine are placed on top of the linens over the altar stone. The idea is that Mass will be celebrated over the remains of the martyrs, just as was done for three centuries when the early Christians had to worship in the catacombs to escape Roman persecution.

Rite of Sprinkling or Penitential Rite

Either the Rite of Sprinkling or the Penitential Rite takes place after the greeting. During Easter time and particularly at Pentecost, the Rite of Blessing and Sprinkling holy water is an appropriate part of the Mass. The holy water reminds the congregation of the waters of Baptism and the invocation of the Holy Spirit.

Water is blessed by the priest, and he may add exorcised salt, because holy water is believed to be a potent weapon against the Devil. The priest then takes a bucket of holy water and sprinkles with a reed of hyssop or a metal aspergillum (special device to hold a few ounces of holy water with holes at the end to allow drops to flow out into congregation).

The Penitential Rite is used on most Sundays and weekdays. If a deacon is present, he may introduce three petitions to which the congregation responds: "Lord, have mercy; Christ, have mercy; Lord, have mercy."

Although in no way a replacement or substitute for individual celebration of the sacrament of Penance and Reconciliation (confession), the Penitential Rite still allows a communal admission of personal sin and the need for divine mercy and forgiveness.

Confiteor

The priest may choose to invoke the *Confiteor* (Latin for "I confess"). This ancient prayer for forgiveness may be used in the confessional during the sacrament of Penance and Reconciliation, but when said at Mass, it does not mean that the sins of the congregants have been absolved. It is not a private or individual confession; rather, it is a communal admission that as human beings, we are all sinners, we all make mistakes, and we all can and ought to do and be better.

> I confess to Almighty God
> and to you, my brothers and sisters,
> that I have greatly sinned,
> in my thoughts and in my words,
> in what I have done and in what I have failed to do,
> **through my fault, through my fault,**
> **through my most grievous fault;**
> therefore I ask blessed Mary ever-virgin,
> all the angels and saints,
> and you, my brothers and sisters,
> to pray for me to the Lord our God.

The big change here is the inclusion of the triple *mea culpa* (Latin for "my fault"), whereas in the former English translation it was only said once.

Kyrie

The Church has used for millennia the ancient petition: "Lord, have mercy; Christ, have mercy; Lord, have mercy." It's called the *Kyrie*.

Kyrios is Greek for *Lord. Christos* is Greek for *Anointed One* (*Messiah* in Hebrew). The original Greek text retained in the Latin Mass is *Kyrie, eleison; Christe, eleison; Kyrie, eleison.*

Gloria

On Sundays (except during Advent and Lent) and holy days, the Gloria is said, chanted, or sung by the celebrant and congregation. It begins with the angelic salutation given to the shepherds at the first Christmas when Jesus was born in Bethlehem, "Glory to God in the highest" (*Gloria in excelsis Deo* in Latin), as found in Luke 2:14.

Just as the Penitential Rite is intended to make congregants contrite and soberly repentant, the Gloria is used to uplift the congregation as a reminder of the hope, salvation, and redemption brought by God's grace. The Gloria is suspended during the penitential seasons of Advent and Lent because these seasons are meant to accentuate sadness for sin and the desire for true repentence, but it returns with Christmas and Easter.

"Peace to his people on earth" has been changed to **"on earth peace to people of good will."** This phrase conforms more accurately to the Latin text *(in terra pax hominibus bonae voluntatis).* The phrase "Lord God, Heavenly King, Almighty God and Father, we worship you, we give you thanks, we praise you for your glory" now reads **"We praise you, we bless you, we adore you, we glorify you, we give you thanks for your great glory, Lord God, heavenly King, O God, Almighty Father."** The meaning is the same, it just has a more accurate sentence structure.

Opening Prayer

The Opening Prayer sets the tone for the liturgical act of divine worship. It reminds the assembly that adoration of God is directed to the Father through the Son and in the Holy Spirit. In other words, it is always Trinitarian because the one God is in Three Persons.

Liturgy of the Word

The next section of the Mass is called the Liturgy of the Word because the emphasis is on the written and spoken Word of God. It includes multiple readings, a sermon, the Creed, and a prayer.

Rather than having Bibles in the pews for the people to follow along, many Catholic parishes have what is known as a *missalette,* an abbreviated form of the lectionary. The lectionary, a liturgical book (see Chapter 11), is the official ceremonial book containing Sacred Scripture. It is the same as the Bible in that it contains only biblical passages; the only difference is the order in which the passages are listed. Instead of being arranged somewhat chronologically, the lectionary's passages are arranged by their assignment in the liturgical year. The Church assigns specific passages from the Old and New Testaments for every weekday, Sunday, and holy day, and the weekly missalette includes the relevant passages from the lectionary for each Mass.

First reading

While everyone is seated, a reader or lector walks up to the ambo or pulpit and reads aloud the assigned passage from Sacred Scripture. Normally, the first reading comes from one of the 46 books of the

Old Testament in the Catholic Bible. The passage is prefaced by the phrase "a reading from . . ." and then the name of the book of the Bible is mentioned.

The precise chapter and verse of the reading are not mentioned. The Bible itself was originally written without any chapter or verse identification. In fact, the Bible had no chapters until 1248 when Archbishop Stephen Langton assigned divisions, and no verse numbers until Robert Stephanus worked out versification in 1555.

When the reader or lector comes to the end of the passage, he or she says "The word of the Lord" and the people respond "Thanks be to God." The book (lectionary) is not to be lifted up as the person says "the word of the Lord," because the spoken and proclaimed word is being affirmed more than the written text.

Protestant Bibles have the same 39 canonical books as Catholic Bibles but do not have the other seven deuterocanonical books (Baruch, Maccabees 1 and 2, Tobit, Judith, Ecclesiasticus, and Wisdom). These books originated in the Greek version of the Hebrew Bible (called the Septuagint), which goes back to between 250 and 150 BC. Christian Bibles had all 46 books until Martin Luther and the other reformers removed the deuterocanonical books (called *Apocrypha* by Protestants) in the 16th century.

Psalm

The Bible includes 150 psalms, and many of them are incorporated into the Sacred Liturgy of the Ordinary form. A psalm is always included in weekday and Sunday Masses.

The only psalms not used in divine worship are the curse or deprecatory psalms, which are requests for harsh retribution against one's enemies. Although they're considered equally inspired revealed Scripture, they don't make for elegant worship of the Almighty.

Either a cantor sings or chants the psalm or a lay reader or lector reads (recites) the verses of the psalm. The congregation repeats the response.

Second reading

The second Scripture reading from the Bible comes from the New Testament. Usually it's an Epistle, or sometimes a passage from the Acts of the Apostles or from the Book of Revelation (Apocalypse).

Weekday Masses don't include this second reading, but Sundays and holy days always do.

Like the first reading, the second is introduced merely by the name of the Book and not by chapter and verse. At the end of the passage, the reader says "The word of the Lord" and the people respond "Thanks be to God."

Gospel

Before the Gospel is proclaimed, the Alleluia is sung or chanted. (It may be omitted during weekday Masses.) The entire congregation stands and stays standing during the proclamation of the Gospel.

If a deacon is present, he takes the Book of Gospels to the ambo, or pulpit. When no deacon is present, the priest proclaims the sacred text. Although both male and female laity and religious can do the first and second readings, only an ordained minister (deacon, priest, or bishop) can read the Gospel at Mass.

If a deacon reads the Gospel, he first goes to the bishop or priest and receives the following blessing:

> May the Lord be in your heart and on your lips that you may proclaim his Gospel worthily and well, in the name of the Father and of the Son ✠ and of the Holy Spirit, amen.

The Gospel is introduced:

> *Deacon/Priest:* The Lord be with you.
>
> *People:* **And with your spirit.**
>
> *Deacon/Priest:* A reading from the holy Gospel according to [Name of the book of the Bible].
>
> *People:* Glory to you, O Lord.

Then after the Gospel is proclaimed:

> *Deacon/Priest:* The Gospel of the Lord.
>
> *People:* Praise to you, Lord Jesus Christ.
>
> *Deacon/Priest:* Through the words of the Gospel may our sins be wiped away.

The deacon (or priest) reverences the book with a kiss before the last line is said quietly. Like the lectionary, the Book of Gospels is not lifted up, because the proclaimed spoken word is what's being affirmed at this moment, not the written text.

On Sundays and solemn feasts, the Book of Gospels can be incensed prior to reading it aloud.

Homily

A *homily* is a sermon preached by an ordained cleric at Mass or any Sacred Liturgy. While canon law allows laity and religious to preach (outside of Mass) in some very rare occasions, only a deacon, priest, or bishop can preach the homily during Mass. Mass includes a homily on all Sundays and holy days of obligation. Parishes are encouraged to include a homily in weekday Masses during Advent, Lent, Easter Season, and on feast days and festive occasions when more people than usual come to Mass.

Usually the celebrant preaches the homily, but he can entrust it to a concelebrant or to the deacon. Special circumstances may also allow a priest or bishop who is present but who is not concelebrating to preach the homily.

The homily may explain the Scripture passages just read or give moral or doctrinal instruction, especially on particular feasts. It also may bring to light certain spiritual aspects for later meditation and consideration.

Profession of Faith (Creed)

On all Sundays and holy days, the Creed must be recited or sung by the celebrant and congregation. A *creed* is a summary of doctrines written in a format meant to be easy to memorize. Long ago when many people were unable to read and write, most learning was done by sheer memory. People memorized passages, chapters, and even whole books of the Bible centuries before they were written down.

Think of the Creed like a blueprint, recipe, or formula for the beliefs of the Catholic Church. The Creed says what is important to Catholic Christianity in terms of basic tenets, which is why it's so important for believers to know and understand the Creed. Every official doctrine of Catholicism is somehow connected to or derived from it.

Some background on the Creed

The current Creed (also called the Profession of Faith) goes back to the year AD 325. At that time, the heresy of Arianism was rampaging Christendom. Arius was a cleric who maintained that Jesus was indeed human but not quite divine. He insisted that Christ had a similar but not the same divine substance as God the Father. In other words, he portrayed God the Son as a hybrid of divinity and humanity. Arianism is the false doctrine that Jesus Christ is not equal to God. He is the highest creature God made, higher than angels or men, but not equal to the Lord God.

Christianity, however, tenaciously clings to the belief that Jesus is not like Mr. Spock, who is half human and half alien. Christians believe that Jesus is true God and true man. Rather than being 50/50, he is 100 percent human and 100 percent divine. That is the mystery of the Incarnation.

The Creed, developed at the Council of Nicea by the bishops of the world in union with the pope in Rome, clearly defined that Christ is God the Son and has the same substance (*homoousios* in Greek, or *consubstantialem* in Latin) as the God the Father. Arius's notion that Christ only had a *similar* substance (*homoiousios* in Greek) was condemned as heresy.

Recent updates to the English translation

When the Mass was translated into English in 1970, the word *consubstantialem* in Latin was rendered as "one in being." The revised translation now retains the more accurate word **consubstantial,** meaning "of the same substance," to convey that God the Son is equal to God the Father (and God the Holy Spirit) because a single divine nature is shared by all three divine Persons of the Trinity.

Another tweak in the text is the phrase **"I believe"** to replace "We believe." The official Latin uses the word *credo,* which is first person singular (I). Were it first person plural (we), it would use the word *credimus.* The emphasis is merely that each believer must affirm for himself that he personally accepts and embraces the faith. While the Church is always a community of believers, each member retains his identity as an individual. Catholic Christians are taught to cultivate personal relationships with God as well as communal relationships with their neighbors.

"Born of the Virgin Mary" has been changed to **"was incarnate of the Virgin Mary."** This new phrase is a more accurate translation of the Latin text *incarnatus est,* and it conveys the doctrine that Jesus's human nature began not at his birth but from the very first moment of his conception within the womb of his mother, Mary.

Catholics show reverence for the Incarnation by bowing at the phrase "and became man." On Christmas (December 25) and the Feast of the Annunciation (March 25) the custom is to genuflect rather than bow.

Which creed?

The most ancient Christian creed (profession of faith) is the Apostles' Creed. While not composed by the original 12 Apostles themselves, this summary of Christian belief can be traced as far back as the Apostolic era — the time in human history when the Apostles or their immediate disciples were still alive (late first and early second century AD). The second most ancient creed is the Nicene Creed, composed in AD 325 at the Council of Nicea. It took the Apostles' Creed and elaborated on it, especially in regards to Christology (the theology of Jesus' humanity and divinity).

The Apostles' Creed was said at Mass until it was replaced by the Nicene Creed, which is longer and has more substance and depth. Both are still learned and prayed, although only the Nicene Creed is prayed at Mass. The Apostles' Creed is prayed to begin the Rosary.

Two other translations have been altered in the Creed for greater accuracy. "He suffered, died and was buried" now reads **"he suffered death and was buried."** The phrase "on the third day he rose again in fulfillment of the Scriptures" has been changed to **"and rose again on the third day in accordance** (*secundum* in Latin) **with the Scriptures."**

Prayer of the Faithful (General Intercessions)

After the Creed on Sundays or after the homily on weekdays, the Prayer of the Faithful follows. The General Instruction on the Roman Missal (#69) says,

> *In the Prayer of the Faithful, the people respond in a certain way to the word of God which they have welcomed in faith and, exercising the office of their baptismal priesthood, offer prayers to God for the salvation of all.*

If a deacon is present, he prays aloud the intercessions; otherwise, in his absence, it is done by a lay reader or the priest celebrant. The petitions presented for prayer should always try to incorporate these concepts:

✔ The needs of the Church, especially the pope and local bishop

✔ Public authorities and the salvation of the whole world

> ✔ Those burdened by any kind of difficulty, especially the poor and the sick
>
> ✔ The local community, especially the members of the parish and those preparing for sacraments
>
> ✔ The faithful departed and the souls in Purgatory

Liturgy of the Eucharist

After the Liturgy of the Word is the part of Mass called the Liturgy of the Eucharist. It is the heart and soul of the Mass, with the zenith being the consecration of the bread and wine into the Precious Body and Blood of Christ.

Preparation of Gifts (Offertory)

On Sundays and holy days, someone from the congregation usually brings the gifts (bread and wine that will become the Holy Eucharist) down the main aisle to the deacon or priest at the altar. On weekdays when the number of people attending is very small, the priest may just leave them on a side table before Mass. The Latin (Roman) tradition is to use only unleavened bread, whereas the Byzantine and other Eastern Catholic Churches use bread cooked with yeast.

The deacon prepares the altar; if he's not present, it's done by the priest. Taking bread and holding it over the altar, the priest celebrant says:

> Blessed are you, Lord God of all creation, for through your goodness we have received the bread we offer you: fruit of the earth and work of human hands; it will become for us the bread of life.

The people respond:

> Blessed be God forever.

Then the deacon or priest pours wine into the chalice(s), saying:

> By the mystery of this water and wine may we come to share in the divinity of Christ who humbled himself to share in our humanity.

Then taking the chalice and holding it over the altar, the priest says:

> Blessed are you, Lord God of all creation, for through your goodness we have received the wine we offer you: fruit of the vine and work of human hands; it will become our spiritual drink.

The people respond:

> Blessed be God forever.

The priest bows and quietly prays:

> With humble spirit and contrite heart may we be accepted by you, O Lord, and may our sacrifice in your sight this day be pleasing to you, Lord God.

Then he washes his fingers, saying:

> Wash me, O Lord, from my iniquity and cleanse me from my sin.

Lastly, the priest says:

> Pray, brethren (brothers and sisters), that **my sacrifice and yours** may be acceptable to God, the Almighty Father.

The change here is the distinction between the sacrifice of the priest (my) and that of the people (yours), whereas in the older translation it merely said *our sacrifice*.

Then the people respond:

> May the Lord accept the sacrifice at your hands for the praise and glory of his name, for our good and the good of all his **holy** Church.

The only change here is the addition of the adjective *holy* (*sanctae* in Latin).

Offertory Prayer

Each Sunday and holy day is assigned a specific prayer to be said over the gifts. On weekdays the celebrant may choose from options. The priest says this prayer, and the people respond with the usual "amen."

Preface and Sanctus

This part of the Mass precedes the Eucharistic prayer and begins as follows:

> *Priest:* The Lord be with you.
>
> *People:* **And with your spirit.**
>
> *Priest:* Lift up your hearts.
>
> *People:* We lift them up to the Lord.
>
> *Priest:* Let us give thanks to the Lord our God.
>
> *People:* **It is right and just.**

The phrase "the Lord be with you" previously had the response "and also with you," but now the response is **"and with your spirit."** The other change is the last response. Previously, it had been "It is right to give him thanks and praise." Now it reads **"It is right and just"** to conform to the official Latin text.

Next, the following lines are either sung or spoken:

> Holy, Holy, Holy Lord God of **hosts.**
> Heaven and earth are full of your glory.
> Hosanna in the highest.
> Blessed is he who comes in the name of the Lord.
> Hosanna in the highest.

The only change here is the replacement of **hosts** for the previous phrase "power and might." Again, this simply conforms the text to the official Latin.

Eucharistic Prayer

At this point, the most important part of the Mass begins: the Eucharistic Prayer. The Eucharistic Prayer has several components to it.

> ✔ **Thanksgiving:** The word *Eucharist* comes from the Greek word for thanksgiving. The priest first gives thanks to God on behalf of the people for all the blessings and gifts the Lord has given. This gratitude is expressed primarily in the Preface prayer of the Mass (the introduction to the Eucharistic Prayer in which the priest begins with "the Lord be with you" and also says "let us give thanks to the Lord our God").

- ✔ **Acclamation:** The congregation affirms their gratitude by singing the thrice-holy angelic hymn, the *Sanctus* (Holy).

- ✔ **Epiclesis:** The priest acting in *Persona Christi* invokes the Holy Spirit to come down from heaven and bless the gifts of bread and wine. This invocation is expressed physically by the stretching out of the celebrant's arms and hands over the gifts.

- ✔ **Institution narrative and Consecration:** The holiest part of the Mass is when the priest acting in *Persona Christi* uses the exact same words used by Jesus at the Last Supper and speaks them over the bread and wine, thereby consecrating them. The prayer includes the narrative of the Last Supper where Jesus took bread and wine and said "This is my body . . . this is my blood."

- ✔ **Anamnesis:** The anamnesis recalls and reaffirms Christ's command to "do this in memory of me" and the recollection of the mystery of Jesus's Passion, Death, and Resurrection.

- ✔ **Offering:** The priest offers the Son *to* the Father *with* the Holy Spirit on behalf of the entire human race and the whole world. Jesus offers himself to God the Father on behalf of the human race. The priest represents both mankind and Christ, so he is able to mystically offer the Son to the Father for us.

- ✔ **Intercessions:** The priest requests that the fruits of the sacrifice be applied to both the living and the dead.

- ✔ **Final doxology:** The glory of God, Father, Son, and Holy Spirit is manifested in this solemn prayer, which is affirmed by the people in their response of "amen."

The Eucharistic Prayer is the chief of the priestly prayers of the Mass. Only the ordained priest or bishop can say them, because only he has the ordained power and authority to consecrate bread and wine into the Body and Blood of Christ.

The previous prayer was missing some of the elegant and beautiful vocabulary the Church used to describe holy and sacred things and persons, like Jesus himself. Hence the revised translation inserts words like *holy, venerable,* and *sacred* where the previous version omitted them.

One significant change among several incidental ones in the Eucharistic Prayer occurs at the Consecration itself.

Over the bread the priest says the first half of *the most important words of the entire missal:*

> **Take this, all of you, and eat of it, for this is my Body, which will be given up for you.**

Over the wine the priest completes the most important part of the Missal:

> **Take this, all of you, and drink from it, for this is the chalice of my Blood, the blood of the new and eternal covenant, which will be poured out for you and for many for the forgiveness of sins. Do this in memory of me.**

Previously, the phrase had been "for you and for *all,*" but now it's more conforming to the Latin, which says "for you and for **many**" *(pro vobis et pro **multis**).*

Memorial Acclamation

After the consecration of the bread and wine into the Body and Blood of Christ, the priest continues the Eucharistic Prayer, saying:

> The mystery of faith.

The people respond based on which option the choir or celebrant chooses:

> We proclaim your Death, O Lord, and profess your Resurrection until you come again.

Or

> When we eat this bread and drink this cup, we proclaim your Death, O Lord, until you come again.

Or

> Save us, Savior of the world, for by your cross and Resurrection, you have set us free.

After the acclamation, the priest continues the Eucharistic Prayer with intercessions to the Virgin Mary and the saints on behalf of the Church and all her members. Particular mention can be made for the deceased person for whom the Mass is being offered.

Doxology and Great Amen

A doxology is a short hymn of praise to God. Following the Eucharistic Prayer is a doxology to the Triune God (Father, Son, and Holy Spirit) as a sign of public thanks for the consecration of the bread and wine into the Body and Blood of Christ. It is also appreciation for the Holy Sacrifice of the Mass where the Son was offered to Father with the Holy Spirit for the salvation of souls.

The priests concludes the Eucharistic Prayer:

> Through him, and with him, and in him, O God, Almighty Father, in the unity of the Holy Spirit, all glory and honor is yours, forever and ever.

The people respond, "Amen."

Pater Noster (Our Father or Lord's Prayer)

When asked by his disciples how to pray, Jesus gave them the Lord's Prayer (also called the *Our Father*). This prayer is said before the reception of Holy Communion, which is truly our daily bread:

> Our Father, who art in heaven, hallowed be thy name; thy kingdom come, thy will be done on earth as it is in heaven. Give us this day our daily bread, and forgive us our trespasses, as we forgive those who trespass against us; and lead us not into temptation, but deliver us from evil.

"For thine is the kingdom, the power, and the glory, forever and ever" is not said at the end of the prayer, because it was never part of the original passage in Matthew 6:13. It is not in the original Greek or in the Latin of St. Jerome (who in AD 400 translated and edited the first one-volume Christian Bible from Hebrew and Greek into Latin). This closing phrase is found in the King James Version of the Bible, however, and is common to Protestant Christians around the world.

However, Catholic Christians are used to saying it at Mass after the priest says (after the Lord's Prayer):

> Deliver us, Lord, we pray, from every evil, graciously grant peace in our days, that, by the help of your mercy, we may be always free from sin and safe from all distress, as we await the blessed hope and the coming of our Savior, Jesus Christ.

Then the people respond:

> For the kingdom, the power, and the glory are yours now and forever.

Sign of Peace

After the *Pater Noster* the priest says, "The peace of the Lord be with you always" and the congregation replies, "And with your spirit." The priest or deacon may then invite everyone to share a sign of peace.

Originally called the Kiss of Peace, this gesture of fraternity or brotherly love flows from the truth that all men and women are made in the image and likeness of God and by Baptism we become brothers and sisters in Christ. It can be done as a solemn and reverent gesture as done in the Extraordinary form or as a simple hand-shake or small bow while placing both hands on shoulder of the other person. Waving and bear-hugs are not appropriate forms.

Fraction Rite — Agnus Dei (Lamb of God)

Agnus Dei is Latin for *Lamb of God,* and while this prayer is said or sung aloud by the congregation, the priest breaks (fractions) the host he just consecrated into two equal parts. Then he places a small fragment into the chalice containing the consecrated wine (Precious Blood). This mingling of the two symbolizes the unity of the Body and Blood of Christ in every drop and every fragment.

The priest holds the consecrated host over the chalice of consecrated wine and says:

> Behold the Lamb of God; behold him who takes away the sins of the world. **Blessed** are those called to the supper **of the Lamb.**

"Of the Lamb" is newly included, but **blessed** is a replacement for *happy*.

The people respond:

> Lord, I am not worthy **that you should enter under my roof,** but only say the word and **my soul** shall be healed.

Here, the change is the addition of words. Previously, the response was "I am not worthy to receive you, but only say the word and I shall be healed." Now it references Matthew 8:8 where a Roman centurion tells Jesus, "I am not worthy to have you enter under my roof."

The other new element is the addition of the word **soul** instead of just saying *I.* Spiritual healing of the soul is the preeminent objective here.

Communion Rite

The priest consumes the host first and then drinks some of the Precious Blood from the chalice. He then gives a host to the deacon, and after he eats it, the priest gives him the chalice to drink. Then the two of them begin to administer Holy Communion to the altar servers and, if needed, to the extraordinary ministers of Holy Communion. Finally, the congregation comes forward and, either standing in a line or kneeling at the altar rail or *prie dieux* (kneeler for one person), receives first the consecrated host and may also be offered the chalice of Precious Blood (consecrated wine).

The minister says, "The Body [or the Blood] of Christ" and the communicant responds, "Amen."

Prayer after Communion

Just as the Opening Prayer begins Mass and the Prayer over the Gifts is in the middle, a Prayer after Communion completes the rite. Each Sunday and holy day has an assigned prayer. It usually ties together the themes mentioned beforehand and asks for divine assistance to live out the Christian life.

At the end of the prayer, the people say, "Amen."

Concluding Rite

The priest gives the final blessing at the end of the Mass:

> May Almighty God bless you, the Father ✠, the Son, and the Holy Spirit.

Then comes the dismissal:

> *Deacon/Priest:* Go in Peace [or go forth], the Mass is ended.
>
> *People:* Thanks be to God.

On Sundays and holy days, a recessional hymn is usually sung as the priest, deacon, and other ministers process from the sanctuary to the back of the church.

Chapter 6

Extraordinary Form: Traditional Latin Mass

*N*o matter what it's called — Traditional Latin Mass (TLM), Tridentine Mass, Old Mass, Extraordinary form of the Roman Rite — this form of Catholic Mass has been around almost as long as the Church itself.

Introducting the Extraordinary Form of the Mass

The Latin Mass goes back to the time of the Roman caesars. Thanks to the missionary efforts of SS. Peter and Paul, many Jews and pagans in Rome converted to Christianity. What is today called the Extraordinary form of the Roman Rite is the offspring of that early period of Church history when there was one church and one state.

Discovering the origins of the Extraordinary form

The Roman Mass took on more prestige during the time of Charlemagne, who was crowned Holy Roman Emperor by Pope Leo III on Christmas day, AD 800. As the secular ruler of a united Christendom, Charlemagne wanted stability and uniformity throughout the realm. One way of doing that was to have a standard Sacred Worship so Mass would be the same anywhere and everywhere within the empire.

Nevertheless, over time nation states emerged and monarchs wanted to be more and more independent. When Martin Luther in Germany and John Calvin in Switzerland began the Protestant Reformation in the 16th century, vernacular (the common, local languages) entered Sacred Worship.

The Council of Trent (1545–1563) was convened to address the issues and concerns raised by the Reformers. One response was to make sure the Holy Mass was meticulously preserved and protected from any attempts to dilute or distort Catholic doctrine especially on the priesthood, the Real Presence in the Holy Eucharist. The Mass of Pope St. Pius (otherwise known as the Tridentine Mass or Traditonal Latin Mass) became the normal and staple form of Catholic worship for Europe and the New World.

Replacing and restoring the Extraordinary form

For more than four hundred years the Tridentine Mass was the typical form of Catholic worship (except in Eastern Europe and the Middle East where Eastern Catholic liturgy was the common form). When Pope John XXIII convened the Second Vatican Council (1962–1965), one of the goals was to present the timeless truths of faith to the modern world in a new voice. Same message but new medium.

The Mass that came out of Vatican II, first called the Mass of Paul VI (who was the pope who closed the Council), was later called the *Novus Ordo* (New Order) to distinguish it from the previous version, then called the Tridentine or the Traditional Latin Mass. The biggest innovation was the introduction of the vernacular (common tongue) into the Mass.

The Ordinary form (the New Mass) became normative around the world in 1970. However, some Catholics, clergy and laity alike, felt that the vernacular language and the changing of the posture of the priest (from facing east, called *ad orientem,* to facing the people, *versus populum*) were not conducive to their spiritual needs. So in 1988 Pope John Paul II issued *Ecclesia Dei,* which permitted priests to celebrate the old Mass in the old tongue and in the old way. Pope Benedict XVI went further and issued *Summorum Pontificum* in 2007, which allowed any and all priests the ability to celebrate the TLM.

Celebrating the Extraordinary Mass today

Not all parishes offer the Extraordinary form, but most dioceses have at least one parish where all the Masses are in Latin and according to the 1962 Missal. (The rest and majority of parishes are using the vernacular Ordinary form according to the 2002 Missal.) The Extraordinary Mass can take the following forms:

- ✔ **Low Mass (Missa Privata):** Mass in which the priest does not chant the proper parts but quietly reads (recites) them instead

- ✔ **High Mass (Solemn High Mass):** Sung Mass assisted by sacred ministers (a deacon and subdeacon)

- ✔ **Missa Cantata:** Sung Mass without any assisting sacred ministers (no deacon or subdeacon)

- ✔ **Pontifical Mass:** Mass celebrated by a bishop (or an archbishop or cardinal)

- ✔ **Pontifical High Mass (Solemn Pontifical Mass):** Mass celebrated by a bishop and assisted by a deacon and subdeacon

- ✔ **Apostolic (Papal) Pontifical High Mass:** Mass celebrated by the pope and assisted by a deacon, subdeacon, and cleric of the Eastern Catholic Church, who chants the Epistle and Gospel in Greek (after they're chanted in Latin by Western Catholic clerics)

Most parishes in the United States and Canada that have the Extraordinary form do either the Low Mass or the Missa Cantata. The Pontifical Mass is rare.

A Rundown of the Entire Mass

In the sections that follow, we describe from start to finish the parts of the Extraordinary form.

The Mass is divided into two main parts, Mass of Catechumens and Mass of Faithful. This division is similar to the Ordinary form designation of the Liturgy of the Word and Liturgy of the Eucharist.

The *Ordinary of the Mass (Ordo Missae)* is the set of liturgical texts that remain constant and invariable. The passages from Sacred Scripture and the prayers specific for the day or season do change and are listed in the Roman Missal for the celebrant's convenience.

The following abbreviations are used to help distinguish the various participants in the Holy Sacrifice of the Mass according to the Extraordinary form of the Roman Rite:

P. Priest

D. Deacon

L. Lector/subdeacon

S. Server/congregation

C. Choir

V. Versicle

R. Response

Asperges (Sprinkling of holy water)

The priest sprinkles holy water over the congregation while this hymn *(asperges me)* is sung/chanted. This act symbolizes the purifying waters of Baptism that wash away Original Sin and venial sins.

P. Asperges me,

P. Thou shalt sprinkle me,

C. Domine, hyssopo, et mundabor: lavabis me, et super nivem dealbabor. Miserere mei, Deus, secundum magnam misericordiam tuam.

C. Lord, with hyssop, and I shall be cleansed; thou shalt wash me, and I shall be made whiter than snow. Have mercy on me, O God, according to thy great mercy.

V. Gloria Patri, et Filio, et Spiritui Sancto.

V. Glory be to the Father, and to the Son, and to the Holy Spirit.

R. Sicut erat in principio, et nunc, et semper, et in saecula saeculorum. Amen.

R. As it was in the beginning, is now, and ever shall be, world without end. Amen.

(Antiphon:) Asperges me, Domine, hyssopo, et mundabor: lavabis me, et super nivem dealbabor.

(Antiphon:) Thou shalt sprinkle me, Lord, with hyssop, and I shall be cleansed; thou shalt wash me, and I shall be made whiter than snow.

Mass of the Catechumens

Before entering the sanctuary, the priest and altar server(s) say preparatory prayers to show great awe of and reverence to the sanctuary where the Holy Sacrifice will take place. They need to adequately prepare for the worship rather than rushing into it too hastily, clumsily, or casually.

Prayers at the foot of the altar

The priest begins by making the sign of the cross and reciting the prayers of Psalm 42:

P. In nomine Patris, et Filii, et Spiritus Sancti.

P. In the Name of the Father, and of the Son, ✠ and of the Holy Spirit.

S. Amen.

S. Amen

P. Introibo ad altare Dei

P. I will go to the altar of God.

S Ad Deum qui laetificat juventutem meam.

S. To God, the joy of my youth.

P. Judica me, Deus, et discerne causam meam de gente non sancta: ab homine iniquo et doloso erue me.

P. Do me justice, O God, and fight my fight against an unholy people: Rescue me from the wicked and deceitful man.

S. Quia tu es, Deus, fortitudo mea: quare me repulisti, et quare tristis incedo, dum affligit me inimicus?

S. For thou, O God, art my strength: Why hast thou forsaken me? And why do I go about in sadness, while the enemy harasses me?

P. Emitte lucem tuam et veritatem tuam: ipsa me deduxerunt et adduxerunt in montem sanctum tuum, et in tabernacula tua.

P. Send forth thy light and thy truth: for they have led me and brought me to thy holy hill and thy dwelling place.

S. Et introibo ad altare Dei: ad Deum qui laetificat juventutem meam.

S. And I will go to the altar of God: to God, the joy of my youth.

P. Confitebor tibi in cithara, Deus, Deus meus quare tristis es anima mea, et quare conturbas me?

P. I shall yet praise thee upon the harp, O God, my God. Why art thou sad, my soul, and why art thou downcast?

S. Spera in Deo, quoniam adhuc confitebor illi: salutare vultus mei, et Deus meus.

S. Trust in God, for I shall yet praise him, my Savior, and my God.

P. Gloria Patri, et Filio, et Spiritui Sancto.

P. Glory be to the Father, and to the Son, and to the Holy Spirit.

S. Sicut erat in principio, et nunc, et semper: et in saecula saeculorum. Amen.

S. As it was in the beginning, is now, and ever shall be: world without end. Amen.

P. Introibo ad altare Dei.

P. I will go to the altar of God.

S. Ad Deum qui laetificat juventutem meam.

S. To God, the joy of my youth.

P. Adjutorium nostrum in nomine
Domini.

P. Our help ✠ is in the name of the
Lord.

S. Qui fecit coelum et terram.

S. Who made heaven and earth.

The priest, by virtue of ordination, represents both God and man
during Sacred Worship. As a fellow human being, the priest is as
much in need of mercy and forgiveness as the rest of sinful humanity. Hence, he confesses his weakness. As an ordained minister, he
represents the loving forgiveness that God bestows on his children.

Confiteor

The priest bows profoundly low and begins the Confiteor (I confess).

P. Confiteor Deo omnipotenti,
beatae Mariae semper Virgini,
beato Michaeli Archangelo,
beato Joanni Baptistae, sanctis
Apostolis Petro et Paulo, omnibus
Sanctis, et vobis fratres: quia
peccavi nimis cogitatione verbo,
et opere: mea culpa, mea culpa,
mea maxima culpa. Ideo precor
beatam Mariam semper Virginem,
beatum Michaelem Archangelum,
beatum Joannem Baptistam, sanctos Apostolos Petrum et Paulum,
omnes Sanctos, et vos fratres,
orare pro me ad Dominum Deum
Nostrum.

P. I confess to Almighty God,
to Blessed Mary ever-virgin, to
Blessed Michael the Archangel,
to Blessed John the Baptist, to the
Holy Apostles Peter and Paul, to all
the angels and saints, and to you
my brothers and sisters, that I have
sinned exceedingly in thought,
word, deed, [he strikes his breast
three times, saying:] through my
fault, through my fault, through
my most grievous fault, and I ask
Blessed Mary ever-virgin, Blessed
Michael the Archangel, Blessed
John the Baptist, the Holy Apostles
Peter and Paul, all the angels and
saints, and you my brothers and
sisters, to pray for me to the Lord
our God.

S. Misereatur tui omnipotens Deus,
et dimissis peccatis tuis, perducat
te ad vitam aeternam.

S. May Almighty God have mercy
on you, forgive you all your sins,
and bring you to everlasting life.

P. Amen.

P. Amen.

The Confiteor continues with the People's Confession. The servers bow profoundly low.

S. Confiteor Deo omnipotenti, beatae Mariae semper Virgini, beato Michaeli Archangelo, beato Joanni Baptistae, sanctis Apostolis Petro et Paulo, omnibus Sanctis, et tibi Pater: quia peccavi nimis cogitatione verbo, et opere: mea culpa, mea culpa, mea maxima culpa. Ideo precor beatam Mariam semper Virginem, beatum Michaelem Archangelum, beatum Joannem Baptistam, sanctos Apostolos Petrum et Paulum, omnes Sanctos, et te Pater, orare pro me ad Dominum Deum Nostrum.

S. I confess to Almighty God, to Blessed Mary ever-virgin, to Blessed Michael the Archangel, to Blessed John the Baptist, to the Holy Apostles Peter and Paul, to all the angels and saints, and to you my brothers and sisters, that I have sinned exceedingly in thought, word, deed, [strike your breast three times, saying:] through my fault, through my fault, through my most grievous fault, and I ask Blessed Mary ever-virgin, Blessed Michael the Archangel, Blessed John the Baptist, the Holy Apostles Peter and Paul, all the angels and saints, and you Father, to pray for me to the Lord our God.

P. Misereatur vestri omnipotens Deus, et dimissis peccatis vestris, perducat vos ad vitam aeternam.

P. May Almighty God have mercy on you, forgive you your sins, and bring you to everlasting life.

S. Amen.

S. Amen.

P. Indulgentiam absolutionem, et remissionem peccatorum nostrorum, tribuat nobis omnipotens et misericors Dominus.

P. May the Almighty and Merciful Lord grant us pardon, ✠ absolution, and remission of our sins.

S. Amen.

S. Amen.

P. Deus, tu conversus vivificabis nos.

P. Turn to us, O God, and bring us life.

S. Et plebs tua laetabitur in te.

S. And your people will rejoice in you.

P. Ostende nobis Domine, misericordiam tuam.

P. Show us, Lord, your mercy.

S. Et salutare tuum da nobis.

S. And grant us your salvation.

P. Domine, exaudi orationem meam.	P. O Lord, hear my prayer.
S. Et clamor meus ad te veniat.	S. And let my cry come to you.
P. Dominus vobiscum.	P. May the Lord be with you.
S. Et cum spiritu tuo.	S. And with your spirit.
P. Oremus.	P. Let us pray.

The priest prays the following words inaudibly while ascending to the altar.

P. Aufer a nobis, quaesumus, Domine, iniquitates nostras ut ad Sancta sanctorum puris mereamur mentibus introire. Per Christum Dominum nostrum. Amen.	P. Take away from us, O Lord, our iniquities, we beseech you, that we may enter with pure minds into the Holy of Holies. Through Christ our Lord. Amen.

The priest kisses the altar where the relics are, praying the following.

P. Oramus te. Domine, per merita Sanctorum tuorum, quorum reliquiae hic sunt, et omnium Sanctorum: ut indulgere digneris omnia peccata mea. Amen.	P. We beseech you, O Lord, by the merits of your saints, whose relics lie here, and of all the saints, deign in your mercy to pardon me all my sins. Amen.

At High Mass, the priest then incenses the altar, saying:

P. Ab illo benedicaris, in cuius honore cremaberis. Amen.	P. May this incense be blessed by him in whose honor it is to be burned. Amen.

Introit

Introit means *to introduce*. The Introit is a psalm that introduces the Mass.

The priest reads the specific Introit from the Roman Missal for the specific Mass from the Epistle (right) side of the altar. When finished, he concludes with:

P. Gloria Patri, et Filio, et Spiritui Sancto. Sicut erat in principio, et nunc, et semper, et in saecula saeculorum. Amen.	P. Glory be to the Father, and to the Son, and to the Holy Spirit, as it was in the beginning, is now and ever shall be. Amen.

The priest then proceeds to the middle of the altar.

Kyrie

Kyrie eleison is Greek for *Lord have mercy,* and *Christie eleison* means *Christ have mercy.*

The priest stands in the middle of the altar and says, alternating with the server(s):

P. Kyrie eleison.	P. Lord, have mercy.
S. Kyrie eleison.	S. Lord, have mercy.
P. Kyrie eleison.	P. Lord, have mercy.
S. Christe eleison.	S. Christ, have mercy.
P. Christe eleison.	P. Christ, have mercy.
S. Christe eleison.	S. Christ, have mercy.
P. Kyrie eleison.	P. Lord, have mercy.
S. Kyrie eleison.	S. Lord, have mercy.
P. Kyrie eleison.	P. Lord, have mercy.

Gloria

Following the somber admission of unworthiness and need for mercy and forgiveness, the tone turns more joyful, and the choir sings the angelic hymn proclaimed to the shepherds at the time of Christ's birth, the Gloria.

The Gloria is omitted for penitential seasons, Masses for the dead, and certain other Masses.

Standing at the middle of the altar, the priest extends and joins his hands, makes a slight bow, says:

P. Gloria in exceslis Deo.	P. Glory to God in the highest.

The priest sits while the choir sings the Gloria:

C. Et in terra pax hominibus bonae voluntatis. Laudamus te. Benedicimus te. Adoramus te. Glorificamus te. Gratias agimus tibi propter magnam gloriam tuam. Domine Deus, Rex coelestis, Deus Pater omnipotens. Domine Fili unigenite, Jesu Christe. Domine Deus, Agnus Dei, Filius Patris, Qui tollis peccata mundi, miserere nobis. Qui tollis peccata mundi, suscipe deprecationem nostram. Qui sedes ad dexteram Patris, miserere nobis. Quoniam tu solus Sanctus. Tu solus Dominus. To solus Altissimus, Jesu Christe. Cum Sancto Spiritu in gloria Dei Patris. Amen.	C. And on earth peace to people of good will. We praise you. We bless you. We worship you. We glorify you. Lord God, Heavenly King, God the Father Almighty. Lord Jesus Christ, the Only Begotten Son. Lord God, Lamb of God, Son of the Father. You who take away the sins of the world, have mercy on us. You who take away the sins of the world, receive our prayer. You who sit at the right hand of the Father, have mercy on us. For you alone are holy. You alone are Lord. You alone are the Most High, Jesus Christ, with the Holy Spirit, in the Glory of God the Father. Amen.

Turning toward the people, the priest says:

P. Dominus Vobiscum.	P. May the Lord be with you.
S. Et cum spiritu tuo.	S. And with your spirit.
P. Oremus.	P. Let us pray.

Collect

In ancient times, Christians would form processions to various churches where the local people would gather. This gathering was known as the *ecclesia collect* (church assembly). At these places, Mass was celebrated with a community prayer for specific intentions.

The Collect is a brief prayer assigned for that day, season, or occasion. It is equivalent to the Opening Prayer in the Ordinary form.

Epistle

The congregation sits for the reading of the Epistle, one of the letters of the New Testament found in the Bible after the Gospel.

The priest stands at the Epistle (right) side of the altar and reads the Epistle from the Mass he is celebrating, after which the server says:

S. Deo gratias.   S. Thanks be to God.

Gradual, Tract, and Sequence

The server begins preparing for the Gospel, moving the Missal from the Epistle (right) side of the alter to the Gospel (left) side of the alter. Meanwhile, the Gradual (similar to a sequence, it is a liturgical hymn or poem) is sung by the choir. The Alleluia is sung along with the proper Sequence: *Paschale victimae* in the Easter Vigil; *Veni, sancte Spiritus* on Pentecost; *Lauda Sion* on Corpus Christi; *Stabat Mater* on Our Lady of Sorrows; *Dies Irae* on All Souls and in Requiem Masses. In Lent and at Masses for the dead, the Alleluia is omitted, and a tract is sung instead.

Before reading the Gospel, the deacon (if a Solemn or High Mass) returns to the center, bows down, joins his hands, and says:

D. Munda cor meum ac labia mea, omnipotens Deus, qui labia Isaiae Prophetae calculo mundasti ignito: ita me tua grata miseratione dignare mundare, ut sanctum Evangelium tuum digne valeam nuntiare. Per Christum Dominum nostrum. Amen. Jube, Domine benedicere.

D. Cleanse my heart and my lips, O Almighty God, who cleansed the lips of the Prophet Isaiah with a burning coal. In your gracious mercy deign so to purify me that I may worthily proclaim your Holy Gospel. Through Christ our Lord. Amen. Lord, grant me your blessing.

P. Dominus sit in corde meo et in labiis meis. ut digne et competenter annuntiem evangelium suum.

P. The Lord be in your heart and on your lips that you may worthily and fittingly proclaim his Holy Gospel. In the name of the Father, and of the Son, ✠ and of the Holy Spirit.

D. Amen.   D. Amen.

If the Mass is a Missa Cantata or Low Mass, no deacon is used, and the priest says the lines above.

Gospel

The Gospel is one of the four accounts of the life, sayings, and deeds of Jesus Christ written by the Evangelists, Matthew, Mark, Luke, and John.

Everyone in the church stands for the Holy Gospel.

P./D. Dominus vobiscum.	P./D. May the Lord be with you.
S. Et cum spiritu tuo.	S. And with your spirit.
P./D. Sequentia (or Initium) sancti Evangelii secundum [N].	P./D. ✠ A continuation of the Holy Gospel according to St. [name].

The Gospel Book is then incensed.

S. Gloria tibi, Domine.	S. Glory to you, O Lord.

The Holy Gospel is sung or read aloud. At the end, the deacon or server says:

D./S. Laus tibi, Christe.	D./S. Praise to you, O Christ.

At High Mass, the deacon takes the Missal to the celebrant, who kisses it and says:

P. Per evangelica dicta deleantur nostra delicta.	P. May the words of the Gospel wipe away our sins.

If laity are present, the priest may go to the pulpit and read the Epistle and the Gospel aloud in the vernacular language. All stand again for the reading of the Gospel.

Homily

After the Epistle and Gospel, the priest goes to the pulpit to deliver a theological or spiritual reflection to inspire the congregation to aspire to heavenly goals and objectives. The people sit for this sermon, the homily.

Credo

The Profession of Faith, or Creed, that was ironed out and codified at the Ecumenical Council of Nicea in AD 325 is a summary of Christian religion. It is sung, chanted, or spoken at this part of the Mass.

After the homily, the priest goes to the middle of the altar and begins the Creed. As with the Gloria, he intones the first words of the Creed and then sits while the choir sings (the people also sit):

C. Credo in unum Deum, Patrem omnipotentem, factorem coeli et terrae, visibilium omnium et invisibilium. Et in unum Dominum Jesum Christum, Filium Dei unigenitum. Et ex Patre natum ante omnia saecula. Deum de Deo, lumen de lumine, Deum verum de Deo vero. Genitum, not factum, consubstantialem Patri: per quem omnia facta sunt. Qui propter nos homines, et propter nostram salutem descendit de coelis. Et incarnatus est de Spiritu Sancto ex Maria Virgine: *et homo factus est.* Crucifixus etiam pro nobis; sub Pontio Pilato passus, et sepultus est. Et resurrexit tertia die, secundum Scripturas. Et ascendit in coelum: sedet ad dexteram Patris. Et iterum venturus est cum gloria judicare vivos et mortuos. cujus regni non erit finis. Et in Spiritum Sanctum, Dominum et vivificantem: qui ex Patre Filioque procedit. Qui cum Patre, et Filio simul adoratur et conglorificatur: qui locutus est per Prophetas. Et unam, sanctam, catholicam et apostolicam Ecclesiam. Confiteor unum baptisma in remissionem peccatorum. Et exspecto resurrectionem mortuorum. Et vitam venturi saeculi. Amen.

C. I believe in one God, the Father Almighty, Maker of heaven and earth, and of all things visible and invisible. And in one Lord, Jesus Christ, the Only Begotten Son of God. Born of the Father before all ages. God of God, Light of Light, true God of true God. Begotten, not made, of one substance with the Father. By whom all things were made. Who for us men and for our salvation came down from heaven. [Here all present kneel.] And became incarnate by the Holy Spirit of the Virgin Mary: *and was made man.* [Here all arise.] He was also crucified for us, suffered under Pontius Pilate, and was buried. And on the third day he rose again according to the Scriptures. He ascended into heaven and sits at the right hand of the Father. He will come again in glory to judge the living and the dead, and his kingdom will have no end. And in the Holy Spirit, the Lord and Giver of life, who proceeds from the Father and the Son. Who together with the Father and the Son is adored and glorified, and who spoke through the prophets. And one holy, Catholic, and Apostolic Church. I confess one Baptism for the forgiveness of sins and I await the resurrection of the dead and the life ✠ of the world to come. Amen.

All stand, and the priest continues:

P. Dominus vobiscum.	P. May the Lord be with you.
S. Et cum spiritu tuo.	S. And with your spirit.
P. Oremus.	P. Let us pray.

The people sit.

At this point, the Mass of the Catechumens ends and the Mass of the Faithful begins. In the ancient Church, the Catechumens (unbaptized persons preparing for conversion) were dismissed here because they could not receive Holy Communion, which happens in the second half of the Mass.

Mass of the Faithful

Historically, when upbaptized people left the church after the Mass of the Catechumens, the people who did remain in church were baptized members of the Church, the faithful. Therefore, the second part of the Mass is called Mass of the Faithful.

This part of the Mass is more than just the second half, though; it is the heart and soul of the Mass. The Mass of the Faithful contains the offertory where the oblation (sacrifice) is made, where the bread and wine are consecrated into the Body and Blood of Christ, and where the faithful are spiritually fed with Holy Communion.

Unbaptized, unchurched, or uncatechized persons are no longer asked to leave or escorted out of church prior to the Mass of the Faithful. Anyone and everyone is welcome to attend the entire Mass. Only those baptized Christians who are in full communion (members of the Catholic Church) can receive Holy Communion, but all are free to be present during the Mass from beginning to end.

Offertory

The priest says the Offertory Prayer, which offers unleavened wheat bread and grape wine. These gifts of the earth also represent the whole human race who unite themselves to the supreme sacrifice made by Jesus, that of his life for the salvation of the world.

The priest says the offertory prayers in a low voice while the choir sings the Offertory Verse, also called the Offertory Antiphon.

All sit during the Offertory.

P. Suscipe, sancte Pater, omnipotens aeterne Deus, hanc immaculatam hostiam, quam ego indignus famulus tuus offero tibi, Deo meo vivo et vero, pro innumerabilibus peccatis, et offensionibus, et negligentiis meis, et pro omnibus circumstantibus, sed et pro omnibus fidelibus Christianis vivis atque defunctis. Ut mihi, et illis proficiat ad salutem in vitam aeternam.

P. Accept, O Holy Father, Almighty and Eternal God, this spotless host, which I, your unworthy servant, offer to you, my living and true God, to atone for my numberless sins, offenses, and negligences; on behalf of all here present and likewise for all faithful Christians living and dead, that it may profit me and them as a means of salvation to life everlasting.

S. Amen.

S. Amen.

P. Deus, qui humanae substantiae dignitatem mirabiliter condidisti, et mirabilius reformasti: da nobis per hujus aquae et vini mysterium, ejus divinitatis esse consortes, qui humanitatis nostrae fieri dignatus est particeps, Jesus Christus Filius tuus Dominus noster: Qui tecum vivit et regnat in unitate Spiritus Sancti Deus. Per omnia saecula saeculorum. Amen.

P. O God, ✠ who established the nature of man in wondrous dignity, and still more admirably restored it, grant that by the mystery of this water and wine, may we come to share in his Divinity, who humbled himself to share in our humanity, Jesus Christ, your Son, our Lord. Who lives and reigns with you in the unity of the Holy Spirit, one God, forever and ever. Amen.

Offerimus tibi, Domine, calicem salutaris tuam deprecantes clementiam: ut in conspectu divinae majestatis tuae, pro nostra et totius mundi salute cum odore suavitatis ascendat. Amen.

We offer you, O Lord, the chalice of salvation, humbly begging of your mercy that it may arise before your Divine Majesty, with a pleasing fragrance, for our salvation and for that of the whole world. Amen.

In spiritu humilitatis, et in animo contrito suscipiamur a te, Domine, et sic fiat sacrificium nostrum in conspectu tuo hodie, ut placeat tibi, Domine Deus.

In a humble spirit and with a contrite heart, may we be accepted by you, O Lord, and may our sacrifice so be offered in your sight this day as to please you, O Lord God.

Veni, Sanctificator omnipotens aeterne Deus. Et benedic hoc sacrificum tuo sancto nomini praeparatum.

Come, O Sanctifier, Almighty and Eternal God, and bless ✠ this sacrifice prepared for the glory of your holy name.

When Mass is sung, the priest blesses the incense, saying:

P. Per intercessionem beati Michaelis Archangeli, stantis a dextris altaris incensi, et omnium electorum suorum, incensum istud dignetur Dominus benedicere, et in odorem suavitatis accipere. Per Christum Dominum nostrum. Amen.

P. Through the intercession of Blessed Michael the Archangel, standing at the right hand of the altar of incense, and of all his elect may the Lord vouchsafe to bless ✠ this incense and to receive it in the odor of sweetness. Through Christ our Lord. Amen.

The priest incenses the offerings and the cross, saying:

P. Incensum istud a te benedictum, ascendat ad te, Domine, et descendat super nos misericordia tua.

P. May this incense blessed by you arise before you, O Lord, and may your mercy come down upon us.

The priest incenses the altar and says:

P. Dirigatur, Domine, oratio mea sicut incensum in conspectu tuo: elevatio manuum mearum sacrificium vespertinum. Pone, Domine, custodiam ori meo, et ostium circumstantiae labiis meis : ut non declinet cor meum in verba malitiae, ad excusandas excusationes in peccatis.

P. Let my prayer, O Lord, come like incense before you; the lifting up of my hands, like the evening sacrifice. O Lord, set a watch before my mouth, a guard at the door of my lips. Let not my heart incline to the evil of engaging in deeds of wickedness.

He then hands back the thurible to the deacon or server, saying:

P. Accendat in nobis Dominus ignem sui amoris, et flammam aeterne caritatis. Amen.

P. May the Lord enkindle in us the fire of his love and the flame of everlasting charity. Amen.

The celebrant, the ministers, the servers, and the people are incensed, in that order.

Lavabo

Lava is Latin for *wash.* The priest washes his hands in a ritual purification symbolizing his own personal unworthiness to offer the Mass. Only by God's grace of the sacrament of Holy Orders is he able to continue and complete the offering and the sacrifice.

Going to the Epistle (right) side of the altar, the priest washes his fingers and says:

P. Lavabo inter innocentes manus meas. et circumdabo altare tuum, Domine. Ut audiam vocem laudis. et enarrem universa mirabila tua. Domine, dilexi decorem domus tuae: et locum habitationis gloriae tuae. Ne perdas cum impiis, Deus animam meam: et cum viris sanguinum vitam meam: in quorum manibus iniquitates sunt: dextera eorum repleta est muneribus. Ego autem in innocentia mea ingressus sum: redime me, et miserere mei. Pes meus stetit in directo: in ecclesiis benedicam te, Domine.

P. I wash my hands in innocence, and I go around your altar, O Lord, giving voice to my thanks, and recounting all your wondrous deeds. O Lord, I love the house in which you dwell, the tenting place of your glory. Gather not my soul with those of sinners, nor with men of blood my life. On their hands are crimes, and their right hands are full of bribes. But I walk in integrity; redeem me, and have pity on me. My foot stands on level ground; in the assemblies I will bless you, O Lord.

Gloria Patri, et Filio, et Spiritui Sancto. Sicut erat in principio, et nunc, et semper: et in saecula saeculorum. Amen.

Glory be to the Father, and to the Son, and to the Holy Spirit. As it was in the beginning, is now, and ever shall be: world without end. Amen.

Facing the middle of the altar, the priest continues.

P. Suscipe sancta Trinitas, hanc oblationem, quam tibi offerimus ob memoriam passionis, resurrectionis, et ascensionis Jesu Christi Domini nostri: et in honorem beatae Mariae semper Virginis, et beati Joannis Baptistae, et sanctorum Apostolorum Petri et Pauli, et istorum, et omnium Sanctorum: ut illis proficiat ad honorem, nobis autem ad salutem: et illi pro nobis intercedere dignentur in coelis, quorum memoriam agimus in terris. Per eumdem Christum Dominum nostrum. S. Amen.

P. Accept, most Holy Trinity, this offering which we are making to you in remembrance of the Passion, Resurrection, and Ascension of Jesus Christ, our Lord; and in honor of Blessed Mary, ever-virgin, Blessed John the Baptist, the Holy Apostles Peter and Paul, and of [name of the saints whose relics are in the altar] and of all the saints; that it may add to their honor and aid our salvation; and may they deign to intercede in heaven for us who honor their memory here on earth. Through the same Christ our Lord.

S. Amen.

S. Amen.

The priest kisses the altar, turns to the people, and says:

P. Orate fratres, ut meum ac vestrum sacrificium acceptabile fiat apud Deum Patrem omnipotentem.

P. Pray brethren, that my sacrifice and yours may be acceptable to God the Father Almighty.

S. Suscipiat Dominus sacrificium de manibus tuis ad laudem et gloriam nominis sui, ad utilitatem quoque nostram, totiusque Ecclesiae suae sanctae.

S. May the Lord receive the sacrifice from your hands to the praise and glory of his name, for our good, and that of all his holy Church.

Secret prayers

With his hands extended, the priest says the secret prayers. They are called *secret* not because the priest is a agent of the CIA or MI6, but because he says them quietly. In the Ordinary form of the Roman Rite, this prayer is called the *Oblation* or *Prayer Over the Gifts*.

The preface to the prayer, which begins "Per ominia saecula saeculorum" (forever and ever), is where we give thanks and praise to God. It concludes with the Sanctus, a prayer of union with the heavenly hosts and of adoration of the most "Holy, Holy, Holy" triune God.

Most often the preface is the Preface of the Most Holy Trinity (below) unless substituted with another, such as the Preface of the Nativity or the Preface of the Epiphany. When using the Preface of the Most Holy Trinity, the priest says (in a louder voice):

P. Per omnia saecula saeculorum.

P. World without end.

S. Amen.

S. Amen.

P. Dominus vobiscum.

P. The Lord be with you.

S. Et cum spiritu tuo.

S. And with thy spirit.

P. Sursum corda.

P. Lift up your hearts.

S. Habemus ad Dominum.

S. We have them lifted up unto the Lord.

P. Gratias agamus Domino Deo nostro.

P. Let us give thanks to the Lord our God.

S. Dignum et justum est.

S. It is meet and just.

P. Vere dignum et justum est, aequum et salutare, nos tibi semper, et ubique gratias agere: Domine sancte, Pater omnipotens, aeterne Deus. Qui cum unigenito Filio tuo, et Spiritu Sancto, unus es Deus, unus es Dominus: non in unius singularitate personae, sed in unius Trinitate substantiae. Quod enim de tua gloria, revelante te, credimus, hoc de Filio tuo, hoc de Spritu sancto, sine differentia discretionis sentimus. Ut in confessione verae, sempiternaeque Deitatis, et in personis proprietas, et in essentia unitas, et in majestate adoretur aequalitas. Quam laudant Angeli, atque Archangeli, Cherubim quoque ac Seraphim: qui non cessant clamare quotidie, una voce dicentes:

P. It is truly meet and just, right and profitable, for us, at all times, and in all places, to give thanks to thee, O Lord, the Holy One, the Father Almighty, the everlasting God: Who, together with thine Only Begotten Son and the Holy Ghost, art one God, one Lord, not in the singleness of one Person, but in the Trinity of one substance. For that which, according to thy revelation, we believe of thy glory, the same we believe of thy Son, the same of the Holy Ghost, without difference or distinction; so that in the confession of one true and eternal Godhead we adore distinctness in persons, oneness in essence, and equality in majesty: Which the angels praise, and the archangels, the cherubim also and the seraphim, who cease not, day by day crying out with one voice to repeat:

Here the bell is rung three times.

Sanctus

The thrice-holy hymn comes from the Old Testament of the Bible, in Isaiah 6:3: "Holy, holy, holy, is the Lord of hosts: the whole earth is full of his glory." It signifies that this is the beginning of the most holy part of the Mass as even the angels in heaven now stand at attention as the priest is about to begin the Eucharistic Prayer.

P. Sanctus, Sanctus, Sanctus, Dominus Deus Sabaoth. Pleni sunt coeli et terra gloria tua. Hosanna in excelsis. Benedictus qui venit in nomine Domini. Hosanna in excelsis.

P. Holy, holy, holy, Lord God of hosts. The heavens and the earth are full of thy glory. Hosanna in the highest. Blessed is he who cometh in the name of the Lord. Hosanna in the highest.

The people kneel at this point of the Mass.

Canon of the Mass

Canon comes from the Greek word for *measuring rod.* The Canon of Scripture is the list of sacred books the Church officially endorses as authentically inspired. The Canon of the Mass is the set of official prayers said by the priest which authentically effect the Holy Sacrifice, and it's the holiest part of the Mass. The celebrant remembers Salvation History and retells the supreme act of divine love, the sacrifice of the Son by the Father, which is made manifest on the altar.

Though the Last Supper and the Death of Jesus on Good Friday occurred two millennia ago, they are made present at this time at the Holy Mass on the altar. The one and same sacrifice of Calvary is reenacted in an unbloody manner. The consecration of the bread into the Body of Christ and the separate consecration of the wine into the Blood of Christ represent the separation of body and blood, which causes death.

Yet, it is not dead flesh and blood the believer receives in Holy Communion, but rather the risen Body and Blood, Soul and Divinity of Christ. Death is reenacted, and so is Resurrection. The priest uses the first person singular "this is *my* body . . . this is *my* blood" because through the sacrament of Holy Orders he is made an *alter Christus* (another Christ) who acts *in persona Christi* (in the person of Christ) whenever the sacraments are celebrated.

The priest then begins the offering prayer *(Hanc Igitur)* of the Mass while holding his hands over the chalice with his thumbs over-lapped in a cross, representing the sins of the world that Christ took upon himself.

Te Igitur

Te igitur are the first two Latin words of the Roman Canon (Eucharistic Prayer). Often the first or first two words of a Latin document or section of it are used to identify it. The opening phrase is *Te igitur clementissime Pater,* which translates to "to you therefore most merciful Father." It signifies that the Holy Sacrifice of the Mass is offered to God the Father, from God the Son, with God the Holy Spirit.

The priest prays silently:

P. Te igitur clementissime Pater, per Jesum Christum Filium tuum Dominum nostrum, supplices rogamus ac petimus, uti accepta habeas, et benedicas haec ✠ dona, haec ✠ munera, haec ✠ sancta sacrificia illibata, in primis quae tibi offerimus pro Ecclesia tua sancta Catholica; quam pacificare, custodire, adunare, et regere digneris toto orbe terrarum: una cum famulo tuo Papa nostro [N.] et Antistite nostro [N.] et omnibus orthodoxis, atque Catholicae et Apostolicae fidei cultoribus.

P. Therefore, we humbly pray and beseech thee, most merciful Father, through Jesus Christ thy Son, our Lord, to receive and to bless these ✠ gifts, these ✠ presents, these ✠ holy unspotted sacrifices, which we offer up to thee, in the first place, for thy holy Catholic Church, that it may please thee to grant her peace, to guard, unite, and guide her, throughout the world: as also for thy servant [name], our pope, and [name], our bishop, and for all who are orthodox in belief and who profess the Catholic and apostolic faith.

Commemoration of the Living

The Mass is for both the living and the dead, hence the church on earth (Church Militant) is specifically identified just as later in the Canon are the dead (Church Suffering, souls in Purgatory, and Church Triumphant, saints in heaven). Before praying to the saints and asking their intercession, the church prays for the living, particularly the poor, homeless, sick, and dying.

P. Memento Domine famulorum, famularumque tuarum [N.] et [N.] et omnium circumstantium, quorum tibi fides cognita est, et nota devotio, pro quibus tibi offerimus: vel qui tibi offerunt hoc sacrificium laudis pro se, suisque omnibus: pro redemptione animarum suarum, pro spe salutis et incolumitatis suae: tibique reddunt vota sua aeterno Deo vivo et vero.

P. Be mindful, O Lord, of thy servants, [names of special persons for whom the Mass may be offered], and of all here present, whose faith and devotion are known to thee, for whom we offer, or who offer up to thee, this sacrifice of praise, for themselves, their families, and their friends, for the salvation of their souls and the health and welfare they hope for, and who now pay their vows to thee, God eternal, living, and true.

Communicantes

Communicantes means *communion,* and in Catholic theology it is not limited to Holy Communion. The root of the word comes from two separate words: *co* (meaning *with*) and *unio* (meaning *union*) combine to form communio (which means *being united with*). The Communion of Saints are all the living on earth, the souls in Purgatory, and the saints in heaven.

P. Communicantes, et memoriam venerantes, in primis gloriosae semper virginis Mariae genitricis Dei et Domini nostri Jesu Christi: sed {et beati Joseph, ejusdem virginis sponsi} et beatorum Apostolorum ac martyrum tuorum, Petri et Pauli, Andreae, Jacobi, Joannis, Thomae, Jacobi, Philippi, Bartholomaei, Matthaei, Simonis et Thaddaei: Lini, Cleti, Clementis, Xysti, Cornelii, Cypriani, Laurentii, Chrysogoni, Joannis et Pauli, Cosmae et Damiani, et omnium sanctorum tuorum: quorum meritis precibusque concedas, ut in omnibus protectionis tuae muniamur auxilio. Per eumdem Christum Dominum nostrum. Amen.

P. Having communion with and venerating the memory, first, of the glorious Mary, ever a virgin, mother of Jesus Christ, our God and our Lord: likewise of Blessed Joseph, spouse of the same virgin, of thy blessed apostles and martyrs, Peter and Paul, Andrew, James, John, Thomas, James, Phillip, Bartholomew, Matthew, Simon and Thaddeus; of Linus, Cletus, Clement, Sixtus, Cornelius, Cyprian, Lawrence, Chrysogonus, John and Paul, Cosmas and Damian, and of all thy saints: for the sake of whose merits and prayers do thou grant that in all things we may be defended by the help of thy protection. Through the same Christ, our Lord. Amen.

Hanc Igitur

The priest extends his hands over the oblation and prays:

P. Hanc igitur oblationem servitutis nostrae, sed et cunctae familiae tuae, quaesumus, Domine, ut placatus accipias: diesque nostros in tua pace disponas, atque ab aeterna damnatione nos eripi, et in electorum tuorum jubeas grege numerari. Per Christum Dominum nostrum. Amen.

P. Wherefore, we beseech thee, O Lord, graciously to receive this oblation which we thy servants, and with us thy whole family, offer up to thee: dispose our days in thy peace; command that we be saved from eternal damnation and numbered among the flock of thine elect. Through Christ our Lord. Amen.

Quam Oblationem

The bell is rung once before this invocative prayer leading up to the consecration, asking him once more to bless what the Church offers here.

P. Quam oblationem tu, Deus, in omnibus, quaesumus benedictam ✠, adscriptam ✠, ratam ✠, rationabilem, acceptabilemque facere digneris: ut nobis Corpus ✠, et Sanguis ✠ fiat dilectissimi Filii tui Domini nostri Jesu Christi.

P. And do thou, O God, vouchsafe in all respects to bless ✠, consecrate ✠, and approve ✠ this our oblation, to perfect it and render it well-pleasing to thyself, so that it may become for us the body ✠ and blood ✠ of thy most beloved Son, Jesus Christ our Lord.

Consecration

The priest repeats the exact words spoken by Christ at the Last Supper over the bread and wine:

P. Qui pridie quam pateretur, accepit panem in sanctas ac venerabiles manus suas: et elevatis oculis in coelum ad te Deum Patrem suum omnipotentem, tibi gratias agens, benedixit ✠, fregit, deditque discipulis suis, dicens: Accipite et manducate ex hoc omnes:

P. Who, the day before he suffered, took bread into his holy and venerable hands, and having lifted up his eyes to heaven, to thee, God, his Almighty Father, giving thanks to thee, blessed it ✠, broke it, and gave it to his disciples, saying: Take ye and eat ye all of this:

The priest then bends over the host and says:

P. Hoc est enim corpus meum. **P. For this is my body.**

Then the priest adores the host by genuflecting and elevates the now sacred host high enough for everyone to see. The bell is rung. The priest then uncovers the chalice and says:

P. Simili modo postquam coenatum est, accipiens et hunc praeclarum Calicem in sanctas ac venerabiles manus suas: item tibi gratias agens, benedixit ✠, deditque discipulis suis, dicens: Accipite et bibite ex eo omnes:

P. In like manner, after he had supped, taking also into his holy and venerable hands this goodly chalice, again giving thanks to thee, he blessed it ✠, and gave it to his disciples, saying: Take ye, and drink ye all of this:

The priest then bends over the chalice and says:

P. Hic est enim calix sanguinis mei, novi et aeterni testamenti: mysterium fidei, qui pro vobis et pro multis effendetur in remissionem peccatorum. Haec quotiescumque feceritis in mei memoriam facietis.

P. For this is the chalice of my blood, of the new and everlasting testament, the mystery of faith, which for you and for many shall be shed unto the remission of sins. As often as ye shall do these things, ye shall do them in memory of me.

The priest then adores by genuflecting and elevates the chalice high enough for everyone to see, and the bell is rung again.

Salvation history

Previous sacrifices by Abel, Abraham, and Melchizadech in the Old Testament are remembered. Their sacrifices were symbols or types of the full and efficacious sacrifice Jesus Christ made on the cross when he died on Good Friday, mystically represented at every Mass.

Oblation

The priest continues:

P. Unde et memores Domine, nos servi tui, sed et plebs tua sancta, ejusdem Christi Filii tui Domini nostri tam beatae passionis, nec non et ab inferis resurrectionis, sed et in coelos gloriosae ascensionis: offerimus praeclarae majestati tuae de uis donis ac datis, hostiam ✠ puram, hostiam ✠ sanctam, hostiam ✠ immaculatam, Panem ✠ sanctum vitae aeternae, et Calicem ✠ salutis perpetuae.

P. Wherefore, O Lord, we, thy servants, as also thy holy people, calling to mind the blessed passion of the same Christ, thy Son, our Lord, his Resurrection from the grave, and his glorious Ascension into heaven, offer up to thy most excellent majesty of thine own gifts bestowed upon us, a victim ✠ which is pure, a victim ✠ which is stainless, the holy bread ✠ of life everlasting, and the chalice ✠ of eternal salvation.

Supra quae propitio ac sereno vultu respicere digneris: et accepta habere, sicuti accepta habere dignatus es munera pueri tui justi Abel, et sacrificium patriarchae nostri Abraham: et quod tibi obtulit summus sacerdos tuus Melchisedech, sanctum sacrificium, immaculatam hostiam.

Vouchsafe to look upon them with a gracious and tranquil countenance, and to accept them, even as thou wast pleased to accept the offerings of thy just servant Abel, and the sacrifice of Abraham, our patriarch, and that which Melchisedech, thy high priest, offered up to thee, a holy sacrifice, a victim without blemish.

Supplices te rogamus, omnipotens Deus; jube haec perferri per manus sancti Angeli tui in sublime altare tuum, in conspectu divinae majestatis tuae: ut quotquot ex hac altaris participatione, sacrosanctum Filii tui Corpus ✠ et Sanquinem ✠ sumpserimus omni benedictione coelesti et gratia repleamur. Per eumdem Christum Dominum nostrum. Amen.

We humbly beseech thee, Almighty God, to command that these our offerings be borne by the hands of thy holy angel to thine altar on high in the presence of thy divine Majesty; that as many of us as shall receive the most sacred ✠ Body and ✠ Blood of thy Son by partaking thereof from this altar may be filled with every heavenly blessing and grace: Through the same Christ our Lord. Amen.

Commemorantes

Commemorantes means to remember or commemorate, and the Church recalls the faithful departed at this part of the Mass. Most Masses are offered specifically for the soul of a deceased person and their names can be mentioned in the space indicated [name].

P. Memento etiam, Domine, famulorum famularumque tuarum [N.] et [N.] qui nos praecesserunt cum signo fidei, et dormiunt in somno pacis. Ipsis Domine, et omnibus in Christo quiescentibus, locum refrigerii, lucis et pacis, ut indulgeas, deprecamur, per eumdem Christum Dominum nostrum. Amen.

P. Be mindful, also, O Lord, of thy servants [name] and [name], who have gone before us with the sign of faith and who sleep the sleep of peace. To these, O Lord, and to all who rest in Christ, grant, we beseech Thee, a place of refreshment, light, and peace. Through the same Christ our Lord. Amen.

The priest strikes his breast, saying:

P. Nobis quoque peccatoribus famulis tuis, de multitudine miserationum tuarum sperantibus, partem aliquam et societatem donare digneris, cum tuis sanctis Apostolis et Martyribus: cum Joanne, Stephano, Matthia, Barnaba, Ignatio, Alexandro, Marcellino, Petro, Felicitate, Perpetua, Agatha, Lucia, Agnete, Caecilia, Anastasia, et omnibus sanctis tuis: intra quorum nos consortium, non aestimator meriti, sed veniae, quaesumus, largitor admitte. Per Christum Dominum nostrum, per quem haec omnia, Domine, semper bona creas, sanctificas ✠, vivificas ✠, benedicis ✠ et praestas nobis. Per ipsum ✠, et cum ipso ✠, et in ipso ✠, est tibi Deo Patri ✠ omnipotenti, in unitate tus ✠ Sancti, omnis honor et gloria.

P. To us sinners, also, thy servants, who put our trust in the multitude of thy mercies, vouchsafe to grant some part and fellowship with thy holy apostles and martyrs; with John, Stephen, Matthias, Barnabas, Ignatius, Alexander, Marcellinus, Peter, Felicitas, Perpetua, Agatha, Lucy, Agnes, Cecilia, Anastasia, and with all thy saints. Into their company do thou, we beseech thee, admit us, not weighing our merits, but freely pardoning our offenses: through Christ our Lord, by whom, O Lord, thou dost always create, sanctify ✠, quicken ✠, bless ✠, and bestow upon us all these good things. Through him ✠, and with him ✠, and in him ✠, is to thee, God the Father ✠ Almighty, in the unity of the Holy ✠ Ghost, all honor and glory.

The priest ends the Roman Canon (Eucharistic Prayer), and then raises his voice and says:

P. Per omnia saecula saeculorum. Amen.

P. World without end. Amen.

Pater Noster

The Lord's Prayer, or Our Father, was taught to the Apostles by Christ himself. It is now said in preparation for the reception of Holy Communion, which is the true "daily bread." All stand.

P. Oremus. Praeceptis salutaribus moniti, et divina institutione formati, audemus dicere:

P. Let us pray. Admonished by salutary precepts, and following divine directions, we presume to say:

Pater noster, qui es in coelis: sanctificetur nomen tuum: adveniat regnum tuum: fiat voluntas tua sicut in coelo et in terra. Panem nostrum quotidianum da nobis hodie: et dimitte nobis debita nostra, sicut et nos dimittimus debitoribus nostris. Et ne nos inducas in tentationem. Sed libera nos a malo. Amen.

Our Father, who art in heaven, hallowed be thy name; thy kingdom come; thy will be done on earth as it is in heaven; give us this day our daily bread; and forgive us our trespasses, as we forgive those who trespass against us, and lead us not into temptation. But deliver us from evil. Amen.

Libera nos, quaesumus Domine, ab omnibus malis praeteritis, praesentibus, et futuris: et intercedente beata et gloriosa semper Virgine Dei Genitrice Maria, cum beatis Apostolis tuis Petro at Paulo, atque Andrea, et omnibus sanctis, da propitius pacem in diebus nostris: ut ope misericordiae tuae adjuti, et a peccato simus semper liberi, et ab omni perturbatione securi.

Deliver us, we beseech thee, O Lord, from all evils, past, present, and to come: and by the intercession of the blessed and glorious Mary, ever a virgin, Mother of God, and of thy holy apostles Peter and Paul, of Andrew, and of all the saints, graciously grant peace in our days, that through the help of thy bountiful mercy we may always be free from sin and secure from all disturbance.

Fractio Panis

The priest breaks a small piece of the consecrated Sacred Host and places it inside the chalice containing the Precious Blood.

P. Per eumdem Dominum nostrum Jesum Christum Filium tuum. Qui tecum vivit et regnat in unitate Spiritus Sancti Deus. Per omnia saecula saeculorum.

P. Through the same Jesus Christ, thy Son, our Lord, who liveth and reigneth with thee in the unity of the Holy Ghost, God, world without end.

S. Amen.

S. Amen.

P. Pax ✠ Domini sit ✠ semper vobiscum ✠.

P. May the peace ✠ of the Lord ✠ be always with ✠ you.

S. Et cum spiritu tuo.

S. And with thy spirit.

P. Haec commixtio et consecratio Corporis at Sanguinis Domini nostri Jesu Christi fiat accipientibus nobis in vitam aeternam. Amen.

P. May this commingling and consecrating of the Body and Blood of our Lord Jesus Christ avail us who receive it unto life everlasting. Amen.

Agnus Dei

Agnus dei, Latin for *lamb of God,* is the title St. John the Baptist affirmed Jesus when he baptized Christ at the River Jordan. Jesus is the Lamb slain for the sins of the world. His blood saved souls just as the blood of the lamb on the doorposts spared lives of the Hebrews the night of Passover before the Exodus, when the angel of death passed over the homes of the people. Jesus is called the Lamb of God because he sheds his blood on the doorpost of the cross and thus frees humanity from the slavery of sin.

Three prayers follow the Agnus Dei, preceding the Communion prayer, which comes from the Roman centurion's plea for Christ to heal his sick servant boy.

Bowing down, the priest says:

P. Agnus Dei, qui tollis peccata mundi, miserere nobis. Agnus Dei, qui tollis peccata mundi, miserere nobis. Agnus Dei, qui tollis peccata mundi, dona nobis pacem.

P. Lamb of God, who takest away the sins of the world: have mercy on us. Lamb of God, who takest away the sins of the world: have mercy on us. Lamb of God, who takest away the sins of the world: grant us peace.

Domine Jesu Christe, qui dixisti Apostolis tuis: pacem relinquo vobis, pacem meam do vobis: ne respicias peccata mea, sed fidem Ecclesiae tuae; eamque secundum voluntatem tuam pacificare et coadunare digneris. Qui vivis et regnas Deus, per omnia saecula saeculorum. Amen.

[Prayer 1:] O Lord Jesus Christ who didst say to thine apostles: Peace I leave you, my peace I give you: look not upon my sins, but upon the faith of thy Church, and vouchsafe to grant her peace and unity according to thy will: Who livest and reignest God, world without end. Amen.

Domine Jesu Christe, Fili Dei vivi, qui ex voluntate Patris cooperante Spritu Sancto, per mortem tuam mundum vivificasti: libera me per hoc sacrosanctum Corpus et Sanguinem tuum ab omnibus iniquitatibus meis et universis malis: et fac me tuis semper inhaerere mandatis: et a te nunquam separari permittas: qui cum eodem Deo Patre et Spiritu Sancto vivis et regnas Deus in saecula saeculorum. Amen.

[Prayer 2:] O Lord Jesus Christ, Son of the living God, who, according to the will of the Father, through the cooperation of the Holy Ghost, hast by thy Death given life to the world: deliver me by this thy most Sacred Body and Blood from all my iniquities, and from every evil; make me always cleave to thy commandments, and never suffer me to be separated from thee, who with the same God, the Father and the Holy Ghost, livest and reignest God, world without end. Amen.

Perceptio Corporis tui, Domine Jesu Christe, quod ego indignus sumere praesumo, non mihi proveniat in judicium et condemnationem: sed pro tua pietate prosit mihi ad tutamentum mentis et corporis, et ad medelam percipiendam. Qui vivis et regnas cum Deo Patre in unitate Spiritus Sancti Deus, per omnia saecula saeculorum. Amen.

[Prayer 3:] Let not the partaking of thy Body, O Lord Jesus Christ, which I, all unworthy, presume to receive, turn to my judgment and condemnation; but through thy loving kindness may it be to me a safeguard and remedy for soul and body; who, with God the Father, in the unity of the Holy Ghost, livest and reignest, God, world without end. Amen.

Reception of Holy Communion

The priest genuflects, rises, and says:

P. Panem coelestem accipiam et nomen Domini invocabo.

P. I will take the bread of heaven, and will call upon the name of the Lord.

Taking the Sacred Host with his left hand, the priest repeats the following prayer three times while striking his breast each time, and the bell is rung each of the three times.

P. Domine, non sum dignus ut intres sub tectum meum: sed tantum dic verbo, et sanabitur anima mea.

P. Lord, I am not worthy that thou shouldst enter under my roof; but only say the word, and my soul shall be healed.

Communion of the Faithful

After the priest receives Holy Communion, he gives it to the clergy in the sanctuary next and then goes to the altar or communion rail to give Holy Communion to the faithful (people in the congregation who are baptized Catholics and in the state of grace — not conscious of any mortal sins).

Holding the Sacred Host in his right hand, the priest makes the sign of the cross with it and says:

P. Corpus Domini nostri Jesu Christi custodiat animam meam in vitam aeternam. Amen.

P. May the Body of our Lord Jesus Christ keep my soul unto life everlasting. Amen.

The priest himself then receives Holy Communion and after a brief meditation continues:

P. Quid retribuam Domino pro omnibus quae retribuit mihi? Calicem salutaris accipiam, et nomen Domini invocabo Dominum, et ab inimicis meis salvus ero.

P. What shall I render unto the Lord for all the things that he hath rendered unto me? I will take the chalice of salvation and will call upon the name of the Lord. With high praises will I call upon the Lord, and I shall be saved from all mine enemies.

The priest takes the chalice in his right hand and makes the sign of the cross with it, saying:

P. Sanguis Domini nostri Jesu Christi custodiat animam meam in vitam aeternam. Amen.

P. May the Blood of our Lord Jesus Christ keep my soul unto life ever-lasting. Amen.

The priest himself then drinks of the chalice.

Here the server recites the *Confiteor* in the name of the communicants, and the priest responds with the *Misereatur* and the *Indulgentiam*.

The priest, holding the ciborium, faces the people and holds up a broken segment from his original host. Before all the communicants, he says:

P. Ecce Agnus Dei, ecce Qui tollit peccata mundi.

P. Behold the Lamb of God, behold him who taketh away the sins of the world.

R: Domine, non sum dignus, ut intres sub tectum meum: sed tantum dic verbo, et sanabitur anima mea. (Repeated three times.)

R: Lord, I am not worthy that thou shouldst enter under my roof; but only say the word, and my soul shall be healed. [Repeated three times.]

Here the lay faithful come forward to the Communion rail to receive our Lord in the Sacrament of Holy Communion. The priest places a host directly on the tongue of each communicant as he kneels. Communicants say nothing and don't take Communion in the hand in the Extraordinary form. While he administers Holy Communion to each person, the priest says:

P. Corpus Domini nostri Jesu Christi custodiat animam tuam in vitam aeternam.	P. May the Body of our Lord Jesus Christ keep your soul unto life everlasting.
R: Amen.	R: Amen.

The Council of Trent (in the 16th century) solemnly defined the dogma that the faithful do not have to receive both the consecrated wine (Precious Blood) and the consecrated host in order to receive Holy Communion because in either the host or in the chalice are *both* the Body and Blood, Soul and Divinity of Christ. In other words, when Catholics receive the host they de facto receive both the Body and the Blood of Christ. Only the priest must consume both elements.

When all have received Communion, the priest returns to the altar and replaces the ciborium in the tabernacle. He then purifies with wine in the chalice, saying:

P. Quod ore sumpsimus Domine, pura mente capiamus: et de munere temporali fiat nobis remedium sempiternum.	P. Into a pure heart, O Lord, may we receive the heavenly food which has passed our lips; bestowed upon us in time, may it be the healing of our souls for eternity.

The priest then goes to the Epistle (right) side of the altar and, while the server pours wine and water over his fingers, says:

P. Corpus tuum, Domine, quod sumpsi, et Sanguis, quem potavi, adhaereat visceribus meis: et praesta, ut in me non remaneat scelerum macula, quem pura et sancta refecerunt sacramenta. Qui vivis et regnas in saecula saeculorum. Amen.	P. May thy Body, O Lord, which I have received, and thy Blood, which I have drunk, cleave to mine inmost parts: and do thou grant that no stain of sin remain in me, whom pure and holy mysteries have refreshed: Who livest and reignest world without end. Amen.

Post Communion Prayer

Before the Communion Prayer, the priest and congregation have the following exchange:

P. Dominus vobiscum. | P. May the Lord be with you.

S. Et cum spiritu tuo. | S. And with thy spirit.

At the Epistle side, the priest recites the Communion Prayer appropriate for the Mass being celebrated.

The priest then returns to the center, kisses the altar, turns toward the people, and says:

P. Dominus vobiscum. | P. The Lord be with you.

S. Et cum spiritu tuo. | S. And with thy spirit.

P. Ite, missa est. | P. Go, the Mass is ended.

S. Deo gratias. | S. Thanks be to God.

The priest bows over the altar and recites the following prayer, known as the *Placeat,* which summarizes the intention of the entire mass:

P. Placeat tibi sancta Trinitas, obsequium servitutis meae; et praesta, ut sacrificium, quod oculis tuae majestatis indignus obtuli, tibi sit acceptabile, mihique et omnibus, pro quibus illud obtuli, sit, te miserante, propitiabile. Per Christum Dominum nostrum. Amen.

P. May the lowly homage of my service be pleasing to thee, O most Holy Trinity: and do thou grant that the sacrifice which I, all unworthy, have offered up in the sight of thy majesty, may be acceptable to thee, and, because of thy loving kindness, may avail to atone to thee for myself and for all those for whom I have offered it up. Through Christ our Lord. Amen.

Blessing

The priest kisses the altar, and at the word *Pater,* turns toward the people, blesses them, saying:

P. Benedicat vos omnipotens Deus, Pater, et Filius ✠, et Spiritus Sanctus.

P. May almighty God, the Father, and the Son ✠, and the Holy Ghost, bless you.

S. Amen. | S. Amen.

Last Gospel

The priest now goes to the Gospel (left) side of the altar; he makes the sign of the cross, first upon the altar, and then upon his forehead, lips, and heart, and then he reads the Last Gospel:

P. Dominus vobiscum.

P. The Lord be with you.

S. Et cum spiritu tue.

S. And with thy spirit.

P. Initium sancti Evangelii secundum Ioannem:

P. The beginning of the Holy Gospel, according to St. John:

In prinicipio erat Verbum, et Verbum erat apud Deum, et Deus erat Verbum. Hoc erat in principio apud Deum. Omnia per ipsum facta sunt, et sine ipso factum est nihil quod factum est. In ipso vita erat, et vita erat lux hominum: et lux in tenebris lucet, et tenebrae eam non comprehenderunt. Fuit homo missus a Deo, cui nomen erat Joannes. Hic venit in testimonium, ut testimonium perhiberet de lumine, ut omnes crederent per illum. Non erat ille lux, sed ut testimonium perhiberet de lumine. Erat lux vera quae illuminat omnem hominem venientem in hunc mundum. In mundo erat, et mundus per ipsum factus est, et mundus eum non cognovit. In propria venit, et sui eum non receperunt. Quotquot autem receperunt eum, dedit eis potestatem filios Dei fieri, his qui credunt in nomine ejus. Qui non ex sanguinibus, neque ex voluntate carnis, neque ex voluntate viri, sed ex Deo nati sunt. (Here all genuflect) *et verbum caro factum est*, et habitavit in nobis et vidimus gloriam ejus, gloriam quasi unigeniti a Patre, plenum gratiae et veritatis.

In the beginning was the Word, and the Word was with God, and the Word was God. The same was in the beginning with God. All things were made by him, and without him was made nothing that was made. In him was life, and the life was the light of men: and the light shineth in darkness, and the darkness did not comprehend it. There was a man sent from God, whose name was John. This man came for a witness to give testimony of the light, that all men might believe through him. He was not the light, but was to give testimony of the light. That was the true light which enlighteneth every man that cometh into this world. He was in the world, and the world was made by him, and the world knew him not. He came unto his own, and his own received him not. But as many as received him, to them he gave great power to become the sons of God: to them that believe in his name: who are born, not of blood, nor of the will of the flesh, nor of the will of man, but of God. And [here all genuflect] *the word was made flesh, and dwelt among us,* and we saw his glory, the glory as of the only begotten of the Father, full of grace and truth.

S. Deo gratias.

S. Thanks be to God.

Prayers after Low Mass

Pope Leo XIII in 1884 asked that the Ave Maria, Salve Regina, and prayer to St. Michael the Archangel be prayed at the end of every Low Mass for the safety of the Church. During that time, the territory of the former Papal States, which had been ruled by the popes since the eighth century, were experiencing great unrest due to the unification of Italy in the late 19th century. The Papal States became part of the new kingdom of Italy, and Vatican City emerged in 1929 as an independent country through a concordat (treaty) signed with Prime Minister Mussolini.

The Leonine Prayers continued even after the Concordat recognized the pope as indepenedent sovereign and Vatican City as a separate nation. The prayers are continued because wars and attacks on the Church still happen around the world from time to time, and prayers for peace should continue.

After Low Mass, the priest kneels at the altar steps and says the following prayers with the people:

Ave Maria

Ave Maria is Latin for *Hail Mary*, which is the prayer taken verbatim from Luke's Gospel when the Archangel Gabriel announces to the Virgin Mary that she is to be the mother of the Savior and she in turn is greeted by her cousin Elizabeth, then pregnant with John the Baptist.

P. Ave Maria, gratia plena, Dominus tecum. Benedicta tu in mulieribus, et benedictus fructus ventris tui, Jesus. Sancta Maria, Mater Dei, ora pro nobis peccatoribus, nunc, et in hora mortis nostrae. Amen. (Repeat three times.)

P. Hail Mary, full of grace, the Lord is with thee. Blessed art thou amongst women, and blessed is the fruit of thy womb, Jesus. Holy Mary, Mother of God, pray for us sinners, now, and at the hour of our death. Amen. [Repeat three times.]

Salve Regina

Hail Holy Queen is the translation of the Latin phrase *salve regina*. This is a hymn to the Virgin Mary that comes from the Middle Ages, when the monks and nuns would chant this before they prayed night prayer.

P. Salve Regina, Mater misericordiae. Vita, dulcedo, et spes nostra, salve. Ad te clamamus exsules filii Hevae. Ad te Suspiramus, gementes et flentes in hac lacrimarum valle. Eja ergo, Advocata nostra, illos tuos misericordes oculos ad nos converte. Et Jesum, benedictum a fructum ventris tui, nobis post hoc exsilium ostende. O clemens, o pia, o dulcis Virgo Maria. Ora pro nobis, sancta Dei Genitrix.

P. Hail, Holy Queen, Mother of mercy, our life, our sweetness, and our hope! To thee do we cry, poor banished children of Eve, to thee do we send up our sighs, mourning and weeping in this valley of tears. Turn then, most gracious Advocate, thine eyes of mercy towards us, and after this our exile show unto us the blessed fruit of thy womb, Jesus. O clement, O loving, O sweet Virgin Mary. Pray for us, O Holy Mother of God.

S. Ut digni efficiamur promissionibus Christi.

S. That we be made worthy of the promises of Christ.

P. Oremus. Deus refugium nostrum et virtus, populum ad te clamantem propitius respice; et intercedente gloriosa et immaculata Virgine Dei Genitrice Maria, cum beato Josepho ejus Sponso, ac beatis Apostolis tuis Petro et Paulo, et omnibus Sanctis, quas pro conversione peccatorum, pro libertate et exaltatione sanctae Matris Ecclesiae, preces effundimus, misericors et benignus exaudi. Per eumdem Christum Dominum nostrum. Amen.

P. Let us pray. O God, our refuge and our strength, look down with favor upon thy people who cry to thee; and through the intercession of the glorious and immaculate Virgin Mary, Mother of God, of her spouse, Blessed Joseph, of thy holy apostles, Peter and Paul, and all the saints, mercifully and graciously hear the prayers which we pour forth to thee for the conversion of sinners and for the liberty and exaltation of holy mother Church. Through the same Christ our Lord. Amen.

St. Michael

The priest prays to St. Michael the Archangel:

P. Sancte Michael Archangele, defende nos in praelio. Contra nequitiam et insidias diaboli esto praesidium. Imperet illi Deus, supplices deprecamur. Tuque princeps militiae caelestis, Satanam aliosque spiritus malignos, qui ad perditionem animarum pervagantur in mundo divina virtute in infernum detrude. Amen.

P. St. Michael, the archangel, defend us in battle. Be our protection against the malice and snares of the devil. We humbly beseech God to command him. And do thou, O prince of the heavenly host, by the divine power thrust into hell Satan and the other evil spirits who roam through the world seeking the ruin of souls. Amen.

Chapter 7

Variations in the Ordinary Form

*T*he Holy Mass is the center of all Catholic worship of Jesus Christ, and in addition to the weekly, obligatory Sunday church services, special liturgies are offered on certain occasions in the lives of the congregants and days of celebration in the Church. These variations on the Mass are spiritual bookmarks in the lives of the faithful.

Many of the Masses covered in this chapter are *Ritual Masses,* which are Sacred Liturgies celebrated on any day of the week. *Ritual* means a set of actions, gestures, or words performed on certain occasions and having symbolic meaning to reaffirm Church teaching. These Masses focus on one of the seven sacraments or the final sacrament possible, a Catholic burial.

Nuptial (Wedding) Mass

Weddings in the Catholic Church may take place with or without a Mass. If both the bride and groom are Catholic, they typically have a Nuptial or wedding Mass, but if one is not Catholic and a majority of the invited guests aren't either, then they usually have a wedding service alone without a Mass, because only Catholics who are *in full communion* with Church teachings and laws are permitted to receive Holy Communion. Which way to go is determined by the pastor after discussion with the bride and groom and based on the policies of the local diocese.

Exchanging vows is the essential part of a Catholic wedding. Mutual consent of the bride and groom is what makes them husband and wife, and therefore the actual ministers of the Sacrament of Matrimony are the couple themselves. The priest or deacon is not the minister; rather, he is the official witness for the Church of this union.

Introductory rites

The arrangement of the entrance procession at a Catholic wedding Mass depends on the diocese and parish where the ceremony takes place. Some bishops and/or priests have policies on how the bridal party comes down the aisle, so the couple should find out before the rehearsal.

The traditional wedding marches by Wagner and Mendelssohn are banned by every Catholic diocese because their sources aren't appropriate to the reverent tone of a Catholic wedding (Wagner's "Bridal Chorus" accompanies characters in an opera to the bedroom, and Mendelssohn's song goes with Shakespeare's comedy *A Midsummer Night's Dream*.) Many other popular musical pieces are considered appropriate by the Church, though, including: "Rondeau" by Mouret, "Trumpet Voluntary" by Stanley, "Jesu, Joy of Man's Desiring" by Bach, and "Canon in D Major" by Pachelbel.

The Mass opens as usual with the sign of the cross and Penitential Rite followed by the Opening Prayer, designed for the Sacrament of Christian Marriage.

Liturgy of the Word

Just as in a regular Sunday parish Mass, the wedding Mass includes a reading from the Old Testament, a psalm (usually sung), a New Testament Epistle, and a Gospel. Only the priest or deacon can proclaim the Gospel, but any layperson or consecrated religious (monk, nun, brother, or sister) can read the other passages.

The Gospel is followed by a homily, which itself is followed by the Rite of Marriage within the wedding (Nuptial) Mass.

Declaration of intention

The bride and groom stand before the priest with their two witnesses (best man and maid/matron of honor). The couple is asked three questions before they exchange their consent:

Have you come here freely and without reservation to give yourselves to each other in marriage?

Will you love and honor each other as man and wife for the rest of your lives?

Will you accept children lovingly from God and bring them up according to the law of Christ and his Church?

Exchange of consent

The priest asks the bride and groom to hold their right hands together. The couple may either repeat their vows after hearing them from the priest or they may be said as a question in which the bride and groom need only reply with "I do."

Blessing and exchange of rings

The bride and groom are the ministers of matrimony, and the priest or deacon is the official witness of the exchange of those vows on behalf of the Universal Church. The exchange of rings is merely a symbolic gesture to remind the couple of their permanent, faithful, and, God-willing, fruitful union.

The priest blesses the rings:

✠ May the Lord bless these rings, which you give to each other as the sign of your love and fidelity.

Then the newly married couple exchanges rings. The bride and groom take turns placing the rings on each other's finger and saying:

[Name], take this ring as a sign of my love and fidelity. In the name of the Father, and of the Son, and of the Holy Spirit.

The Prayers of the Faithful (General Intercessions) follow the exchange, and then the Mass continues as usual.

Liturgy of the Eucharist

The priest and congregation proceed with the Preparation of the Gifts and Offertory Hymn, and the normal Mass continues. During a wedding Mass, however, the priest has the option of inserting a special *Hanc Igitur* (a part of Eucharistic Prayer I, also known as Roman Canon):

Father, accept this offering from your whole family and from [name of bride] and [name of groom], for whom we now pray. You have brought them to their wedding day: Grant them the gift of children and a long and happy life together.

Nuptial Blessing

This unique part of a Nuptial Mass occurs after the *Pater Noster* (Our Father or Lord's Prayer). The priest asks the couple to kneel, and then he gives the Nuptial Blessing:

My dear friends, let us turn to the Lord and pray that he will bless with his grace this woman now married in Christ to this man and that through the sacrament of the body and blood of Christ, he will unite in love the couple he has joined in this holy bond.

Father, by your power you have made everything out of nothing. In the beginning you created the universe and made mankind in your own likeness. You gave man the constant help of woman so that man and woman should no longer be two, but one flesh, and you teach us that what you have united may never be divided. Father, you have made the union of man and wife so holy a mystery that it symbolizes the marriage of Christ and his Church.

Father, by your plan man and woman are united, and married life has been established as the one blessing that was not forfeited by original sin or washed away in the flood. Look with love upon this woman, your daughter, now joined to her husband in marriage. She asks your blessing. Give her the grace of love and peace. May she always follow the example of the holy women whose praises are sung in the Scriptures. May her husband put his trust in her and recognize that she is his equal and the heir with him to the life of grace. May he always honor her and love her as Christ loves his bride, the Church. Father, keep them always true to your commandments. Keep them faithful in marriage and let them be living examples of Christian life.

Give them the strength which comes from the Gospel so that they may be witnesses of Christ to others. Bless them with children and help them to be good parents. May they live to see their children's children. And, after a happy old age, grant them fullness of life with the saints in the kingdom of heaven. We ask this through Christ our Lord. Amen.

The Mass then proceeds with the Sign of Peace, the *Agnus Dei* (Lamb of God), Holy Communion, and Prayer after Communion.

A final blessing is given. Finally, the priest makes the formal announcement (presents the newly married couple by name). The newlyweds exchange the customary kiss before they process out of the church hand in hand.

Requiem (Funeral) Mass

The death of a loved one is always painful and difficult, and more than any other occasion needs the spiritual support and strength of the Church through the Holy Mass. The funeral rites of the Catholic Church are first and foremost for the assistance of the departed person and secondarily for the surviving family and friends.

The funeral Mass is offered for the soul of the deceased. Even if this person lived a virtuous and holy life and went straight to heaven when he or she died, the Mass is not in vain. The spiritual benefits are still given to the family and friends who attend.

Funeral wakes usually take place the night before the burial services. Typically, Catholics either have a Rosary prayed at the funeral parlor the night before the burial or have a formal vigil service, also called a wake. The custom in some countries is to hold the wake in the deceased person's home and then have the body transferred to the church for the Mass the next day.

The Sacred Liturgy for the Deceased is much like a Sunday parish Mass in that there are two readings from Scripture before the Gospel, the psalm is usually sung, and a cantor or choir (or both) is usually present to help sing the hymns and acclamations.

The following sections describe the sequence of a traditional funeral Mass.

Introductory rites

The body is brought to the church in a casket from the funeral home. The family follows immediately behind as pallbearers carry or wheel the casket into the vestibule of the church. (Pallbearers are persons selected, usually by the family, to carry the casket at the church and cemetery.) Before entering the church proper, the priest greets the congregation at the back of the church with the following words:

> The Grace of Our Lord Jesus Christ and love of God and the fellowship of the Holy Spirit be with you all.

The people respond:

> And also with you.

In November of 2011, the response will change to *And with your spirit.*

The priest then sprinkles holy water on the casket as a reminder of the Baptism, which made the deceased a child of God:

> In the waters of Baptism, [name] died with Christ and rose with him to new life. May he/she now share with him eternal glory.

A funeral pall (cloth covering the entire casket) and a Bible or Book of the Gospels are sometimes placed on the casket. Altar servers carrying the processional cross and candles then lead the procession from the back of the church to the front. The family typically sits in the first pew on one side with pallbearers seated opposite.

The pallbearers bring the casket forward in front of the sanctuary and position it so that the feet point toward the altar. The paschal (Easter) candle stands immediately next to the casket, symbolizing Christ the Light breaking the darkness of death. At this point in the Mass the cantor usually leads the congregation with an opening hymn.

Liturgy of the Word

After the funeral Mass's introductory rites, Mass continues as usual with an Opening Prayer followed by the Liturgy of the Word (Scripture readings and homily), which remind the celebrant that the sermon is a prayerful reflection on the Christian understanding of life, death, and resurrection of every believer.

The General Intercessions (Prayer of the Faithful) are tailored for the funeral Mass and include prayers not only for the deceased but for their family and friends and for the needs of all the world church.

Liturgy of the Eucharist

The Liturgy of the Eucharist proceeds like in any other Mass with the Preparation of the Gifts and Offertory Hymn. Often, family members or friends of the deceased bring up the gifts of bread and wine that are to be consecrated by the priest at Mass to become the Body and Blood of Christ. The Prayer Over the Gifts and the Preface to the Eucharistic Prayer are also tailored for funeral Masses.

Final Commendation

After Holy Communion and the Final Prayer, the priest goes to the casket for the Final Commendation. He uses incense to represent the prayers being offered for the deceased, and like the rising smoke from the incense burner, the prayers rise up to heaven.

The altar servers with cross and candles lead the procession out of church followed by the pallbearers with the casket and then family. If the deceased was a United States veteran, the funeral pall is removed and replaced with the American flag. After placing the body in the hearse, the funeral entourage proceeds to the cemetery for burial. At the cemetery, the priest offers some brief prayers blessing the grave and reminding the survivors about the resurrection of the dead on the Last Day.

Mass with Baptism

Baptism is the first sacrament a Catholic receives and is called the gateway to the other sacraments, because only a baptized person can receive them. It is the first of three Sacraments of Initiation into the Church and makes you an adopted Child of God.

Catholicism considers Baptism the spiritual process of being "born again of water and the Spirit." The sacrament removes the Original Sin of Adam and Eve and infuses Sanctifying Grace which allows the soul the possibility of heaven, but it is not a get-out-of-hell-for-free card. More than a cultural or symbolic act, Baptism makes an indelible mark on the soul. That is why no one can be *un*-baptized or *re*-baptized. Once is forever.

Most babies in Catholic families are baptized within two to five weeks of their birth, as soon as mommy and daddy are confident enough to take their bundle of joy out of the house and into the public. Parents and godparents sit with the child to be baptized and are accompanied by friends and family as well.

When done within Mass, the Rite of Baptism is divided into parts: the reception of the child, anointing, blessing of the baptismal water, renunciation of sin and Profession of Faith, Baptism, second anointing, clothing with the white garment, and lighting the candle.

Reception of the child

The reception of the child takes place during the introductory rites of the Mass, before the Liturgy of the Word.

Priest: What name do you give your child?

Parents: [Child's name].

Priest: What do you ask of God's Church for your child?

Parents: Baptism.

Priest: You have asked to have your child baptized. In doing so, you are accepting the responsibility of training him/her in the Catholic faith. It will be your duty to keep God's commandments as Christ taught us, by living God and our neighbor. Do you clearly understand what you are undertaking?

Parents: We do.

Priest: Godparents, are you ready to help the parents of this child in their duties as Christian parents?

Godparents: We are.

The priest then makes a small sign of the cross on the forehead of the baby and says

[Name], the Christian community welcomes you with great joy. In its name I claim you for Christ our Savior by the sign of his cross. I now trace the cross on your forehead and invite your parents and godparents to do the same.

The Liturgy of the Word continues as usual, and the Rite of Baptism continues after the homily. Intercessions and Prayer of Exorcism are said on behalf of the child who is to be baptized:

Almighty and ever-living God, you sent your only Son into the world to cast out the power of Satan, spirit of evil, to rescue man from the kingdom of darkness, and bring him into the splendor of your kingdom of light. We pray for this child: Set him/her free from original sin, make him/her a temple of your glory, and send your Holy Spirit to dwell with him/her. We ask this through Christ our Lord.

Anointing

The child is anointed with the oil of catechumens *(oleum sanctorum)* before Baptism as a sign of being set apart as a child of God. The priest dips his thumb in oil and makes a small cross on the child's breast, just below the neck, saying:

We anoint you with oil of salvation in the name of Christ our Savior; may he strengthen you with his power, who lives and reigns forever and ever. Amen.

Blessing of baptismal water

The person being baptized is born again by water and Holy Spirit. The water to be used for Baptism is blessed, and images of water in the Bible are remembered during the prayer:

- In Genesis, water is mentioned as the world is being created, so water is symbolic of life.

- Water is also seen as symbolically cleansing sin and evil, both during Noah's flood and with Moses's parting of the Red Sea to deliver the Hebrews from slavery.

- Jesus was baptized at the River Jordan by his cousin, St. John the Baptist.

- Water flowed with blood from the sacred heart of Jesus when he died on the cross and a Roman soldier thrust a spear into his chest to make sure he was dead.

Renunciation of Sin and Profession of Faith

The main elements of the Creed, also known as the Profession of Faith, are asked of the parents and godparents:

Priest: Do you reject Satan?

People: I do.

Priest: And all his works?

People: I do.

Priest: And all his empty promises?

People: I do.

Priest: Do you believe in God, the Father Almighty, Creator of heaven and earth?

People: I do.

Priest: Do you believe in Jesus Christ, his only Son, our Lord, who was born of the Virgin Mary, was crucified, died, and was buried, rose from the dead, and is now seated at the right hand of the Father?

People: I do.

Priest: Do you believe in the Holy Spirit, the Holy Catholic Church, the Communion of Saints, the forgiveness of sins, the resurrection of the body, and life everlasting?

People: I do.

Baptism

The priest again asks if it is the parents' will that their son or daughter be baptized. Then the parents hold their baby over the water of the baptismal font, and the priest pours water over the baby's head. Alternatively, the infant may be immersed three times. The priest says

> I baptize [name] in the name of the Father, and of the Son, and of the Holy Spirit, amen.

Second anointing

The newly baptized child is anointed with the chrism oil. This second anointing represents the assimilation into the Body of Christ, the Church. A baptized Christian is one who is anointed in the Lord. The priest does this anointing on the head of the child, saying

> God the Father of our Lord Jesus Christ has freed you from sin, given you a new birth by water and the Holy Spirit, and welcomed you into his holy people. He now anoints you with the chrism of salvation. As Christ was anointed Priest, Prophet, and King, so may you live always as a member of his body, sharing everlasting life.

Clothing with the white garment

Even if the baby is already dressed in white, many parishes use baptismal bibs or minigarments at this place in the ceremony. It represents the white cloths found in the empty tomb on Easter Sunday which had wrapped the body of Jesus after his death. They signify the resurrection of the body at the end of time.

> [Name], you have become a new creation and have clothed yourself in Christ. See in this white garment the outward sign of your Christian dignity. With your family and friends to help you by word and example, bring that dignity unstained into the everlasting life of heaven.

Lighting the candle

The priest takes a small candle and lights it from the already lit Easter (paschal) candle and says

Receive the light of Christ. Parents and godparents, this light is entrusted to you to be kept burning brightly. This child of yours has been enlightened by Christ. He/she is to walk always as a child of the light. May he/she keep the flame of faith alive in his/her heart. When the Lord comes, may he/she go out to meet him with all the saints in the heavenly kingdom.

The candle is blown out and the family sits down again in their pew. Mass returns to the Liturgy of the Eucharist with the Preparation of the Gifts.

Confirmation Mass

Confirmation is the second Sacrament of Initiation and confirms what was done in Baptism. The Creed is repeated and the questions formerly answered by the parents and godparents are now answered by the young man or young woman about to be confirmed. While the Holy Trinity (Father, Son, and Holy Spirit) fill the soul of the newly baptized, the Holy Spirit is one who fills the soul of the newly confirmed.

The Sacrament of Confirmation is done at different times in the Eastern and Latin (Western) Catholic Church. In the Eastern Church, the three Sacraments of Baptism, Confirmation (also called Chrismation), and Holy Eucharist are done at the same time, usually in infancy. In the Latin Church, the three events are separated by several years. Usually the bishop visits each parish annually to confirm its teenagers.

The pastor formally presents those to be confirmed, the *confirmandi,* to the bishop. Most bishops ask a few questions of each of the young men and women, such as: What are the Seven Sacraments? What are the Ten Commandments? What are the gifts and fruits of the Holy Spirit? What are the Beatitudes?

Renewal of baptismal promises

After the homily, in which the bishop usually questions the confirmandi on their knowledge of the faith, the sacrament itself begins with the renewal of promises made when the young men and women were baptized as babies. Because they could not answer for themselves, their parents and godparents answered on their behalf, and now as young adults, they renew those promises themselves before the bishop.

Laying on of hands

Laying on of hands is the first of two necessary actions for a valid sacrament of Confirmation (along with anointing with chrism oil; see the next section). These two actions are called *the essential matter.*

The bishop begins,

> My dear friends, God our Father gave the new birth of eternal life to his chosen sons and daughters. Let us pray to our Father that he will pour out the Holy Spirit to strengthen his sons and daughters with his gifts and anoint them to be more like Christ the Son of God.

The bishop then extends his hands either over the whole group of confirmandi or on the head of each one individually. He says the following prayer:

> All-powerful God, Father of our Lord Jesus Christ, by water and the Holy Spirit you freed your sons and daughters from sin and gave them new life. Send your Holy Spirit upon them to be their helper and guide. Give them the spirit of wisdom and understanding, the spirit of right judgment and courage, the spirit of knowledge and reverence. Fill them with the spirit of wonder and awe in your presence. We ask this through Christ our Lord.

Anointing with chrism (Sanctum Chrisma)

Chrism is olive oil blessed by the bishop each year on Holy Week (just before Easter) and used in Confirmation as well as Baptism and Holy Orders. The candidates for Confirmation stand before the bishop, and each child's sponsor places a hand on the child's right shoulder. The bishop anoints by dipping his right thumb into the chrism oil and pressing it to the forehead (in the form of a cross) of each candidate, mentioning the Confirmation name chosen by the person.

Unlike the Eastern Catholic church that confirms (chrismates) at Baptism, the Latin Rite Catholic Church separates the two sacraments in time. Baptizing the infant means that mom and dad chose the name of their son or daughter. Confirmation years later allows the baptized person to choose his own Confirmation name (which becomes his third name, falling between his middle name and surname). *Confirmandi* choose the name of a saint who they wish to emulate and follow in example, who then becomes their patron saint.

> *Bishop:* [Name], be sealed with the gift of the Holy Spirit.
>
> *Candidate:* Amen.

The bishop then places his right hand on the left cheek of the newly confirmed and says

> *Bishop:* Peace be with you.
>
> *Confirmed:* And also with you.

The response of the confirmed will change to *And with your spirit* in November 2011.

The Mass continues with the Prayer of the Faithful or General Intercessions, the Liturgy of the Eucharist, and so on.

Mass for Anointing of the Sick

Not everyone who's sick is in a hospital or nursing home — some are homebound. For these faithful, the Church offers an optional Mass of Anointing that takes place in the home. St. James said in his epistle in the New Testament,

> *If there are any sick among you, then let them call for the priests of the church and the priest will pray over them and anoint the sick person with oil and the prayer of faith will save the sick person.* (James 5:14)

The Mass begins with the usual introductory rites, and then the priest may welcome all the sick together by saying:

> Christ taught his disciples to be a community of love. In praying together, in sharing all things, and in caring for the sick, they recalled his words: "Insofar as you did this to one of these, you did it to me." We gather today to witness to this teaching and to pray in the name of Jesus the healer that the sick may be restored to health. Through this Eucharist and anointing we invoke his healing power.

The Mass then continues with the Confiteor or other Penitential rite options as listed in the Missal.

Opening prayer

After the opening prayer, the priest says:

> Father, you raised your Son's cross as the sign of victory and life. May all who share in his suffering find in these sacraments a source of fresh courage and healing. We ask you this through our Lord Jesus Christ, your Son, who lives with you and the Holy Spirit, one God, forever and ever. Amen.

The Liturgy of the Word proceeds with the Scripture readings and homily.

Anointing

The priest anoints the sick persons with the oil of the sick *(oleum infirmorum)*. If several sick people are at the Mass, other priests may assist the celebrant. Each priest anoints some of the sick, using the sacramental formula. First he anoints the forehead, saying:

> Through this holy anointing may the Lord in his love and mercy help you with the grace of the Holy Spirit. Amen.

Then he anoints the open palms of the person, saying:

> May the Lord who frees you from sin save you and raise you up. Amen.

If the sick person is a priest, he is anointed on the *back* of his hands, as the palms were anointed when he was ordained.

After anointing, the following prayer is offered:

> Father in heaven, through this holy anointing grant our brothers and sisters comfort in their suffering. When they are afraid, give them courage, when afflicted, give them patience, when dejected, afford them hope, and when alone, assure them of the support of your holy people. We ask this through Christ our Lord. Amen.

The Mass continues with the Liturgy of the Eucharist. A special Prayer Over the Gifts is said:

> Merciful God, as these simple gifts of bread and wine will be transformed into the risen Lord, so may he unite our sufferings with his and cause us to rise to new life. We ask this through Christ our Lord. Amen.

A special preface can be used at a Mass for Anointing of the Sick:

> Father, all-powerful and ever-living God, we do well always and everywhere to give you thanks, for you have revealed to us in Christ the healer your unfailing power and steadfast compassion. In the splendor of his rising, your Son conquered suffering and death and bequeathed to us his promise of a new and glorious world, where no bodily pain will afflict us and no anguish of spirit. Through your gift of the Spirit, you bless us, even now, with comfort and healing, strength and hope, forgiveness and peace. In this supreme sacrament of your love you give us the risen body of your Son: a pattern of what we shall become when he returns again at the end of time. In gladness and joy we unite with the angels and saints in the great canticle of creation, as we sing (say): Holy, Holy, Holy . . .

Eucharistic Prayer

Special embolisms may also be used at Mass of Anointing. These are unique prayers inserted into the Eucharistic prayer, which is the most solemn part of the Mass and spoken only by the Priest.

This *Communicantes* is said if the Roman Canon (Eucharistic Prayer I) is used:

> Father, accept this offering from your whole family, and especially from those who ask for healing of body, mind, and spirit. Grant us your peace in this life, save us from final damnation, and count us among those you have chosen.

The following embolism is said when Eucharistic Prayer II is used:

> Remember also those who ask for healing in the name of your Son, that they may never cease to praise you for the wonders of your power.

And with Eucharistic Prayer III:

> Hear especially the prayers of those who ask for healing in the name of your Son, that they may never cease to praise you for the wonders of your power.

The Mass continues as usual with the *Pater Noster* (Our Father), *Agnus Dei* (Lamb of God), and Holy Communion.

Final prayer

This final prayer is said by the priest:

> Merciful God, in celebrating these mysteries your people have received the gifts of unity and peace. Heal the afflicted and make them whole in the name of your only Son, who lives and reigns for ever and ever. Amen.

Weekday Mass

Weekday Mass is just like Sunday Mass except that only one Scripture reading is done before the Gospel instead of two. The congregation attending the weekday Mass is typically much smaller than on Sundays, so hymns may be omitted. No offering is collected during the week in parishes.

Holy Day Mass (Solemnities)

Holy day Masses are treated like Sundays. Two readings from Scripture are done before the Gospel reading, and chanting and incense are typically part of the Mass, as well. The celebrant may also wear more formal albs at these special Masses.

Easter and Christmas are two most important solemnities and holy days of the Church year, followed by the feasts of the Lord (Corpus Christi, Ascension Thursday, Epiphany), feasts of the Virgin Mary (Immaculate Conception, Assumption, Nativity), and feasts of some of the more significant saints (St. Joseph, SS. Peter and Paul, Holy Apostles, All Saints, patron saint of the parish, patron saint of the diocese). You can find out more about special celebrations of the liturgical year in Chapter 3.

Some holy days have proper sequences (poetic verses) recited before the Gospel listed in the lectionary (the Catholic book of Bible readings for Mass). The *Stabat Mater* is read on the feast of Our Lady of Sorrows (September 15); *Veni Sancte Spiritus* on Pentecost (50 days after Easter); *Victimae paschali laudes* on Easter; *Lauda Sion Salvatorem* on Corpus Christi. The Extraordinary form of the Roman Rite also includes the *Dies Irae* on All Souls Day.

Chapter 8

Extending the Mass: Liturgy of the Hours and Eucharistic Devotions

In This Chapter

▶ Praying throughout the day: The Liturgy of the Hours

▶ Adoring the Eucharist outside of Mass: Eucharistic devotions

The word *liturgy* comes from the Greek word *leitourgia,* meaning public worship. The most obvious example of liturgy is the Sacred or Divine Liturgy, which is called the Holy Mass (or Holy Sacrifice of the Mass) in the Latin Rite of the Catholic Church. But other forms of liturgy exist in Catholic worship and are connected to the Mass, including the Liturgy of the Hours and Exposition and Benediction of the Blessed Sacrament.

Today, *liturgy* describes all the official services of the Church. Traditional Sunday Mass may be the most well-known service, but liturgy extends throughout the week in various forms that are practiced by ordained clergy, consecrated religious, and devout laity. In this chapter we explore the Liturgy of the Hours, a ritual of prayer and Scripture reading done eight times a day, and Eucharistic devotions, everyday adoration of the host practiced in various forms and circumstances. These extensions of the Mass bring worship to members of the Church throughout their daily lives.

The Liturgy of the Hours

Known as the *Divine Office* or the *Breviary* before the Second Vatican Council (1962–1965), the Liturgy of the Hours is the public praying of the 150 psalms of the Bible and many readings from the other books of the Bible by clergy and religious around the world. The day is divided into several liturgical hours, and at each, at least three psalms and a few other scriptural passages are read. Over the course of one year, almost all the psalms and a good portion of the Bible (when combined with the daily Mass readings) are read and prayed by bishops, priests, deacons, religious sisters and brothers, monks and nuns, and laity alike.

The Mass is the highest form of prayer, so the Liturgy of the Hours is considered an extension of the Sacred or Divine Liturgy because the word of God is being used for public worship day in and day out. The Catechism of the Catholic Church says public prayer of the Church (the *Divine Office*) is structured to make the full day and night holy in praise to God.

The Biblical foundation for what Catholics currently call the *Liturgy of the Hours* is in the ideal Jesus gave to his followers in the New Testament of setting aside particular hours for prayer. Prayer was a constant part of Jesus's earthly life, and the Church continues that practice, using the Liturgy of the Hours as a way of fulfilling Christ's call to "pray always." The Liturgy of Hours is prayed in union with Jesus, inspired by his spirit and directed to his Father. By following the Liturgy of the Hours, the Church unites itself with the hymn of praise of angels and saints. God doesn't need the praise of human beings, but humans need to praise God to be fully human.

The Liturgy of the Hours consists of different prayers said at different times of the day. The prayer of the first hour, typically at 6 a.m., is *Prime.* The third hour prayer, at 9 a.m., is *Terce,* and *Sext* is the prayer of the sixth hour, at noon. The ninth hour prayer at 3 p.m. is *None.* Catholic monasteries ring bells every three hours beginning at midnight to remind the monks and nuns of the time to pray.

As they evolved in the monasteries, the hours of prayer came to include Matins, Prime, Lauds, Terce, Sext, None, Vespers, and Compline. *Matins* was recited or sung at night, and *Prime* and *Lauds* were the morning prayers. *Terce, Sext,* and *None* were prayed throughout the day, and *Vespers* and *Compline* were evening and night prayers.

This schedule was easy to keep in the monasteries, where everyone has to follow the same time schedules, but the difficulty outside the monastery (for parish priests and lay faithful at home) meant some of the hours were not observed. Some monastic or more traditional churches (that likely still use the Extraordinary form of the Mass) still use the longer observance (every three hours), but today, clergy, religious, and laity use a shortened schedule with some flexibility. They're asked to pray the principal hours of morning prayer, evening prayer, night prayer, Office of Readings, and one of the midday or midafternoon prayers.

Matins

Matins, now called the *Office of Readings,* was originally prayed by monks in the dead of night or wee hours of the morning. It is still a night prayer done in choral recitation, but now it may be prayed in personal prayer at any time, and the first hour of prayer may now be celebrated either as the Office of Readings (Matins) or Lauds, a morning prayer.

The Office of Readings starts with the Invitatory, an invitation to praise God. After the Invitatory, those in prayer sing or recite a hymn and then the psalms. On Sundays, the *Te Deum* (a hymn) is prayed after the psalms. Each day's psalms and other scriptural passages from the Bible are predetermined and assigned based on liturgical calendar (Sanctoral or Temporal cycle). There is no variety or choice, because these are the official prayers of the church and everyone is supposed to be praying the same passages.

Lauds

Lauds, from the Latin *Laudes,* meaning *praise,* is the morning prayer of Christ and his Church. The prayer marks the beginning of the day and reminds the faithful of the Resurrection of Jesus. The texts of the Lauds, particularly on Sunday, focus on the risen Savior and the triumph of light over darkness.

Lauds begins with an invitational prayer that also rejoices in the Lord's Resurrection, which is followed by a hymn that focuses on the liturgical season or particular feast day. The main focus is on the psalms that follow the hymn, where the priest or leader of prayer expresses the primary focus of the prayer.

When not prayed in common (that is, when not accompanied by others), the individual alone says all the parts. When prayed with others (in common), a leader says specific parts.

The first psalm is read and followed by the Canticle of Lauds, which is taken from the Old Testament. Psalms two and three are read; the third psalm of Lauds is always one of praise.

Then comes the Canticle of Zechariah, which forms a bridge between the Hebrew and the Christian Covenants, between the Old and the New Testaments. The prayers of intercession that follow are praises and petitions that are followed by the Lord's Prayer. Finally, the presider's prayer gathers the intentions of the entire Church and ends with a blessing.

Vespers

Vespers, from the Latin word *vesper,* which means *evening,* is usually a prayer of gratitude.

The reform initiated by Vatican II called for evening prayer to consist of two psalms and one canticle from the New Testament, which is what gives Vespers its Christ-centered focus.

Vespers follows the same format as Lauds, concluding with the intercessions for the entire church and the particular needs of the local people, and then ends with the prayer of the presider and the blessing.

Parishioners pray Psalm 41 on the first Friday of the month, reminding them of the sufferings of Christ on Good Friday. The psalm expresses the humiliation, betrayal, and abandonment that Jesus endured to win our salvation.

The Canticle of Mary, commonly known as the Magnificat, is at the heart of the Church's official evening prayer. The Blessed Virgin of Nazareth praises God's goodness to her and to those who accept God's will in their lives. The poor will be exalted and the rich will be sent away empty. Pope Paul VI, in his papal letter on Marian devotion, wrote that "the Canticle of the Virgin has become the prayer of the whole Church for all times." This fervent prayer expresses Mary's enduring attitude before the throne of God in heaven.

The full congregation stands for the Magnificat and makes the sign of the cross as the incense is spread through the church where they are gathered. The canticle is one of joy and devotion.

Compline

Compline, now called *Night Prayers* (but not to be confused with Matins), is the final prayer of the day and should be prayed right before bedtime.

The prayer begins like the others but includes an examination of conscience, followed by one or two psalms assigned for each day. There is a reading, and the responsory (response done in verse) for night prayers follows the quotes of the dying Jesus on the cross: "Into your hands I commend my spirit." The Canticle of Simeon with its antiphon leads to the concluding prayer. After the blessing has been given by the presider, the congregation sings or recites one of the antiphons in honor of the Blessed Virgin Mary.

Eucharistic Devotions

Catholics perform devotions to the Holy Eucharist (consecrated bread and wine that the faithful believe are the Real Body and Blood of Christ) because of its importance. The Eucharist is three things: sacrifice, sacred meal, and sacrament.

✔ It is foremost the holy sacrifice of Jesus Christ, the Son of God, who freely offered his life for the salvation of mankind. The sacrifice of the cross on Calvary on Good Friday and the sacrifice of the Mass are one and the same.

✔ The Holy Eucharist is also a sacred meal by which the believer's soul is nourished with the Real Body and Blood of Christ. The Eucharist is thus a reenactment of the Last Supper on Holy Thursday.

✔ Finally, the Holy Eucharist is the Real Presence of Christ under the appearances of bread and wine. As the Real Body and Blood, soul and divinity of Christ, the Blessed Sacrament deserves all the adoration and worship due God alone. Because Christ is the Second Person of the Holy Trinity, his Real Presence deserves the same worship given to any of the Persons of the One Triune God.

Since the earliest days of Christianity, the adoration of the Holy Eucharist outside of the context of the Mass commonly took place when Christians brought Holy Communion to the sick and dying members of their congregations. At the same time, ancient Christians (during the time of Roman persecution) did not reserve the Eucharist for the purpose of private or public adoration; it was reserved in a separate place under the care of the deacons and kept from the sight of the faithful. This was to protect it from harm and abuse by enemies of the church.

Today, the Eucharist can be viewed, and private prayer before the Blessed Sacrament is one of the treasures of the Western tradition. The place of Eucharistic reservation should foster a sense of the spiritual recollection and silent prayer that are inspired by participation in the Mass.

Eucharistic Exposition and Benediction

In the Old Testament Book of Numbers, God's chosen people wandering in the desert became embittered and angry against God and Moses and, as a result, were attacked by poisonous serpents. The people soon repented and asked Moses to pray that God would remove the serpents. God ordered Moses to make a bronze serpent and hang it on a pole so that anyone who looked at it would be saved from death from the venomous bite.

Just as with the bronze statue, Christians wanted to be able to *see* the sacramental host. It was that need to see the host that led to the practice of the priest lifting the Eucharist after it has been consecrated. The elevation of the host remains an important part of Mass, and in many churches bells are rung at this moment to remind the people it is happening.

Eucharistic Exposition and Benediction are an extension of the elevation of the host and chalice at Mass. It is a time of adoration and worship rather than a time of being spiritually fed by Holy Communion (which takes place at Mass).

Blessing the people with the Holy Eucharist is seen as a blessing from Jesus himself, so the priest or deacon wears a humeral veil over his shoulders and covers his hands as he holds the monstrance (a sacred vessel that contains the consecrated bread behind a pane of crystal or glass that allows the sacrament to be seen). The use of the veil symbolizes that the blessing is not from the cleric but from Christ himself in the Blessed Sacrament.

The Eucharistic Exposition, Adoration, and Benediction should include a time of quiet prayer as well as some scriptural passages from the Bible and a sermon from a priest or deacon. This holy hour represents the hour Jesus asked his disciples to pray with him in the Garden of Agony just before his arrest and Crucifixion on Good Friday.

The culmination is the Benediction, when the priest or deacon takes the monstrance and makes the sign of the cross over the congregation. Bells are rung, incense is burned, and people bless themselves. It is the equivalent of getting a blessing from the Lord himself.

While only an ordained cleric (bishop, priest, or deacon) can do the Benediction of the Blessed Sacrament, other members of the faithful may be given permission to expose the Holy Eucharist (take the consecrated host from the tabernacle and place it on the altar in the monstrance) to allow the faithful time for private prayer before the Real Presence.

Eucharistic processions

Any march of persons in front of the Blessed Sacrament in a monstrance that begins at one point (church or chapel) and proceeds to another point is a *procession.* It can be around the inside of a church, it can be around the block where the church is located, or it can be from one church or shrine to another.

The physical walking about with the Holy Eucharist in the monstrance in a formal procession is a symbol of the journey of faith, the pilgrimage all believers are to have in this world as they prepare for the next. Formal processions with the Blessed Sacrament came out of the practice of bringing Viaticum to the sick and dying. From *viaticus,* which means *going with you, Viaticum* is the Latin name given to the Eucharist that's brought to a dying Christian. It indicates that the Lord himself accompanies the soul through the gates of death.

Historically, bringing Holy Communion to sick or dying persons was conducted very solemnly. The server rang a small bell warning faithful Christians to kneel in adoration as the priest passed by carrying the Blessed Sacrament to those who were suffering. But those healthy Christians wanted and needed an affirmation on the Real Presence of Christ in the Holy Eucharist, too, so a custom arose in the Middle Ages of having a procession move from one church to the next. Everyone was encouraged to join in the procession, which was seen as a mini-pilgrimage. Going to the Holy Land or other holy shrines was not always possible logistically, economically, or otherwise. Making a walk from one parish church to the next, however, was much more convenient.

To this day, popes acting as Bishops of Rome have processions from the Basilica of St. John Lateran (the actual cathedral church of the Diocese of Rome) to the Basilica of St. Peter (otherwise known as the Vatican, the residence of the pope). Many churches have Eucharistic Processions outside to temporary altars when neighboring churches are too far to walk to.

On Holy Thursday, an abbreviated procession occurs when the Holy Communion is taken from the tabernacle at the end of Mass and brought to the repository where it stays until midnight. Another shorter procession is the annual 40 Hours parish devotion when a procession takes the Blessed Sacrament around the outside of the church or up and down the aisles inside. This procession can also take place on the Feast of Corpus Christi.

The Feast of Corpus Christi

The Holy Eucharist was instituted by Jesus at the Last Supper, and the Church commemorates the gift of Jesus on Holy Thursday. Christ gives himself in the Eucharist to feed, comfort, and strengthen his faithful followers with his Real Presence, remaining with them even in his absence while they await his return in glory.

The Feast of the Body and Blood of Christ (*Corpus Christi* in Latin) is celebrated in the United States on the Sunday after Trinity Sunday in order to solemnly commemorate the institution of the Holy Eucharist. Some believe the feast's origin was a miracle in Bolsena, Italy, in which a consecrated host actually shed blood, convincing an unbeliever of the Real Presence of Christ in the Eucharist. The cloth or corporal stained with the sacred blood is now displayed behind a pane of glass in the Cathedral of Orvieto in central Italy. (For more examples of Eucharistic miracles, turn to Chapter 15.)

Pope Urban IV, a great admirer of Eucharistic devotion, extended this feast to the entire Church in 1264. He asked St. Thomas Aquinas to compose an official celebration for the Divine Office (the Breviary, or now called Liturgy of the Hours) of Corpus Christi, which is today one of the most beautiful in the Liturgy of the Hours. A Eucharistic procession was not required on the day the Feast of Corpus Christi is celebrated with Mass in church, but soon processions of the Holy Eucharist became very popular throughout the European countries. The Blessed Sacrament was initially carried in a glass or crystal reliquary before the use of a monstrance became common. While optional, it is now not uncommon to have at least several parishes have processions at the end of the Mass on Corpus Christi.

40 Hours Devotion

The 40 Hours Devotion is a period of continuous prayer before the Blessed Sacrament, which is solemnly exposed for veneration. This devotion encourages faithful Catholics to sacramental and spiritual communion with our Savior. It is practiced from the time that the last Sunday Mass ends until 40 hours later, sometime on Tuesday. Consecrated host from Sunday Mass is placed in a monstrance, and traditionally at least one person remains present with the monstrance at all times.

Where 40 Hours Devotions are practiced, the local bishop or diocese assigns the dates to parishes. It was commonly done around the patronal feast of the parish (that is, near the feast day of the patron saint in whose honor the church was built).

Eucharistic congresses

The goals of a Eucharistic congress are

- ✔ Seeking a deeper reflection on the Eucharist as the mystery of Jesus working in the Church

✔ Promoting more active participation in the liturgy as a means of evangelization and a way of deepening a sense of community among Christians

✔ Focusing on the early Church's example of sharing material goods and promoting the many areas of human progress while not losing focus on the Eucharist Presence as a promise of future sharing with Christ in glory

Eucharistic congresses are clearly influenced by the piety of a particular society and the politics of the local situation. Though a relatively recent phenomenon, their international character, or *universality,* is one of the four marks of the Church. The first congress took place at Lillie in France in 1873, and 43 international Eucharistic congresses have since taken place. These gatherings were extremely popular in times and places where Eucharistic devotion flourished among ordinary Catholics.

The Eucharistic congress movement and the growing liturgical movement began a fertile positive relationship at the Eucharistic congress held in Munich in 1960. Since that time, the Eucharistic sacrifice has been the primary focus of each congress, and the spirit of Eucharistic devotion inspired by the Second Vatican Council has prevailed.

Perpetual adoration chapels

Because Catholic Christians believe the Holy Eucharist is the Real, true and substantial Presence of Christ, naturally they want to spend time with him. Christians of all denominations profess Jesus as Lord and Savior. Catholics are no different in that regard. What is different is that they have perpetual adoration chapels that provide an opportunity to spend quality time in a special place with the Presence of Christ 24/7.

Some religious communities have perpetual adoration of the Holy Eucharist as the center of their spirituality. Cloistered Dominican Nuns, Poor Clare Nuns, Carmelite Nuns, and others have the Blessed Sacrament perpetually exposed outside of the celebration of Mass.

But in the average parish church, keeping the Blessed Sacrament (Holy Eucharist) in the monstrance on the altar all day and night is not practical. One reality is that the place is used for daily Mass and often for weddings, funerals, Baptism, Confirmation, and other services. Additionally, the cost of keeping the entire church lit and at a comfortable temperature can be prohibitive for an around-the-clock schedule.

The practical solution is to have a separate, dedicated location for the perpetual adoration of Christ in the Eucharist, and that's an adoration chapel. It can be a separate room from the larger body of the church or be adjacent to it. Some places are even in separate buildings. It can thus be kept warm in winter and cooled easily during the summer months. People often feel more comfortable in a smaller space that creates an atmosphere of quiet intimacy with the Lord.

The most important aspect of a perpetual adoration chapel is that it be reverent and conducive to quiet prayer. Some neighborhoods may not be suitable for all-night devotions because of the safety factor. But perpetual adoration is a Eucharistic devotion in which members of a particular parish or other institution commit themselves to taking hours of adoration before the Blessed Sacrament seven days a week, both during the day and throughout the night.

If you divide the time of devotion into hours, that's 168 hours to fill in a week. Having at least 200 volunteers for this devotion is safest so that a substitute can take the place of another adorer in an emergency situation.

Lay involvement encouraged by the Second Vatican Council is at the heart of any program of perpetual adoration. Volunteers have no rules beyond behaving in a reverent manner appropriate to spending time with the Lord in the Eucharist. The many spiritual benefits and graces that may be gained by individual Catholics and the entire parish by the establishment of a program of perpetual adoration far outweighs any inconvenience that may be encountered.

Chapter 9

Eastern Catholic Divine Liturgy

· ·

In This Chapter

▶ Understanding the origins of the Divine Liturgy

▶ Preparing for the main liturgies

▶ Celebrating the public part of Mass with the Liturgy of Catechumens

▶ Receiving the Eucharist in the Liturgy of Faithful

· ·

*T*he largest of the Eastern Catholic Rites is the Byzantine Rite, which is used by a number of Eastern Catholic Churches. The Divine Liturgy of St. John Chrysostom is the most predominant liturgy used, so we examine it in this chapter.

The liturgies of the Eastern and Western Churches have substantial similarities. Both East and West require readings from Sacred Scripture (Bible) in the first half of the Mass, and both have the Last Supper narrative (including the exact words of Christ) in the second half, where the bread and wine are consecrated into the Body and Blood of Christ and where Holy Communion is given to the faithful. Both Churches have the same beliefs, and both are in unity with the pope.

Some differences distinguish the two Churches, though. Western (Latin) Catholicism emphasizes the sacrificial nature of the Mass, particularly the Last Supper on Holy Thursday and the Death of Christ on the cross on Good Friday, but Eastern Catholicism emphasizes the mystery and glory of the Resurrection of Jesus Christ from the dead on Easter Sunday. Both Churches affirm the same elements; the difference is merely one of liturgical perspective.

Elements of the Masses differ as well. The deacon is very integral to Eastern Catholic liturgy, and Mass rarely takes place without a deacon, whereas in the Latin Rite, deacons are very helpful but only mandatory at Masses with a bishop. Also, instead of using statues in the churches, as in the West, the East uses icons (paintings on wood). The Eastern Rite also uses lots and lots of incense and chanting during the Mass.

All Eastern Catholic liturgies have preparatory rites (the Liturgy of Preparation) followed by the main liturgy itself. Like in the Western Church, the main liturgy is divided into two parts: The Mass or Liturgy of Catechumens is first, followed by the Mass or Liturgy of the Faithful (in which Communion takes place). In this chapter we take you through these parts of the Mass, but first we give you some background on the history of this rite.

History of the Byzantine Rite and Liturgy of St. John Chrysostom

Catholic worship can be divided into the four major liturgical families: Roman, Byzantine (Constantinopolitan), Antiochian, and Alexandrian. Each form originated in the ancient cities of their patriarchs, which were the key centers of Christianity in Apostolic times and the pre-medieval era. Five patriarchates, called the Pentarchy, centered on the cities of Jerusalem, Rome, Antioch, Alexandria, and Constantinople.

Four of the five patriarchates established liturgical families that were continued in several liturgical rites (traditions), and these rites further generated about 20 Churches within Catholicism (before the Schism with the Eastern Orthodox Church in 1054). Jerusalem was the only patriarchate that didn't give birth to a unique liturgical tradition. The Roman Rite developed as the basis of the Western Church, and the remaining three patriarchates became what's considered the Eastern Church. The largest descendent comes from the Church of Constantinople, and is now called the Byzantine Rite.

The Divine Liturgy of St. John Chrysostom was devised by the first Archbishop and Patriarch of Constantinople, John (AD 349–407). He was well aware of an ancient axiom, *lex orandi, lex credenda,* which translates from Latin into *the law of prayer is the law of belief.* In other words, sacred worship of God, especially the Divine Liturgy (Holy Mass), being the highest form of prayer, must also reflect, inform, and support the doctrines and teachings of the Christian religion. John wanted to ensure that the beliefs were properly and accurately portrayed in sacred worship. As a priest and then a bishop, John preached so eloquently that he was given the moniker *Chrysostom,* which means *golden mouthed* in Greek, by his peers and his parishioners.

Peeking at heaven through icons

Byzantine Divine Liturgy is filled with awesome and magnificent Christian art, particularly icons, hand-painted pictures depicting Jesus, the Blessed Virgin Mary, and other saints on wood panels. Veneration of the icons is an important part of sacred worship. The icons are considered windows into heaven, and they're purposely not made to look three-dimensional or too lifelike, because we're peeking into heaven from our position on earth. Heaven is pure and holy, but Earth is imperfect and sinful.

St. John Chrysostom contended with one of the first and most pernicious of the Christian heresies, that of *Arianism*. These Arians were not skinheads with swastikas (as the term *Aryan* is sometimes applied today). The Arians John dealt with were Christians following the priest Arius (AD 250–336). Arius's theology was so obsessed with defending the doctrine of *monotheism* (the belief in only one God in the universe, not many) that it committed the heresy of denying the doctrine of the Holy Trinity (one God in Three Persons) and the doctrine of the divinity of Christ. Arianism taught that Jesus Christ, the Son of God, has a similar but not same divine nature as God the Father.

Christian dogma (Catholic, Orthodox, and Protestant) firmly believes that Jesus is both God and Man, human and divine. He has a human nature and a divine nature united under one divine person. The Ecumenical Councils of Nicea (AD 325) and Constantinople I (AD 381) solemnly defined these teachings on the nature of Christ. The Liturgy of St. John Chrysostom and most other Byzantine Catholic liturgies support and affirm each other, particularly on the idea of the divinity of Christ.

Liturgy of Preparation

The introductory part of the Byzantine Divine Liturgy is called the *Liturgy of Preparation*. It's also called *Prothesis* (setting forth) or *Proskomedia* (an offering).

This ceremony is unique and has no corresponding part in the Latin or Roman Rite of the Western Catholic Church. In the West, the bread and wine and the sacred vessels which contain them are merely prepared by a sacristan or acolyte or by the deacon or priest himself. No particular prayers are said, and no particular ceremony is used for the prep work. However, both rites involve prayers for vesting of the celebrant (in the West, this step is obligatory for the Extraordinary form and optional for the Ordinary form).

The bread used for the Liturgy of Preparation is called *Prosphora*. A round loaf of leavened bread is baked in two layers to represent the two natures (human and divine) of Christ. A square seal with a cross and the Greek letters ICXC and NIKA (standing for *Jesus Christ Conquers*) is made on the top of the loaf. Unlike the Latin or Roman Rite, which only uses unleavened bread, the Byzantine and other Eastern Catholic Rites use yeast in their recipes to produce leavened bread for Divine Worship. The yeast symbolizes the Risen Lord, because the Hebrews were not permitted to use yeast in the Passover (Seder) Meal as they were fleeing in haste from slavery into the Promised Land.

Byzantine Rites uses only grape wine that is red, not only because it was used by Christ at the Last Supper (the first Divine Liturgy), but also to accentuate the fact that the wine will be consecrated into the very Blood of Christ. The Latin Rite, while firmly believing in the changing into the Precious Blood, uses either red or white grape wine.

The Liturgy of Preparation has three main parts, which we describe in the following sections:

- ✔ Prayers before the Holy Doors
- ✔ Vesting prayers
- ✔ Preparing the oblations

Kairon (Prayers before the Holy Doors)

The priest and deacon are admonished in the ritual texts to be in the state of grace — that is, to be free of mortal sin — when they celebrate the Divine Mysteries of Sacred Worship. It is gravely sinful for ordained ministers to offer the holy gifts while in an unworthy spiritual state, but this sin does not affect the validity of the sacrament or sacrifice. The same applies for the Latin Rite and all other Eastern Rites as well.

The priest and deacon enter the church and stand before the iconostasis (wall of icons separating sanctuary from the nave where the congregation sits) wearing their clerical attire (cassock). They pray together before the icon of Christ and the icon of the Virgin Mary.

Deacon: Give the blessing, Father.

Priest: Blessed is our God at all times, now and always and forever. Heavenly King, Consoler, the Spirit of Truth, present in all places and filling all things, the Treasury of blessings and the Giver of life, come and dwell in us, cleanse us of all stain, and save our souls, O Good One.

Deacon: Holy is God! Holy the Mighty One! Holy the Immortal One! Have mercy on us. [Three times]

Glory be to the Father, and to the Son, and to the Holy Spirit, now and always and forever. Amen.

All-Holy Trinity, have mercy on us. Lord, forgive our sins. Master, pardon our transgressions. Holy One, look upon us and heal our infirmities for your name's sake.

Lord, have mercy. [Three times]

Glory be to the Father, and to the Son, and to the Holy Spirit, now and always and forever. Amen.

Our Father, who art in heaven, hallowed be thy name. Thy kingdom come, thy will be done on earth as it is in heaven. Give us this day our daily bread, and forgive us our trespasses as we forgive those who trespass against us, and lead us not into temptation, but deliver us from evil.

Priest: For thine is the kingdom and the power and the glory, of the Father, and the Son, and the Holy Spirit, now and always and forever.

Deacon: Amen.

Have mercy on us, Lord. Have mercy on us. At a loss for any defense, we sinners offer this prayer to you, the Master: Have mercy on us.

Priest: Glory be to the Father, and to the Son, and to the Holy Spirit.

Deacon: Lord, have mercy on us, for we have put our trust in you: Rise not in anger against us, remember not our transgressions, but in the depth of your mercy look upon us even now and save us from our enemies: for you are our God and we are your people, we are all the work of your hands and we constantly call upon your name.

Priest: Now and always and forever. Amen.

Deacon: Blessed Mother of God, open the portal of your deep mercy to us who put our trust in you, so that we may not be brought to confusion, but through you may be delivered from adversity, for you are the salvation of the Christian fold.

Priest: Before your most pure image we bow in worship, O Good One, begging forgiveness for our stumblings, Christ God: because you chose of your own free will to ascend upon the cross in the flesh in order to deliver from the enemy's yoke those you had created. For this reason we cry out to you in thanksgiving: "You, our Savior have filled all things with joy when you came to save the world."

The priest and deacon kiss the icon of Christ. Then they go before the icon of the Mother of God for the troparion:

> *Priest:* Mother of God, since you became a fountain of mercy, count us worthy of your compassion; look upon a people that has sinned, show forth your power as you always do. Because we have put our trust in you, we hail you as once did Gabriel, the captain of the angels.

The priest and deacon kiss the icon of the Theotokas, and then bow their heads.

> *Priest:* Lord, stretch forth your hand from your dwelling place on high, and strengthen me for your ministry now forthcoming, so that I may stand without condemnation before your awesome judgment seat and complete the unbloody sacrifice. For yours is the power and the glory forever. Amen.

Both priest and deacon make three reverences before the holy doors, and then bow to the two choirs. They go into the sanctuary, the priest through the north door and the deacon through the south door, saying as they go:

> *Priest and Deacon:* I shall enter into your dwelling place; before your holy temple I shall bow in fear of you.
>
> O Lord, be my guide in your justice because of those who oppress me: Make my way level before your sight. Indeed, in their mouth there is no truth; in their heart, there is nothing but decay. Their throat is but a gaping tomb, while their tongue is honeyed. Be you their judge, O God: May they founder in their evil plots. Cast them out, for their crimes are countless, and they have risen against you, Lord. But as for those who put their trust in you, they shall rejoice and feast forevermore.
>
> You will dwell among them, and all who love your name shall rejoice, For you, Lord, do bless the just and do cover him as with a shield of grace.

Once in the sanctuary, they make three reverences before the holy table and the holy Gospel Book, saying:

> *Priest and Deacon:* O God, be propitious to me a sinner and have mercy on me. [Three times]

Vesting of the deacon

Particular prayers are said as the clerics (deacon and priest) vest after completing the Entrance Prayers before the Holy Doors. The deacon, holding his liturgical vestments on the palm of his right hand, comes to the priest, bows his head, and says:

> *Deacon:* Bless the sticharion and the orarion, Father.
>
> *Priest:* Blessed is our God ✠ at all times, now and always and forever.
>
> *Deacon:* Amen.

The deacon kisses the right hand of the priest. Then the deacon withdraws to another part of the sanctuary and puts on his vestments, saying the proper prayers:

> My soul shall rejoice in the Lord, for he has clothed me with a robe of salvation and covered me with a tunic of happiness; he has crowned me as a bridegroom and as a bride, adorned me with jewels.

And the deacon kisses the orarion (prayer stole) and puts it on his left shoulder, saying nothing. Then he slips the epimanikia (cuffs) over his hands. For the right hand he says:

> Your right hand, Lord, is made glorious in might; your right hand, Lord, has crushed the enemies; and in the fullness of your glory, you have routed the adversary.

And for the left:

> Your hands have made me and fashioned me: Give me understanding and I shall learn your commandments.

Then, going to the prothesis (altar of offering), the deacon arranges the holy objects, each in its proper place.

Vesting of the priest

The priest likewise, vests. Taking in his right hand the tunic and making three reverences toward the east, he blesses it:

> Blessed is our God ✠ at all times, now and always and forever. Amen.

Then the priest puts it on, saying:

> My soul shall rejoice in the Lord, for he has clothed me with a robe of salvation and covered me with a tunic of happiness; he has crowned me as a bridegroom and adorned me with jewels as a bride.

Then, taking the epitrachelion (stole), the priest blesses and kisses it and puts it on, saying:

> Blessed is God ✠ who pours out grace upon his priests: as the chrism upon the head, which ran down unto the beard, the beard of Aaron, ran down even to the hem of his garment, at all times, now and always and forever. Amen.

Then the priest takes the zone (cincture), blesses it, and girds himself, saying:

> Blessed is God ✠ who girds me with strength and makes my way blameless and strengthens my feet like the hart's, at all times, now and always and forever. Amen.

He blesses and kisses the epimanikia (cuffs), then pulls them on, saying for the right hand:

> Your right hand, ✠ Lord, is made glorious in might; your right hand, Lord, has crushed the enemies; and in the fullness of your glory, you have routed the adversary.

And for the left:

> Your hands ✠ have made me and fashioned me: Give me understanding and I shall learn your commandments.

Then, if the priest has been given the honor and rank, he takes the epigonation (genual), blesses and kisses it, and puts it on, saying:

> Gird your sword ✠ at your side, Mighty One, in your splendor and beauty. String your bow; go forth, reign for the sake of truth, meekness and righteousness. Your right hand shall lead you wonderfully, at all times, now and always and forever. Amen.

Finally, taking the phelonion (chasuble), the priest blesses and kisses it and puts it on, saying:

> Your priests, ✠ Lord, shall clothe themselves with righteousness, and your saints shall rejoice in joy, at all times, now and always and forever. Amen.

Washing of the hands

The priest and deacon go to the basin and wash their hands, saying together:

> I shall wash my hands in innocence, Lord, and go around your altar; I shall listen to the sound of your praise and declare all your wonderful works. Lord, I love this house, your dwelling place and the tent where your glory abides.

> Link not my souls with the lost ones, nor my life with men of blood. They carry shame within their hands and their right hand is filled with bribes.

> As for me, I have walked in my innocence: Redeem me and have mercy on me.

> My foot is set upon the rightful road: In the assemblies, I will bless you, Lord.

Prothesis (Ceremony of preparation of the oblations)

The priest and deacon go to the altar of offering and make three reverences before it, saying:

> O God, be propitious to me a sinner and have mercy on me. [Three times]

The deacon wipes the diskos and chalices.

> *Priest:* You have redeemed us from the curse of the law by your Precious Blood: By being nailed to the cross and wounded with the lance, you have become for men the fountain of immortality : glory to you, our Savior.

> *Deacon:* Bless, Master.

> *Priest and Deacon:* Blessed is our God ✠ at all times, now and always and forever. Amen.

The deacon, standing at the right hand of the priest and holding his orarion with the three fingers of his right hand, points to the bread. The priest takes the Prosphora (bread that is used in Divine Liturgy; some will be consecrated into the Body of Christ while the rest is given after the liturgy as blessed bread) in his left hand and the holy lance in his right, and blessing the bread three times over the seal, he says:

> In remembrance of our Lord and God and Savior Jesus Christ. [Three times]

Then he thrusts the holy lance into the right side of the seal and makes an incision, saying:

> *Priest:* As a sheep, he was led to the slaughter.
>
> *Deacon:* Let us pray to the Lord.

He thrusts the lance into the left side of the seal, saying:

> *Priest:* As a spotless lamb silent before its shearer, he opens not his mouth.
>
> *Deacon:* Let us pray to the Lord.

The priest makes an incision in the top of the seal, saying:

> *Priest:* In his humiliation, his judgment was taken away.
>
> *Deacon:* Let us pray to the Lord.

And then thrusting the lance into the bottom of the seal, he says:

> *Priest:* And who shall declare his generation?
>
> *Deacon:* Let us pray to the Lord.

The priest, thrusting the holy lance obliquely into the right side of the bread, lifts out the *amnos* (Greek for *lamb*), the bread that will definitely be consecrated. (The leftover bread that is not consecrated is called *antidoron*.)

> *Deacon:* Lift up, Master.
>
> *Priest:* For his life was taken away from the earth.

The priest puts the amnos upside down on the diskos (paten).

> *Deacon:* Immolate, Master.

The priest immolates (sacrifices) by cutting the amnos crosswise and saying:

> *Priest:* The Lamb of God who takes away the sins of the world is immolated for the life and salvation of the world.
>
> *Deacon:* Pierce, Master.

The priest turns over the amnos, with the side bearing the cross upwards, and pierces it on the right side, below the letters *IC*, saying:

One of the soldiers pierced his side with a lance, and at once there came forth blood and water; and he who saw it bore witness, and his witness is true.

The deacon pours wine and a few drops of water into the poterion (chalice), and says to the priest:

Bless this holy union, Father.

The priest blesses it and says:

Blessed ✠ is the union of your holy things, at all times, now and always and forever. Amen.

Then the priest takes a second Prosphora and says:

In honor and memory of our most highly blessed and glorious Lady the Mother of God and ever-virgin Mary, through whose prayers do you, Lord, receive this sacrifice upon your altar in heaven.

The priest then removes particles of bread from the lamb and arranges them one by one in rows on either side of the lamb. He takes the particles from five different Prosphoras. Each particle he removes and places gets its own specific blessing, all of which are listed below:

At your right stood the Queen, clothed in an embroidered mantle of gold.

In honor and memory of the great captains of the angelic armies, Michael and Gabriel, and of all the heavenly bodiless powers.

Of the honorable and glorious prophet and forerunner John the Baptist. Of the holy glorious prophets Moses and Aaron, Elias and Eliseus, David son of Jesse; of the Three Holy Youths and the prophet Daniel, and of all the holy prophets.

Of the holy, glorious and illustrious apostles Peter and Paul and of all the holy apostles.

Of our fathers among the saints the great pontiffs and universal doctors Basil the great, Gregory the Theologian and John Chrysostom; Athanasius and Cyril, Nicholas of Myra, the holy hieromartyr Josaphat, Nikita, Bishop of Novgorod and Leontius, Bishop of Rostov. Cyril and Methodius, the Teachers of the Slavs, and of all holy pontiffs.

Of the holy first martyr and archdeacon Stephen; of the holy great martyrs Demetrius, George and Theodore of Tyre, and of all holy martyrs. Of the holy women martyrs Thecla, Barbara,

Cyriaca, Euphemia, Parasceva, and Catherine, and of all holy women martyrs.

Of our saintly fathers the God-bearers Anthony, Euthymius, Sabbas, Onupbrius, Athanasius of Athos, Anthony and Theodore of the Caves, Sergius of Radonets and Barlaam of Khutintk, and of all the saintly fathers. Of our venerable mothers in God Pelagia, Theodosia, Anastasia, Eupraxia, Febronia, Theodulia, Euphrosyne, Mary of Egypt, and of all holy and venerable mothers.

Of the holy wonderworkers laboring without pay Cosmas and Damian, Cyrus and John, Pantaleimon, and Hermolaus, and of all the holy ones laboring without pay.

Of the holy and righteous ancestors of God Joachim and Anne, [of the patron saint of the church or monastery, and of the saint of the day], of the holy grand duke Vladimir, the Equal of the Apostles and of all the saints, through whose prayers visit us, O God.

Of our father among the saints John Chrysostom, Archbishop of Constantinople.

Remember, Master who love mankind, all Orthodox Bishops, our Patriarch [name], our Most Reverend Bishop [name], the reverend priests, the deacons in Christ and all the clergy, [in monasteries, our Superior (name)], our brothers and fellow ministers, priests, deacons, and all our brethren whom in the depth of your compassion you have called to communion with you, all-good Master.

After placing this first group of particles, the priest takes particles to commemorate certain living people by name, starting with the bishop who ordained him, if he's still alive.

Remember, Lord, [name]. [Repeat for other people the priest wants to name]

In memory and for the remission of sins of the blessed founders of this holy church (or monastery).

Then the priest commemorates by name deceased people who he wants to include, starting with the bishop who ordained him, if no longer alive. For each name, he removes a particle and says:

Remember, Lord, [name]. [Repeat for other people the priest wants to name]

Remember all our Orthodox Fathers and brethren who have fallen asleep in the hope of resurrection to eternal life and in communion with you, O Lord who love mankind.

Then the deacon likewise remembers the living and dead people he wants to acknowledge. The priest removes a final particle and says:

> Remember also, Lord, my unworthiness and pardon my transgressions, deliberate and indeliberate.

The priest, blessing the censer, recites the Prayer of Incensing:

> *Deacon:* Bless the incense, Master. Let us pray to the Lord.
>
> *Priest:* We offer you incense, Christ our God, for an odor of spiritual fragrance: receive it on your altar in heaven, and send down on us in return the grace of your All-Holy Spirit.
>
> *Deacon:* Let us pray to the Lord.

And having incensed the asteriskos (star cover), the priest places it over the holy bread.

> *Priest:* And the star came and stood over the place where the child was.
>
> *Deacon:* Let us pray to the Lord. Adorn, Master.

And having incensed the first veil, the priest covers the holy bread with it and says:

> *Priest:* The Lord is King, he has put on splendor; the Lord has put on might and has girded himself, for he has strengthened the universe so that it cannot be moved.
>
> *Deacon:* Let us pray to the Lord. Veil, Master.

And having incensed the second veil, the priest covers the holy chalice and says:

> *Priest:* Your power, O Christ, has covered the heavens and the earth is filled with your praise.
>
> *Deacon:* Let us pray to the Lord. Cover, Master.

Having incensed the third veil, called the *aer,* the priest places it over both and says:

> Cover us over with the cover of your wings; drive away from us every alien and enemy; make life peaceful for us. Lord, have mercy on us and on your world, and save our souls, O Good One who loves mankind.

Then the priest, taking the censer, incenses the offering three times, saying:

Priest: Blessed are you, our God, who were pleased so to do. Glory to you.

Deacon: Now and always and forever. Amen. [Both lines repeated three times]

The priest bows respectfully three times, saying:

With a view to the offering of the precious gifts, let us pray to the Lord.

If a bishop is celebrating the liturgy, the priest doesn't complete the Rite of Preparation. Instead, after removing the particles of the Mother of God and those of the saints, he covers the paten and the chalice with the aer, saying nothing. The celebrating bishop then says the remaining lines of the Rite of Preparation. The cherubic hymn is then sung before the great entrance.

Blessing of the Holy Gifts

The next part of the Mass is the Blessing of the Holy Gifts. The priest says the Prayer of Offering:

Priest: O God, our God, who sent forth the Heavenly Bread, food for the whole world, our Lord and God Jesus Christ, as a Savior, Redeemer, and Benefactor to bless and sanctify us: Be pleased to bless ✠ this offering and to accept it on your altar in heaven. In your goodness and love for mankind, remember both those who offer it and those for whom it is offered. Hold us uncondemned in the celebration of your Divine Mysteries, for hallowed and glorified is your most noble and magnificent name, of the Father, the Son, and the Holy Spirit, now and always and forever.

Deacon: Amen.

The priest concludes the Prothesis (Prayer of Offering), saying:

Priest: Glory to you, Christ God, our hope, glory to you.

Deacon: Glory be to the Father, and to the Son, and to the Holy Spirit, now and always and forever. Amen.

Deacon: Lord, have mercy. [Three times]

Deacon: Give the blessing, Master, in the name of the Lord.

Priest: May Christ our true God, (who is risen from the dead, [if it is a Sunday]) through the prayers of his all pure Mother, of our father among the saints John Chrysostom, Archbishop of Constantinople, and of all the saints, have mercy on us and save us, for he is good and loves mankind.

Deacon: Amen.

The Great Doxology and troparian

The Great Doxology is a hymn that is also sung at Orthros (the Eastern Church's word for Matins).

> Glory to you, who show forth the light! Glory to God in the highest. Peace on earth and good will among men.
>
> We praise you, we bless you, we worship you, we glorify you, and we give thanks to you for the splendor of your glory.
>
> O Lord King, O Heavenly God, Father Almighty, O Lord, Only Begotten Son, Jesus Christ, and you, All Holy Spirit.
>
> O Lord God, O Lamb of God, O Son of the Father, who takes away the sin of the world, have mercy on us, O you who take away the sins of the world.
>
> Accept our supplication, O you who are enthroned at the right hand of God the Father, and have mercy on us.
>
> For you alone are Holy, you alone are the Lord Jesus Christ, in the glory of God the Father. Amen.
>
> Every day will I bless you, and sing to your name, always and forever.
>
> Deign, O Lord, to keep us this day without sin.
>
> Blessed are you O Lord, God of our Fathers; praised and glorified is your name forever. Amen.
>
> O Lord, let your mercy rest upon us for we have placed our trust in you.
>
> Blessed are you, O Lord, teach me your statutes. [Three times]
>
> O Lord, you have been for us a refuge from age to age. I said: Lord, have mercy on me and heal my soul, for I have sinned against you.
>
> O Lord, to you I come for shelter, teach me to obey your will, for you are my God.
>
> For with you is the fountain of life, and in your light we shall see light.
>
> Extend your mercy upon those who confess you.
>
> Holy God, Holy Mighty One, Holy Immortal One, have mercy on us. [Three times]
>
> Glory be to the Father and to the Son and to the Holy Spirit, now and always and forever. Amen.
>
> Holy Immortal One, have mercy on us.
>
> Holy God, Holy Mighty One, Holy Immortal One, have mercy on us.

The doxology is followed by the troparion (hymn) of Sunday or the feast being commemorated. For ordinary Sundays, if it is the 1st, 3rd, 5th, or 7th tone, the following troparion is chanted in the 2nd tone (musical setting) or in the same tone as the doxology:

> *Priest:* Today salvation has come to the world; let us sing to him who is risen from the tomb, the author of our life, for he has crushed death by his death and bestowed upon us victory and great mercy.

If it is the 2nd, 4th, 6th, or 8th tone, the following troparion is chanted in the 2nd tone or in the same tone as the doxology:

> *Priest:* When you rose from the tomb and broke the fetters of Hades, you abolished the sentence of death, O Lord, and thus delivered all men from the snares of the enemy. Appearing to the Apostles, you sent them out to preach, and through them, bestowed your peace upon the world: O you who alone are full of mercy.

Liturgy of Catechumens

In the Byzantine Rite of the Catholic Church, the bread and wine used for the Divine Liturgy (the Holy Sacrifice of the Mass) are prepared by the priest at a small table located on the left side of the altar (the table of preparation). After he has completed this rite (called *Proskomedia*) the priest leaves the prepared chalice and paten on the table of preparation and goes to the altar to begin the Divine Liturgy.

The congregation stands. The priest kisses the Holy Gospel on the altar and then makes the sign of the cross over the altar with the Gospel Book, and begins:

> *Priest:* Blessed is the Kingdom of the Father, and of the Son, and of the Holy Spirit, now and forever.
>
> *People:* Amen.

Response during Eastertide

> *Priest and People:* Christ is risen from the dead, by death he conquered death, and to those in the graves, he granted life. [Three times]

The congregation then sits.

Litany of Peace

Also called the Great Litany, the Litany of Peace is so named because it begins with three petitions concerning peace. The priest or deacon speaks, and the congregation responds.

> *Priest/ Deacon:* In peace, let us pray to the Lord.

> *People:* Lord, have mercy.

> *Priest/Deacon:* For peace from on high, and for the salvation of our souls, let us pray to the Lord.

> *People:* Lord, have mercy.

> *Priest/Deacon:* For peace in the whole world, for the well-being of the holy Churches of God and for the union of all, let us pray to the Lord.

> *People:* Lord, have mercy.

> *Priest/Deacon:* For this holy church and for all who enter it with faith, reverence and the fear of God, let us pray to the Lord.

> *People:* Lord, have mercy.

> *Priest/Deacon:* For our holy ecumenical Pontiff Benedict, the Pope of Rome, let us pray to the Lord.

> *People:* Lord, have mercy.

> *Priest/Deacon:* For our most Reverend Archbishop and Metropolitan [name], for our God-loving Bishop [name], for the venerable priesthood, the diaconate in Christ, for all clergy and the people, let us pray to the Lord.

> *People:* Lord, have mercy.

> *Priest/Deacon:* For our civil authorities and all in the service of our country, let us pray to the Lord.

> *People:* Lord, have mercy.

> *Priest/Deacon:* For this city, for every city, and countryside, and for those living within them in faith, let us pray to the Lord.

> *People:* Lord, have mercy.

> *Priest/Deacon:* For seasonable weather, for an abundance of the fruits of the earth, and for peaceful times, let us pray to the Lord.

> *People:* Lord, have mercy.

> *Priest/Deacon:* For the safety of those who travel by sea, air, and land, and for the salvation of the sick, the suffering, and the captive, let us pray to the Lord.

> *People:* Lord, have mercy.

Special intentions are added at this time, such as rain during time of drought, end of famine or war, or work for the unemployed.

Litany for the Departed

The following petitions are said by the priest or deacon at this point only during Requiem (funeral) liturgies.

> *Priest/Deacon*: For the servant(s) of God [name of the deceased], and for his (her/their) blessed memory, and that his (her/their) every transgression, voluntary and involuntary, be forgiven, let us pray to the Lord.

> *People:* Lord, have mercy.

> *Priest/Deacon*: That he (she/they) may stand uncondemned before the dread judgment seat of Christ, and that his (her/their) soul(s) may be included in the realm of the living, in the place of light, where all the saints and righteous repose, let us pray to the Lord.

> *People:* Lord, have mercy.

> *Priest/Deacon*: That we be delivered from all affliction, wrath, and need, let us pray to the Lord.

> *People:* Lord, have mercy.

> *Priest/Deacon*: Protect us, save us, have mercy on us and preserve us, O God, by your grace.

> *People:* Lord, have mercy.

> *Priest/Deacon*: Remembering our most holy, most pure, most blessed and glorious Lady, the Mother of God and ever-virgin Mary with all the saints, let us commend ourselves and one another, and our whole life, to Christ, our God.

> *People:* To you, O Lord.

> *Priest* [silently]: Lord our God, whose might is beyond utterance, and glory is incomprehensible, whose mercy is measureless, and love of man is ineffable: Yourself O Master, look down with your mercy upon us, and upon this holy house, and grant to us, and to those who pray with us, the riches of your mercy and of your compassion.

> *Priest:* For to you, Father, Son, and Holy Spirit, is due all glory, honor, and worship, now and forever.

> *People:* Amen.

First antiphon

The antiphon is one of 150 psalms from the Bible. It is recited or sung (chanted) and if possible, done antiphonally, meaning, alternating from left side to right side or alternating between cantor and congregation.

The congregation sings the following antiphon on Sundays:

> Shout joyfully to the Lord, all the earth, sing praise to his name, give to him glorious praise, through the prayers of the Mother of God, O Savior, save us. Glory be to the Father, and to the Son, and to the Holy Spirit, now and forever. Amen.

> Through the prayers of the Mother of God, O Savior, save us.

The following antiphon is sung on weekdays:

> It is good to give thanks to the Lord, and to sing praises to your name, O Most High.

> Through the prayers of the Mother of God, O Savior, save us. Glory be to the Father, and to the Son, and to the Holy Spirit, now and forever. Amen.

> Through the prayers of the Mother of God, O Savior, save us.

Second antiphon

The congregation sings the additional following antiphon on Sundays:

> Be gracious to us, O God, and bless us; let your face shine upon us, and have mercy on us. O Son of God, risen from the dead, save us who sing to you: Alleluia!

And on weekdays, the following antiphon comes second:

> The Lord reigns. He is clothed in majesty; robed is the Lord and girt about with strength. Through the prayers of your Saints, O Savior, save us.

Hymn of the Incarnation and little entrance

The congregation stands for the hymn of the Incarnation and the procession of the priest.

> Glory be to the Father, and to the Son, and to the Holy Spirit, now and ever and forever. Amen.

> O Only Begotten Son and Word of God, who, being immortal, deigned for our salvation to become incarnate of the Holy Mother of God and ever-virgin Mary, and became man without change; you were also crucified, O Christ, our God, and by death have trampled death, being One of the Holy Trinity, glorified with the Father and the Holy Spirit, save us.

The priest makes three bows, and then a procession is formed (all clergy — priest, deacon, and subdeacon) and the priest carries the Gospel Book around the altar.

Priest [silently]: O Lord, our Master and God, who in heaven established orders and armies of angels and archangels for the service of your glory, make this our entrance to be an entrance of holy angels, serving together with us, and with us glorifying your goodness. For to you is due all glory, honor, and worship, Father, Son, and Holy Spirit, now and forever. Amen.

Making the sign of the cross toward the altar, the priest says:

Blessed is the entrance of your saints, always, now, and forever.

The priest kisses the Gospel Book, elevates it, and says aloud:

Wisdom! Be attentive!

On Sundays, the people then say:

Come, let us worship and bow before Christ. O Son of God, risen from the dead, save us who sing to you: Alleluia!

On weekdays, the people instead say:

Come, let us worship and bow before Christ. O Son of God, wondrous in your saints, save us who sing to you: Alleluia!

Troparions and kontakions

Troparions are hymns of one stanza, and *kontakions* are very lengthy hymns often only sung in parts. Both are liturgical pieces of music meant to teach the people theological truths of the faith.

The people say the tropars and kondaks proper to the day. Then the priest prays silently:

O holy God abiding in the saints, praised by the thrice-holy hymn of the seraphim, glorified by the cherubim and adored by all the heavenly powers, you brought all things out of nothingness into being, and created man to your own image and likeness, and adorned him with your every gift; you give wisdom and understanding to him who asks, and despising not the sinner, you ordain repentance for salvation. You have allowed us, your humble and unworthy servants, to stand at this time before the glory of your holy altar and to offer to you due adoration and praise. Accept, O Master, from the lips of us sinners the thrice holy hymn, and visit us in your goodness. Forgive us every offense voluntary and involuntary, sanctify our souls and bodies and grant that we may serve you in holiness all the days of our life; through the prayers of the holy Mother of God and all the saints, who have pleased you throughout the ages.

The priest then speaks aloud:

> *Priest:* For you, our God, are Holy, and to you we give glory, to the Father, Son, and the Holy Spirit, now and forever.
>
> *People:* Amen.

Prayer of the Thrice-Holy God (Trisagion)

At Mass during most of the year, the people say the following prayer:

> Holy God, Holy and Mighty, Holy and Immortal, have mercy on us.
>
> Holy God, Holy and Mighty, Holy and Immortal, have mercy on us.
>
> Holy God, Holy and Mighty, Holy and Immortal, have mercy on us.
>
> Glory be to the Father, and to the Son, and to the Holy Spirit, now and forever. Amen.
>
> Holy and Immortal, have mercy on us.
>
> Holy God, Holy and Mighty, Holy and Immortal, have mercy on us.

During Easter Week, the congregation says the following prayer:

> All you who have been baptized into Christ, have put on Christ. Alleluia.
>
> All you who have been baptized into Christ, have put on Christ. Alleluia.
>
> All you who have been baptized into Christ, have put on Christ. Alleluia.
>
> Glory be to the Father, and to the Son, and to the Holy Spirit, now and forever. Amen.
>
> Have put on Christ, Alleluia.
>
> All you who have been baptized into Christ, have put on Christ. Alleluia.

The priest first prays silently:

> Blessed is he who comes in the name of the Lord. Blessed are you on the throne of the glory of your kingdom, enthroned upon the Cherubim, always, now, and forever.

And then he says out loud:

> Let us be attentive! Peace be with all! Wisdom! Be attentive!

Following which, the people sing the Prokimenon proper to the day.

Priest: Wisdom!

Reader: The reading of the Epistle of [name].

Priest: Let us be attentive!

The congregation sits. The reader begins by addressing the congregation as "Brethren," and then he reads the Epistle for the day. When he's finished, the priest says:

Peace be with you. Wisdom! Be attentive!

The congregation again stands.

People: Alleluia! Alleluia! Alleluia!

Priest [silently]: O Gracious Master, pour forth into our hearts the spotless light of your divine knowledge and open the eyes of our minds that we may understand the teachings of your Gospel. Instill in us also the fear of your blessed commandments, so that, having curbed all carnal desires, we may lead a spiritual life, both thinking and doing everything that pleases you. For you, O Christ, our God, are the enlightenment of our souls and bodies, and to you we render glory, together with your eternal Father, and with your all holy, good and life-creating Spirit, now and forever. Amen.

Priest: Wisdom, let us stand upright and listen to the Holy Gospel according to St. [name].

People: Glory be to you, O Lord, glory be to you.

Priest: Let us be attentive!

Gospel

The priest or deacon chants the Gospel. After the reading, the priest kisses the closed Gospel Book and places it in the middle of the altar. Before sitting again, the people say:

Glory be to you, O Lord, glory be to you.

Sermon

The priest gives the day's sermon. Clergy are admonished to preach on the inspired and revealed word of Sacred Scripture. When possible, they should also explain the moral and doctrinal truths of the Catholic religion, particularly showing the biblical foundation.

Litany of Supplication

After the sermon, the priest gives the Litany of Supplication:

> *Priest:* Let us all say with our whole soul, and with our whole mind, let us say:
>
> *People:* Lord, have mercy.
>
> *Priest:* O Lord Almighty, God of our fathers, we pray you, hear and have mercy.
>
> *People:* Lord, have mercy.
>
> *Priest:* Have mercy on us, O God, according to your great mercy; we pray you, hear and have mercy.
>
> *People:* Lord, have mercy. [Three times]
>
> *Priest* [silently]: Accept, O Lord our God, this fervent prayer from your servants and have mercy on us according to your great mercy, and send down your benefits upon us and upon all your people, who expect from you abundant mercies.
>
> *Priest:* We also pray for our holy ecumenical Pontiff, Benedict, the Pope of Rome, and for our most reverend Archbishop and Metropolitan [name], for our God-loving Bishop [name], for those who serve and have served in this holy church, for our spiritual fathers, and for all our brethren in Christ.
>
> *People:* Lord, have mercy. [Three times]
>
> *Priest:* We also pray for our civil authorities and all in the service of our country.
>
> *People:* Lord, have mercy. [Three times]

Special intentions (special topical needs of the day and local area) may be added here.

> *Priest:* We also pray for the people here present who await your great and abundant mercy, for those who showed us mercy, and for all Christians of the true faith.
>
> *People:* Lord, have mercy. [Three times]
>
> *Priest:* For you are a merciful and gracious God, and we render glory to you, Father, Son, and Holy Spirit, now and forever.
>
> *People:* Amen.

Second Litany for the Departed

The priest continues with a second Litany for the Departed:

> *Priest:* Have mercy on us, O God, according to your great mercy; we pray you hear and have mercy.

People: Lord, have mercy. [Three times]

Priest: We also pray for the repose of the souls of the departed servants of God [name] and that his (her/their) every transgression, voluntary and involuntary, be forgiven them.

People: Lord have mercy. [Three times]

Priest: May the Lord God commit his (her/their) soul(s) to the place where the just repose.

People: Lord, have mercy. [Three times]

Priest: For the mercy of God, for the kingdom of heaven, and for the remission of their sins, let us beseech Christ, the Immortal King and our God.

People: Grant it, O Lord.

Priest: Let us pray to the Lord.

People: Lord, have mercy.

Priest [silently]: O God, of spirits and of all flesh, who has trampled death, and vanquished the devil, and has granted life to your world; do you, O Lord, give rest to the souls of your departed servant [name], in a place of light, a place of refreshment, a place of repose, where there is no pain, sorrow, or sighing. As a good and gracious God, forgive every sin committed by him (her/them), in word or deed or thought for there is no man living who does not sin. For you alone are without sin, your righteousness is everlasting righteousness and your word is truth.

Priest: For you are the resurrection, and the life, and the repose of your departed servant [name], O Christ our God, and to you we render glory, with your eternal Father, and your all holy, gracious and life-creating Spirit, now and forever.

People: Amen.

If any catechumens (people who are not yet baptized members of the Church) are present, at this time the Litany of Catechumens takes place, followed by the dismissal of catechumens before the Liturgy of the Faithful.

Liturgy of the Faithful

After the exit of the catechumens, the Liturgy of the Faithful begins.

Priest: All we faithful, again and again in peace let us pray to the Lord.

People: Lord, have mercy.

First Prayer of the Faithful

The priest silently prays:

> We thank you, O Lord God of Powers, for having deemed us worthy to stand, at this time, before your holy altar, and to prostrate ourselves before your mercy, for our sins and for the people's misgivings. Accept our prayer, O God, and make us worthy to offer to you prayers and supplications, and unbloody sacrifices for all your people, and enable us, whom you have placed in this your ministry through the power of your Holy Spirit, to call upon you at all times and in all places, without condemnation and offense, with a pure testimony of our conscience, that hearing us, you may be merciful to us according to the magnitude of your goodness.

Second Prayer of the Faithful

The priest again prays silently:

> Again, as so many times before, we fall down before you and entreat you, O gracious Lover of mankind, that you may regard our supplication, cleanse our souls and bodies from every defilement of flesh and spirit, and grant that we may stand blameless and without condemnation before your Holy Altar. Grant also, O God, to those who are praying with us, betterment of life, faith, and spiritual understanding. Grant that they may serve you always with fear and love, that they may blamelessly and without condemnation partake of your Holy Mysteries and become worthy of your heavenly kingdom.

He then speaks aloud:

> *Priest:* That being ever protected by your power, we may render glory to you, Father, Son, and Holy Spirit, now and forever.

> *People:* Amen.

> *Priest* [silently]: No one who is bound by carnal desires and pleasures is worthy to come to you, to approach you, or to minister to you, the King of Glory, for to minister to you is great and awesome, even to the heavenly powers themselves. Yet, because of your ineffable and boundless love for mankind, though in nature unchanged and unchangeable, you became man and were made our high priest and, as Master of all, gave into our keeping the holy office of this liturgical and unbloody sacrifice. For you alone, O Lord our God, rule over all things in heaven and on earth, and are borne on the cherubic throne, and are the Lord of the Seraphim and King of Israel, who alone are holy and dwell in the saints. Therefore, I beseech you, who alone are gracious and ready to hear me; look favorably upon me, your sinful and unprofitable servant, and cleanse my heart

and soul of an evil conscience, and by power of your Holy
Spirit, enable me, clothed with the grace of the priesthood,
to stand before this, your holy altar, and offer the sacrifice of
your sacred and most pure Body and Precious Blood. With
bowed head, I approach you and implore you, turn not your
face away from me, nor exclude me from among your children,
but allow these gifts to be offered to you by me, your sinful and
unworthy servant; for it is you, O Christ, our God, who offer
and are offered, who receive and are received, and to you we
render glory, with your eternal Father, and your all holy, gracious, and life-creating Spirit, now and forever. Amen.

Cherubic hymn

The congregation stands and sings together:

Let us, who mystically represent the Cherubim, and sing the
thrice-holy hymn to the life-creating Trinity, now set aside all
earthly cares . . .

Then the priest says the same prayer quietly three times, raises up
his hands, and silently says the Cherubic Hymn three times.

The great entrance

The great entrance marks the procession of the clergy through the
Holy Doors as the chalice and diskos are carried to the Altar of
Oblation (Holy Table).

The priest goes to the table of preparation (Prothesis), takes the
diskos and chalice, and makes the great entrance.

Priest: May the Lord God remember in his kingdom, Our Holy
Ecumenical Pontiff Benedict, the Pope of Rome, our most
reverend Archbishop and Metropolitan [name], and our God-
loving Bishop [name], and the entire priestly, diaconal, and
monastic order, our civil authorities, and all our armed forces,
the noble memorable founders and benefactors of this holy
Church, and all you Christians of the true faith, always, now,
and forever.

People: Amen. That we may welcome the King of all, invisibly
escorted by angelic hosts. Alleluia, alleluia, alleluia.

Priest [silently]: The noble Joseph took down your most pure
body from the cross, wrapped it in a clean shroud, and with
fragrant spices laid it in burial in a new tomb.

Covering the holy gifts, the priest continues silently:

In your goodness, show favor to Sion: rebuild the walls of
Jerusalem. Then you will be pleased with lawful sacrifice,

(burnt offerings wholly consumed), then you will be offered young bulls on your altar.

Litany of the Offertory

The priest silently says:

> O Lord God Almighty, who alone are holy and receive the sacrifice of praise from those who call upon you with their whole heart, accept the prayer also of us sinners; bring us to your holy altar, enable us to offer to you gifts and spiritual sacrifice for our sins, and for the people's transgressions; and deem us also worthy to find favor in your sight, that our sacrifice may be pleasing to you, and that the good Spirit of your grace may rest in us and upon these gifts here present, and upon all your people.

He then says aloud:

> *Priest:* Peace be with all.
>
> *People:* And with your Spirit.
>
> *Priest:* Let us love one another, so that with one mind we may confess.
>
> *People:* The Father, and the Son, and the Holy Spirit, the Trinity, one in substance and undivided.

The priest makes three bows, kisses the holy gifts covered with the holy veil, the diskos, the chalice, and the edge of the altar, and prays each time:

> *Priest* [silently]: I will love you, O Lord, my strength, the Lord is my fortress and my refuge.
>
> *Priest:* The doors, the doors. In wisdom, let us be attentive!

Nicene Creed

This creed was formulated by the Ecumenical Council of Nicea in AD 325. Both the Eastern and Western Catholic and Orthodox churches make this profession of faith. The wording is slightly different in the Eastern Church because it's directly translated from the original Greek whereas the Roman Church uses an English translation of the Latin version.

> *People:* I believe in one God, the Father Almighty, creator of heaven and earth, and of all things visible and invisible. And in one Lord, Jesus Christ, Son of God, the Only Begotten, born of the Father before all ages. Light of Light, true God of true God, begotten, not made, of one substance with the Father, through whom all things were made. Who for us men and for

our salvation came down from heaven, and was incarnate from the Holy Spirit and Mary the Virgin, and became man.

He was also crucified for us under Pontius Pilate, and suffered, and was buried. And he arose again on the third day, according to the Scriptures. And he ascended into heaven and sits at the right hand of the Father. And he will come again with glory, to judge the living and the dead, and of his kingdom there will be no end. And in the Holy Spirit, the Lord and Giver of Life, who proceeds from the Father. Who together with the Father and the Son is worshipped and glorified, who spoke through the prophets. In one holy, Catholic, and Apostolic Church. I profess one Baptism for the forgiveness of sins. I expect the resurrection of the dead; and the life of the world to come. Amen.

Priest: Let us stand aright, let us stand in awe, let us be attentive, to offer the holy oblation in peace.

People: The offering of peace, the sacrifice of praise.

Priest: The grace of our Lord Jesus Christ, and the love of God and Father, and the communion of the Holy Spirit, be with all of you.

People: And with your spirit.

Priest: Let us lift up our hearts!

People: We have lifted them up to the Lord.

Priest: Let us give thanks to the Lord.

People: It is proper and just to worship the Father, and the Son, and the Holy Spirit, the Trinity, one in substance and undivided.

Priest: It is proper and just to sing hymns to you, to bless you, to praise you, to thank you, to worship you in every place of your kingdom; for you are God ineffable, inconceivable, invisible, incomprehensible, ever existing, yet ever the same, you, and your Only Begotten Son, and your Holy Spirit; you brought us forth from nonexistence into being, and raised us up again when we had fallen, and left nothing undone, until you brought us to heaven and bestowed upon us your future kingdom. For all this we give thanks to you, and to your Only Begotten Son, and to your Holy Spirit, for all that we know and that we do not know, the manifest and the hidden benefits bestowed upon us. We thank you also for this ministry, which you have willed to accept from our hands, even though there stand before you thousands of archangels, myriads of angels, cherubim and seraphim, six winged, many-eyed, soaring aloft on their wings.

Consecration

The priest begins the consecration:

Singing, shouting, crying out, and saying the triumphal hymn.

The congregation kneels and begins:

> *People:* Holy, Holy, Holy is the Lord of hosts. Heaven and earth are full of your glory, hosanna in the highest. Blessed is he who comes in the name of the Lord, hosanna in the highest.

> *Priest* [in a low voice]: With these blessed powers we also, O Master, Lover of men cry and say: Holy are you and all holy, you, and you; Only Begotten Son, and your Holy Spirit; holy are you and all holy and magnificent is your glory, who so loved your world that you gave your Only Begotten Son, that everyone who believes in him should not perish, but should have life everlasting; who, having come and having fulfilled the whole Divine Plan concerning us, on the night when he was betrayed, or rather, when he surrendered himself for the life of the world, he took bread into his holy and all pure and immaculate hands, gave thanks and blessed, [here the priest blesses the bread] sanctified, broke and gave it to his holy disciples and apostles, saying:

> *Priest:* Take, eat, this is my body, which is broken for you for the remission of sins.

> *People:* Amen.

> *Priest* [silently]: In like manner he [here the priest blesses the chalice] took the cup, after the supper, saying:

> *Priest:* Drink of this all of you, this is my blood of the new testament, which is shed for you and for many for the remission of sins.

> *People:* Amen.

> *Priest* [silently]: Remembering, therefore, this salutary command, and all that was done in our behalf: the cross, the tomb, the Resurrection on the third day, the Ascension into heaven the sitting at the right hand, the second and glorious coming.

The priest lifts the chalice and diskos up and makes the sign of the cross with them, saying:

> We offer to you, yours of your own, in behalf of all, and for all.

The congregation stands and says:

> We praise you, we bless you, we thank you, O Lord, and we pray to you, our God.

The Epiclesis (Invocation of the Holy Spirit)

The priest says the following invocation silently:

Again we offer to you this spiritual and unbloody sacrifice, and we implore and pray, and entreat you, send down your Holy Spirit upon us and upon these gifts here present. [Here the priest blesses the bread.] And make this bread the precious body of your Christ. [Here the priest blesses the chalice.] And that which is in this chalice, the precious blood of your Christ. [The priest blesses both.] Having changed them by your Holy Spirit:

So that to those who partake of them, they may be for the purification of the soul, for the remission of sins, for the communion in your Holy Spirit, for the fullness of the heavenly kingdom, for confidence in you, not for judgment or condemnation.

Moreover, we offer to you this spiritual sacrifice for those who departed in the faith; the forefathers, fathers, patriarchs, prophets, apostles, preachers, evangelists, martyrs, confessors, ascetics, and for every righteous spirit who has died in the faith.

Hymn to the Blessed Virgin

The priest says:

Especially for our most holy, most pure, most blessed and glorious Lady, the Mother of God and ever-virgin Mary.

During most of the year, the people and priest then say the following lines:

It is truly proper to glorify you, who have borne God, the ever-blessed and immaculate and the Mother of our God. More honorable than the cherubim and beyond compare more glorious than the seraphim, who, a virgin, gave birth to God the Word, you, truly the Mother of God, we magnify.

During Eastertide, the following lines are said by the people and priest:

Priest and People: The Angel greeted the Blessed Mother: "Hail, O pure Virgin." And he said again: "Hail, for after three days your Son rose from the grave, and lifted up the dead. Wherefore, O people, rejoice."

"Shine in Splendor, O new Jerusalem, for the glory of the Lord is upon you. O Sion, exult and rejoice today. And you, O pure Mother of God, glory in the resurrection of him whom you bore."

Priest [silently]: For the holy prophet, precursor and Baptist John, for the holy glorious and illustrious apostles, for St. [name], whose memory we celebrate, and for all your saints, through whose prayers, O God, visit us. Remember also all who have departed in the hope of resurrection unto eternal life. [Here the priest mentions those deceased he wishes to remember.] And grant them rest where the light of your face shines. Moreover, we pray you, O Lord, remember the entire episcopate of the orthodox, who faithfully dispense the word of your truth, the entire priesthood, the diaconate in Christ, and all others in holy orders. We further offer you this spiritual sacrifice for the whole world, for the holy, Catholic, and Apostolic Church, for those who live in chastity and venerable conduct; for our civil authorities and for all the armed forces. Grant them, O Lord, a peaceful rule, that we also, sharing their tranquility, may lead a tranquil and calm life in all piety and dignity.

Priest: Among the first, O Lord, remember our holy Ecumenical Pontiff Benedict, the Pope of Rome, our most reverend Archbishop and Metropolitan [Name], our God-loving Bishop [Name], preserve them for your holy churches, in peace, safety, honor, and health, for many years, as they faithfully dispense the word of your truth.

People: And remember all your people.

Priest [silently]: Remember, O Lord, this city in which we dwell and every city and country, and those who live with faith therein. Remember, O Lord, those who travel by sea, air and land, the sick, the suffering, the captive, and their safety and salvation. Remember, O Lord, those who bear offerings and perform good deeds in your holy churches, and those who remember the poor, and upon all of us send down your mercies. [Here the priest mentions those of the living whom he wishes to remember.]

Priest: And grant that we, with one voice and one heart, may glorify and praise your most honorable and sublime name, Father, Son, and Holy Spirit, now and forever.

People: Amen.

Priest: And may the mercies of our great God and Savior Jesus Christ, be with all of you.

People: And with your spirit.

The congregation sits.

Litany of Intercession

The priest continues with the Litany of Intercession.

Priest: Now that we have remembered all the saints, again and again, let us pray to the Lord.

People: Lord, have mercy.

Priest: For the precious gifts offered and consecrated. Let us pray to the Lord.

People: Lord have mercy.

Priest: That our God, in his love for man, may receive them on his Holy and heavenly and spiritual altar, as an aroma of spiritual fragrance, and send down upon us in return the divine grace and gift of the Holy Spirit, let us pray to the Lord.

People: Lord, have mercy.

Priest: That we may be delivered from all affliction, wrath, and need, let us pray to the Lord.

People: Lord, have mercy.

Priest's prayer for a worthy Communion

Priest [silently]: In you, O Gracious Master, we place our whole life and hope, and we beseech, pray, and implore you: make us worthy to partake with a pure conscience of your heavenly and awesome mysteries from this sacred and spiritual altar, for the remission of sins, for the pardon of transgressions, for the fellowship of the Holy Spirit, for the inheritance of the kingdom of heaven, for confidence in you, and not for judgment, nor condemnation.

Priest: Protect us, save us, have mercy on us, and preserve us, O God, by your grace.

People: Lord, have mercy.

Priest: That this whole day may be perfect holy, peaceful, and without sin, let us beseech the Lord.

People: Grant it, O Lord.

Priest: For an angel of peace, a faithful guide, a guardian of our souls and bodies, let us beseech the Lord.

People: Grant it, O Lord.

Priest: For the pardon and remission of our sins and offenses, let us beseech the Lord.

People: Grant it, O Lord.

Priest: For what is good and beneficial to our souls and for peace of the world, let us beseech the Lord.

People: Grant it, O Lord.

Priest: That we may spend the rest of our life in peace and repentance, let us beseech the Lord.

People: Grant it, O Lord.

Priest: For a Christian, painless, unashamed, peaceful end of our life, and for a good account before the fearsome judgment seat of Christ, let us beseech the Lord.

People: Grant it, O Lord.

Priest: Asking for unity in faith, and for communion in the Holy Spirit, let us commend ourselves and one another, and our whole life to Christ, our God.

People: To you, O Lord.

Priest: And grant, O Lord, that we may with confidence and without condemnation dare call upon you, the God of heaven, Father, and say:

The congregation stands as the priest finished this introduction to the Our Father.

The Our Father

After the priest's introduction, the congregation says the Our Father:

People: Our Father who art in heaven, hallowed be thy name. Thy kingdom come, thy will be done on earth, as it is in heaven. Give us this day our daily bread. And forgive us our trespasses, as we forgive those who trespass against us. And lead us not into temptation, but deliver us from evil.

Priest: For thine is the kingdom, and the power, and the glory, Father, Son, and Holy Spirit, now and forever.

People: Amen.

Priest: Peace be with all.

People: And with your spirit.

Priest: Bow your heads to the Lord.

People: To you, O Lord.

Priest [silently]: We give you thanks, O invisible King, who by your immeasurable power has fashioned all things, and in the greatness of your mercy has brought all things out of nonexistence into being. Look down from heaven, O Lord, upon those who have bowed their heads unto you, for they do not bow to flesh and blood, but to you, the awesome God. Therefore, O Master, grant us of these gifts present before us for our good, according to the need of each; sail with those who sail, travel with those who travel, cure those who are sick, O Physician of souls and bodies.

Priest: Through the grace, the mercies and the loving kindness of your Only Begotten Son with whom you are blessed, together with your all-holy, gracious, and life-giving Spirit, now and forever.

People: Amen.

Priest [silently]: Look down, O Lord Jesus Christ, our God, from your holy dwelling place and from the throne of glory of your kingdom, and come to sanctify us, you who are seated on high with the Father, and dwell here invisibly among us, and deem it proper to impart to us, with your mighty hand, your most pure body and precious blood, and through us, to all your people.

Priest and Deacon: O God, be merciful to me, a sinner. [Three times]

Priest: Let us be attentive. Holy things to the holy.

The congregation kneels and says:

One is holy, One is Lord, Jesus Christ, for the glory of God the Father. Amen.

Sunday Communion hymn

The cantor or choir sings:

Praise the Lord from the heavens, Praise him in the highest. Alleluia! Alleluia! Alleluia!

Requiem liturgy

The congregation says the following lines at this point only during a Requiem liturgy:

Blessed are they whom you have chosen and taken to yourself, O Lord, and their memory endures throughout all generations. Alleluia, alleluia, alleluia.

Response during Eastertide

During the Easter season the people respond:

Receive the Body of Christ, taste of the Source of life. [Three times]

Holy Communion

The priest reverently breaks the Lamb (consecrated bread) into four parts and says silently:

Broken and distributed is the Lamb of God, broken yet not divided, ever eaten yet never consumed, but sanctifying the communicants.

He then takes the Holy Eucharist, also silently saying:

The precious and most holy body of Our Lord and God and Savior Jesus Christ, is given to me [name], a priest, for the remission of my sins and life everlasting. Amen.

The priest and people then say together:

O Lord, I believe and profess that you are truly Christ, the Son of the living God, who came into the world to save sinner, of whom I am the first. Accept me as a partaker of your mystical supper, O Son of God; for I will not reveal your mysteries to your enemies, nor will I give you a kiss as did Judas, but like the thief I confess to you:

Remember me, O Lord, when you shall come into your kingdom.

Remember me, O Master, when you shall come into your kingdom.

Remember me, O Holy One, when you shall come into your kingdom.

May the partaking of your Holy Mysteries, O Lord, be not for my judgment or condemnation, but for the healing of soul and body.

O Lord, I also believe and profess that this, which I am about to receive, is truly your most precious Body and your life-giving Blood, which I pray, make me worthy to receive for the remission of all my sins and for life everlasting. Amen.

O God, be merciful to me, a sinner.

O God, cleanse me of my sins and have mercy on me.

O Lord, forgive me, for I have sinned without number.

The priest partakes of the Precious Blood and says silently:

I the servant of God, priest [name], partake of the Precious and Holy Blood of our Lord and God and Savior Jesus Christ, for the remission of my sins and for life everlasting. Amen.

He wipes his lips and the edge of the chalice with the towel and says silently:

Behold, this has touched my lips, and shall take away my iniquities, and shall cleanse my sins.

The priest then turns to people and says out loud:

> Approach with fear of God and with faith.

The people who are going to take Communion go to the altar and say:

> Blessed is he who comes in the name of the Lord: God the Lord has revealed himself to us.

The priest giving Communion to each says:

> The servant of God, [name], partakes of the precious, most holy and most pure Body and Blood of our Lord, God and Savior Jesus Christ for the remission of his (her) sins and for life everlasting. Amen.

While the priest gives Communion to the people, the congregation sings an appropriate hymn. Afterward, the priest continues:

> *Priest:* Save your people, O God, and bless your inheritance.

> *People:* We have seen the true light, we have received the heavenly Spirit, we have found the true faith, and we worship the undivided Trinity; for the Trinity has saved us.

> *Priest* [silently]: Be you exalted, O God, above the heavens, and your glory all over the earth.

> *Priest:* Blessed is our God always, now and forever.

> *People:* Amen.

The congregation stands and declares:

> May our lips be filled with your praise, O Lord, so that we may sing of your glory, for you have deemed us worthy to partake of your holy, divine, immortal, and life-creating mysteries. Keep us in your holiness, so that all the day long we may live according to your truth. Alleluia! Alleluia! Alleluia!

They then sit.

> *Priest:* Having received the divine, holy, most pure, immortal, heavenly, and life-creating, awesome mysteries of Christ, arise, let us worthily thank the Lord.

> *People:* Lord, have mercy.

> *Priest:* Protect us, save us, have mercy on us and preserve us, O God, by your grace.

> *People:* Lord, have mercy.

Priest: Asking that the whole day be perfect, holy, peaceful, and without sin, let us commend ourselves and one another and our whole life to Christ, our God.

People: To you, O Lord.

Prayer of thanksgiving

The priest silently prays:

We give thanks to you, O Master, lover of mankind, Benefactor of our souls, that this day you have deemed us worthy of your heavenly and immortal mysteries. Make straight our path, confirm us in our fear of you, guard our life, make firm our steps, through the prayers and intercessions of the glorious Mother of God and ever-virgin Mary, and of all your saints.

He makes the sign of the cross with the Gospel Book, saying:

Priest: For you are our sanctification, and we render glory to you. Father, Son, and Holy Spirit, now and forever.

People: Amen.

At this point the congregation stands.

Priest: Let us go forth in peace.

People: In the name of the Lord.

Priest: Let us pray to the Lord.

People: Lord, have mercy.

Priest: O Lord, who bless those who bless you, and sanctify those who trust in you, save your people and bless your inheritance, preserve the fullness of your Church, sanctify those who love the beauty of your house; glorify them by your divine power, and do not forsake us who hope in you. Grant peace to your world, to your churches, to the priests, to our civil authorities and to all your people. For every good bestowal and every perfect gift is from above, coming down from you, the Father of lights; and we render glory, thanksgiving, and adoration to you, Father, Son, and Holy Spirit, now and forever.

People: Amen. Blessed be the name of the Lord, now and forever. [Three times]

Priest [silently]: You, O Christ, our God, who are the fulfillment of the law and the prophets, have fulfilled the whole plan of the Father, fill our hearts with joy and gladness, always, now, and forever. Amen.

Priest: The blessing of the Lord be upon you, through his grace and loving kindness, always, now, and forever.

People: Amen.

Priest: Glory be to you, O Christ, our God, our Hope: Glory be to you.

During most of the year, the people give the following response:

Glory be to the Father, and to the Son, and to the Holy Spirit, now and forever. Amen.

Lord, have mercy. Lord, have mercy. Lord, have mercy. Give the blessing!

During Eastertide, the people use the following response:

Christ is risen from the dead, by death he conquered death, and to those in the graves, he granted life.

Lord, have mercy. Lord, have mercy. Lord, have mercy. Give the blessing!

Dismissal

The priest then gives the dismissal:

May Christ our true God, risen from the dead, have mercy on us and save us through the prayers of his most holy Mother, of the holy, glorious, and illustrious Apostles; through the prayers of our holy Father, John Chrysostom, Archbishop of Constantinople, of St. [name (patron/patroness of this church)], and of St. [name (whose feast it is)], and of all the saints, for he is gracious and loves mankind.

Chapter 10

Other Catholic Rites

· ·

· ·

Almost 2,000 years have passed since Jesus celebrated the Last Supper with his Apostles. As with everything else, much has changed in the Church in that time. As historical events shaped the Church and its faithful, the religious within the Church began to recognize their differences, and different rites within the Church formed.

In this chapter we look at the two main categories that these rites fall into; what Pope John Paul the Great often called "the two lungs" of the Catholic Church: the Eastern and Western Churches. Although all Catholics accept the authority of the Bishop of Rome as visible head of the Church, not all Catholics celebrate divine worship (the sacred liturgy) exactly the same as Rome.

This chapter shows the different flavors of Catholic worship that are categorized not only as Eastern or Western but also by ethnic and cultural expressions. This unity amidst diversity is the hallmark of Catholicism; the word *catholic* even comes from the Greek word for *universal (katholikos)*.

Eastern Catholic Churches

The Catholic Church spans both east and west, as did the ancient Roman Empire long ago. Geography and language distinguish the two parts. Historically and liturgically, Western Europe followed the lead of the Latin Church in Rome, while Eastern Europe and Asia Minor were influenced by the Greek Church in Constantinople and followed several traditions connected to the patriarchates of Alexandria (Egypt), Antioch (Syria), and Constantinople (Turkey).

Within the many Eastern Rites in Catholic Christianity are several Eastern Churches with different and distinct liturgical rites. Those Churches united with the Bishop of Rome (the pope) are called *Eastern Catholic;* if separated from the pope, they are called *Eastern Orthodox.* Each of the Orthodox Churches (which are not Catholic) has its own respective patriarchs and metropolitans (high-raking archbishops). Eastern Catholic Churches, however, have just one final authority: the pope. Substantially, the worship is the same. In all Catholic rites, Catholic liturgy (called the Holy Mass in the Western or Latin Rite) is the liturgical celebration of the Paschal Mystery (Death and Resurrection of Christ).

The following sections address some of the largest and most significant branches of the Eastern Church. (Turn to Chapter 9 to find out more about the Byzantine Rite, the largest Eastern Church.)

Alexandrian Rite

The Alexandrian Rite originated in the Egyptian city of Alexandria. Since the first century AD, the city had a strong Jewish community, and it became a logical area for Christian missionaries to seek converts.

A strong rivalry grew up between Alexandria and the imperial city of Constantinople. Constantinople was deeply involved in spreading the liturgy of St. John Chrysostom, a liturgy that eventually became known as the Byzantine Rite (see Chapter 9). Constantinople was clearly the political center of the Eastern Empire, but other Churches strongly resisted having its liturgical language and style foisted on them. This resentment eventually encouraged and strengthened the growth of other liturgical variations.

Coptic

Byzantine Christians began referring to the Alexandrian Rite as the *Coptic* Rite. The word *Copt* reflects both Greek and Arabic words for *Egyptian.* The Egyptian or Coptic Christian Church traces its origin to the tradition that St. Mark the Evangelist was the first missionary to preach the message and Person of Jesus to Egyptians during the reign of Emperor Nero in Rome. Egypt was receptive, because the Holy Family (Jesus, Mary, and Joseph) once fled into Egypt during the reign of King Herod, who sought to kill the Christ-child.

Today the majority of Christians in Egypt are Coptic Orthodox (not Catholic). That church is headed by its own pope, the Patriarch of Alexandria, who lives in Egypt. They reject the Council of Chalcedon's teaching in AD 451 that Christ has two natures (human and divine) united to one divine Person. A Catholic Patriarchate (highest ranking prelate in the Eastern Church, equivalent in honor and rank to a cardinal) was reestablished in 1895 by Pope Leo XIII for those Coptic Christians seeking reunion with Rome.

Discussions between Coptic and Eastern Orthodox theologians show an interest in a unified church, with both groups acknowledging that the controversies of the past were provoked by verbal differences. However, belief in the single "fused" nature of Christ is still affirmed by the Coptic Church, which is not in communion with Rome.

Ethiopian: The Ge'ez Rite

Another Eastern Christian church using the Alexandrian Rite is the Ethiopian Church. The Ethiopian Church previously had a close affinity with the Coptic Church in Egypt, and as a result, it is often mistakenly called the Coptic Church.

St. Athanasius of Alexandria sent missionaries from Egypt to preach the faith to the Ethiopians in the fourth century at the request of a man named Frumentius, who had traveled in Ethiopia. St. Athanasius ordained Frumentius as the first bishop of the Ethiopian Church. To facilitate conversions, the now-obscure Ge'ez language was used in the Ethiopian liturgies. Frumentius was very successful in this mission, and with the cooperation of the King Ezana, Ethiopia was soon converted to Christianity.

The Ethiopian Church held tightly to the earliest customs of Christianity, such as circumcision and Sabbath observance. Monks have always played a strong role in Alexandrian and Ethiopian Christianity, but they were often Monophysites (from *mono,* meaning one, and *physus,* meaning nature) who held that the human and divine natures of Jesus were "fused" or joined into a single nature at his birth. This belief was condemned by the Council of Chalcedon, but the Churches in Egypt and Ethiopia, as well as the smaller churches in Syria, Turkey, and Armenia, have been so deeply tied to ancient tradition that they refused to accept any innovations like the teaching of Chalcedon.

The Ethiopians were pressured in the 16th century to convert to Islam, but they resisted. They also resisted attempts by the invading Portuguese to force them to adopt the Latin Rite.

The 17th century saw the continued efforts to force an end to their ancient customs of circumcision and the observance of the Sabbath. In the 19th century, Ethiopia was again pressured by Muslim forces, and the monks retreated even more deeply to inaccessible places. Toward the end of that century, the country was revitalized by its king, Menelik II, who rebuffed the Italian attempts to colonize Ethiopia. In 1959, the Ethiopian Church declared itself independent from the Coptic Patriarch of Alexandria.

In 1961, part of the Ethiopian Church achieved unity with Rome when Rome established a metropolitan see in the Ethiopian capital of Addis Ababa.

Antiochian (West Syrian) Rite

Christ's followers were first called Christians in the city of Antioch (Acts 11:26), and it became a center for Christians in AD 70 after the destruction of Jerusalem. According to tradition, St. Peter was the first Bishop of Antioch before he went to Rome, and the man known for writing the earliest extant letters (after the Epistles of the New Testament) was St. Ignatius of Antioch, who was its third bishop.

Maronite

Of all the Eastern Catholic Churches, the Maronite Church is the only one known by the name of a human person, St. Maron. This fourth-century hermit established the groundwork and foundation for the Christian religion to take root in modern-day Syria and Lebanon.

The Maronite Rite followed the liturgical ceremonies of Antioch, accepting the teaching of the Council of Chalcedon while at the same time resisting the Byzantine rituals. The Maronite Church developed in central Syria and was strongly influenced by monastic communities that reverenced the memory of Mar Maron, a saintly Syriac monk of the fourth and early fifth centuries who died in AD 410.

Those monastic communities formed an autonomous Church and eventually migrated to Lebanon, Cyprus, and the region of Aleppo. Unique among the Eastern churches, the Maronites have never been separated from Rome and have maintained unity, even in the aftermath of the East-West Schism in 1054. Their union with the Vatican was recognized as early as the sixth century by Pope Hormisdas (AD 514–523) and ratified officially in the year 1215.

The Maronite liturgy continues to express and reflect its rural and monastic origins. This rite has suffered greatly over the years from many efforts to Latinize and Westernize its liturgical rituals. Besides attacks from some Muslim extremists in Lebanon, there have also been attempts from some unscrupulous Latin Christians to get the Maronites to abandon their traditions.

The Divine Liturgy in the Maronite Church has three main parts.

- ✔ Preparation of the offerings, priest, and faithful
- ✔ Consecration of the bread and wine (the offering)
- ✔ Holy Communion

The Holy and Divine Trinity are invoked throughout the service but especially at the Consecration, when thanks are given to God the Father, remembrance is given to God the Son, and invocation is made to God the Holy Spirit.

Although originally spoken in Aramaic and later in Arabic, most Maronite Divine Liturgies are in the liturgical Syriac language. The priest celebrates *ad orientem,* which means facing east rather than facing the people.

Syriac

The liturgy of the Syriac Rite, used in Antioch (present-day Syria) is attributed to St. James the Apostle. After the Council of Chalcedon, many bishops broke away and stopped using the Greek language in their liturgies. The Aramaic dialect of Hebrew known as Syriac had an emotional impact on Christians because it was Jesus' language, so it was used instead.

Through the efforts of Catholic missionaries, many members of this rite, including the patriarch, returned to union with Rome in 1791. Syriac remained the official liturgical language of most of the churches of western Asia until the modern era. Colloquial Arabic is often used for readings, songs, and some of the prayers.

Syro-Malankara

St. Thomas the Apostle traveled to India and founded Christian churches there in the first century AD, and members of the Syro-Malankar Rite trace their origin to St. Thomas' efforts.

This rite belonged to the early Chaldean Church [see the later section "Chaldean (East Syrian) Rite"] that had fallen into the heresy of Nestorius after the Council of Ephesus in AD 431. Nestorius maintained that Christ had two persons and that his mother, the Virgin Mary, was only mother of his human person and not of his divine person. Ephesus affirmed what Nicea said in AD 325 and what was later restated by Chalcedon: Jesus Christ has two natures, human and divine, that he is true God and true man but that his two natures are united to One Divine Person. Hence, Mary can be called (analogously) the Mother of God since her son Jesus is simultaneously the Son of God.

The Syro-Malankar Church broke from the Chaldean Church in 1653, but it was not until 1772 that they obtained a valid hierarchy. Attempts were made by Jesuit missionaries to bring the Syro-Malankar Christians into full communion with Rome, but it didn't actually happen until 1930. Formal ties with the Malankara-Syrian Orthodox Church were dissolved, and four Syro-Malankar bishops were reunited with Rome, bringing many of their Church members with them. This rite is now based in the state of Kerala, India, where St. Thomas is also credited with the development of churches following his arrival there in AD 52.

The Syro-Malankara use the West Syrian form of liturgy. Pope Pius XI established a Catholic hierarchy for the Malankara after an appeal by Malankaran Archbishop Mar Ivanios in 1930, and Pope John Paul II helped with the ecumenical movement with a Papal visit on February 8, 1986.

Armenian Rite

Christianity was officially named the religion of Armenia in the fourth century under the influence of Gregory the Illuminator, who was a Catholic in union with Rome. The Metropolitan Bishop of Caesaria ordained its bishops for several centuries, but in the sixth century, it rejected the decrees of Chalcedon and became Monophysite (following a heresy that maintains that Christ has one nature rather than both human and divine) in faith.

Five hundred years later, at the time of the Crusades, many of the Armenians who were members of the Orthodox Church sought union with Rome. Continued efforts by Catholic missionaries through the centuries have brought a large number of Armenians to the Catholic Church. Most Armenians today remain Orthodox Christians, not in union with Rome, but the number of Armenian Catholics continues to grow.

The Armenian liturgy has its roots in the Churches of Jerusalem and is considered by some to be an early version of the Byzantine Church. Many changes have affected the rite through the years, resulting in a liturgy that resembles the Byzantine but has Latin liturgical characteristics.

The Armenian Catholic Church liturgical calendar celebrates feasts of the Lord on Sundays and those of the saints on other days of the week. In the structure of its rituals, the Armenian Church closely follows the traditions of Jerusalem and Constantinople, but the liturgical vestments and the physical arrangements of the altar bear a close resemblance to the Western usage of the Middle Ages.

Armenians take their religion with them wherever they go, and many Armenians now live in the United States and throughout the world. Of the Eastern Churches, the Armenian Rite is the second-largest group after the Orthodox Christians. Large communities of Armenian Catholics are found in Beirut, Lebanon, and Aleppo, Syria.

Chaldean (East Syrian) Rite

The Chaldean Rite comes from the ancient East Syrian Rite, the Church of ancient Mesopotamia thought to be formed by missionaries from Antioch. It is currently used by two Catholic subdivisions: the Chaldean Catholic and the Syro-Malabar Catholic Churches.

Chaldean Catholic

Christianity was established in Mesopotamia (the modern-day area of Iraq and Iran) at a very early date, but most Christians fell into the heresy of Nestorius in the fifth century (see the earlier section "Syro-Malankara"). Catholic missionaries helped many of these Christians return to union with Rome 1,000 years later, and these reunited Christians were called *Chaldeans*. The pope named the first Chaldean Patriarch Mar Shimun VIII (Yohannan Sulaqa) in 1553. The current patriarch is Cardinal Mar Emmanuel III Delly, elected in 2003. Today he resides in Baghdad, Iraq, together with most of the members of his rite. Chaldean Catholics are also found in Iran, Lebanon, Egypt, Syria, Turkey, and the United States.

The liturgy is of the East Syrian or Chaldean Rite. Dialogue between the Chaldean Catholic Church and the Assyrian Church of the East (the Christians in Mesopotamia who did not reunite with Rome) has improved since Pope John Paul II signed a Christological agreement with the Assyrian Patriarch in Rome in 1994.

Syro-Malabar Catholic

Like the Syro-Malankar Church covered earlier in this chapter, the Syro-Malabar Church is based in India, and it, too, traces its origin to the missionary work of St. Thomas the Apostle and the liturgy of the East Syrian Rite. Despite conflicts with Portuguese missionaries in the 16th century, members of the Syro-Malabar Rite have never broken unity with Rome. Although an ancient rite, it never had its own patriarch until Pope John Paul II named a major archbishop in 1992.

The Syro-Malabar call themselves St. Thomas Christians. In the early church, members of this rite were in communion with the East Syrian Church of Persia but were Westernized with

Portuguese bishops and Latin Rites in the 16th century. That Westernization led to a rebellion in 1653, and though this rite had lost some of its Eastern ways, it didn't come into communion with Rome until 1923 when Pope Pius XI established the Syro-Malabar Catholic hierarchy.

Pope John Paul II elevated the Church to Major ArchEpiscopal status on December 16, 1992, helping the Oriental rite's restoration. The Syro-Malabar Catholic Church is now the second-largest Eastern Catholic Church, with 3.9 million members in India, the United States, and Canada.

Western Catholic Churches

Since the days when SS. Peter and Paul preached to the first Jewish and Roman converts of city of Rome in the middle of the first century, Catholicism has had a strong presence and eventual majority of the imperial city. As capital of the empire, the city of Rome proved at times to be the worst enemy of the Catholic Church and at other times to be her loyal son. Three hundred years of persecution were followed by more than 1,700 years of faithful adherence. The liturgies of Rome began in underground catacombs (Christian tombs) and then emerged to take over pagan temples and transform them into elegant basilicas and cathedrals.

Latin (Roman) Rite

Though *Latin* is often used interchangeably with *Western* when discussing the variations of the Church, *Latin* can also refer to a specific rite within the Western Church.

The Latin Rite developed in ancient Rome. Most texts for Mass and the Divine Office were taken from the Bible in early Roman liturgy, and nonscriptural text started appearing in the eighth century. With the leadership of St. Gregory the Great, monasteries were developed around the Roman basilicas and the monks who chanted and sang the Mass had a deep influence on Roman liturgy.

At the same time that nonscriptural texts started to appear, the Holy Roman Emperor Charlemagne decreed that the Roman liturgical books should replace the Gallican rituals used in the kingdom of the Franks. During his reign, the first musical notations for liturgical singing were created, which up until then had been sung from memory.

The Council of Trent profoundly influenced Western Masses with the Roman Rite; during the second millennium the liturgy of Rome was unanimously adopted by almost all the Western Churches with some minor additions and adaptations.

A large number of the world's more than one billion Catholics use the Latin Rite, which has undergone many changes within the latter half of the 20th century. Commonly called the "New Mass," these changes included some major differences from the old rite, such as the use of the vernacular in the liturgy, how the celebrant is positioned during the Eucharistic Prayer, and the Offertory procession. Congregants have a more active role in the liturgy, and Communion is distributed in the form of both bread and wine.

As these changes came from the pope and the hierarchy in 1970, the people in the pews responded with some anger and resistance, as well as frustration with the return to the use of Latin in the Mass. Pope Benedict XVI has allowed priests to celebrate the "old Mass," and what is now called the *Extraordinary form* of the Roman Rite may now be celebrated by the priest and the people without the permission of the local bishop.

As in the many Eastern Rites, some special rites and practices in the Catholic Church of the West are very old and have therefore been allowed to survive more or less intact.

Ambrosian Rite

Although a wide variety of liturgical rites were likely practiced in northern Italy before Charlemagne's rule, the only one that survived is the Ambrosian liturgy. St. Ambrose had succeeded an Arian bishop to the See of Milan in AD 374, but no direct evidence actually links him to what is now the Ambrosian Rite. He was known to follow the Roman liturgy but was involved in the creation of some liturgical innovations in the composition of hymns for the Mass.

What's more likely to have contributed to his name being attached to the rite was Ambrose's involvement in significant corrections to the liturgical books used by his Arian predecessor. During the Middle Ages, several attempts were made to alter the rite and bring it in line with the now-extinct Gallican Rite and, especially, the Roman Rite. Even St. Peter Damian and some of the popes tried to accomplish these changes. These attempts have resulted in riots and minor disruptions, but the Ambrosian Rite has managed to weather the storms and survive.

The Council of Trent insisted on the spread of the Roman liturgical rituals, but it made exceptions for those local liturgical practices that could prove they had been in existence for more than two centuries. St. Charles Borromeo made some small alterations in the direction of Roman ways, but even he was careful not to destroy the characteristics of this rite. Both the Ambrosian Missal and Breviary were revised after the Second Vatican Council, but scholars have determined that the Ambrosian Rite of today has not been altered since the eighth century (the time of the earliest extant manuscripts).

Dominican Rite

Sometimes considered a variation of the Roman Rite or a relic of the Gallican Rite, the Dominican Rite was composed in the 13th century by member of the Religious Order of Preachers, or Dominicans. (However, no record suggests that creating a unified liturgy for the Dominicans came from St. Dominic.)

In Dominicans' early days, local liturgical differences were typical of all the churches. However, having many liturgies was highly impractical, especially at times when the brothers would assemble together. Unity of prayer and worship were essential to the serene community envisioned by their holy founder.

Both Blessed Jordan of Saxony and John the German worked to make some changes toward a common rite, but it wasn't until Humbert of Romains was elected master general in 1254 that a normative common rite was established.

In the Dominican Rite, the most noticeable differences from the Roman Rite may be seen in the positions and gestures of the celebrant and the fact that some actions happen simultaneously. For example, the deacon unfolds the corporal during the singing of the Epistle and the ministers are incensed during the singing of the Preface.

When the liturgical revisions from the Second Vatican Council appeared in 1968, the Dominicans decided to adopt the renewed Roman Rite of Mass and the Liturgy of the Hours. They retained some of the elements of their own rite, such as the Rite of Profession. Just one traditionalist Dominican Fraternity was allowed to continue using the full Dominican Rite in its earlier form.

Anglican Use

The Anglican Use is a recent innovation within Catholicism and has been carefully modeled on the liturgy of the traditional Episcopalian form of worship. The Anglican Use is a new Catholic form used by formerly Protestant Anglican churches, which, circularly, have their roots in Catholicism.

King Henry VIII of England established the Anglican Church in 1531. He split from the Catholic Church and the pope by declaring himself supreme head of the Church of England. Anglicanism became the new state religion, forcing Catholicism underground as an illegal religion.

Liturgically, the Anglican form of worship was basically the same as the Latin Rite. That changed, however, when Thomas Cranmer, the Archbishop of Canterbury, initiated the Protestant Reformation into English liturgy. He wrote the Book of Common Prayer, which set the tone for Anglican worship.

The Anglican Communion has grown and evolved around the world over the last 500 years, particularly in the United States, where both Protestant Episcopalian and High Church Anglican expressions of the faith can be found. Some Anglicans, such as Blessed John Henry Cardinal Newman, have converted and became Roman Catholic.

Recently, entire Anglican (or Episcopalian) parishes have sought reunion with Rome and at the same time requested permission to keep much of their Anglican form of worship. These newly Catholic parishes practice the *Anglican Use*. The Anglican Use liturgy is derived from many sources, including the Sarum Rite, the English Missal, the 1928 and 1979 versions of the Episcopal Book of Common Prayer, and the Roman Missal. The Eucharistic Prayer and the various rituals of the (Catholic) Anglican Use are found in the *Book of Divine Worship*. The Sunday Mass is similar to that of Protestant Anglican churches that embrace their Catholic origins. These churches are the parts of the Church of England or Anglican Communion that follow the traditions of the Oxford Movement began in 1833. At that time some Anglican scholars sought to promote a more liturgical form of Anglicanism (Episcopalian in the United States) that resembled the Roman Catholic traditions and seemed less mainline Protestant in comparison to other denominations. The altar is situated against the wall and the priest celebrates the Mass with his back to the congregation.

In the Sacred Congregation for the Doctrine of the Faith on July 22, 1980, Pope John Paul II issued the *Pastoral Provision,* which allowed married Anglican clergymen who converted to Catholicism to be ordained as Catholic priests without being obliged to be celibate. Unmarried clergy must take an oath of celibacy prior to ordination, and married clergy must agree not to remarry after ordination. Additionally, married clergy cannot be consecrated bishops. (The same rule applies in ancient tradition still followed by Byzantine Catholic and Eastern Orthodox Christians.) Candidates are judged on an individual basis, and no man is considered to have any right to Catholic ordination.

The Pastoral Provision and the permission to celebrate the Anglican Use are separate entities and are not necessarily linked together. But because of the relaxation of priestly celibacy that the Anglican Use entails, it remains a somewhat controversial innovation within Roman Catholicism (especially among Latin Rite celibate priests).

In 2009, Pope Benedict XVI further structured the Anglican Usage in the Catholic Church by forming personal ordinariates (jurisdiction without territory, like the Military Archdiocese, which composes clergy and laity not by location but by profession). In this case, the Anglican Usage ordinariate is the sum of all former Anglican clergy and laity now reunited to Rome living anywhere in the world. These ordinariates are led by a bishop or priest and are made up of formerly Anglican Catholics. They're to be treated as more or less independent dioceses with their own liturgical practices within the Latin Rite.

Part III
Tools of the Trade

The 5th Wave   By Rich Tennant

In this part . . .

We examine the physical items used for the Mass, such as the books, garments, and other paraphernalia. What the priest and deacon wear, what texts are said, and what artifacts are used for worship are all described and explained.

Chapter 11

Liturgical Books

*I*n this chapter we look at the different manuals and textbooks used in Catholic worship. The books that document official rituals have been painstakingly researched and translated so that they conform to Catholic doctrine and are faithful to Catholic liturgy. The Holy Mass is the most central act of Catholic prayer, and the books used at Mass are most important.

Lectionary

The lectionary is a collection of selected passages from the Bible used as Scripture readings for the Mass. The current Catholic lectionary is contained in two books. Volume I is readings for Sundays, solemnities, and feasts of the Lord and the saints, and Volumes II–IV are readings for weekdays and other Masses.

The scriptural readings and responsorial chants used in the Liturgy of the Word during Mass are all contained in the lectionary. The readings from the Bible and chants between the readings are the main part of the Liturgy of the Word. Both the selection and the arrangement of texts follow the Roman *Ordo Lectionem Missae* that was authorized in the apostolic constitution *Missale Romanum* of April 3, 1969, and published by decree of the Congregation for Divine Worship on May 29, 1969. The National Conference of Catholic Bishops later authorized it for use in the diocese of the United States.

The Scripture during the Mass

The practice of reading passages from the Bible in liturgical settings dates back to the Jewish tradition in Old Testament times.
In those days, and today, the reading from the Torah, the sacred
scroll containing the word of God, was and is the central feature
in the liturgy of the synagogue. In the Temple of Jerusalem, the
people of Israel had a tradition of reading excerpts from the Bible
and singing the psalms. The fourth chapter of Luke's Gospel indicates that Jesus went into the local synagogue in Nazareth and,
during the Sabbath service, stood up and read to the people a messianic passage from the Book of the Prophet Isaiah which Jesus
dramatically applied to himself when he said "today this Scripture
has been fulfilled in your hearing."

The early Christians quickly adapted the Jewish custom of reading passages from the Old Testament in their liturgical assemblies.
The New Testament book the Acts of the Apostles refers to the use
of readings from Scripture by early Christians when they gathered
for the liturgy.

The readings cycles

Until the Second Vatican Council (1962–1965), Western (Latin Rite)
Catholic Christians used a single-volume Missal that had all the
Scripture readings assigned in a one-year format. The same readings were repeated every year for every weekend and weekday.
After the Council, the Missal was divided into two separate books,
the lectionary (which contains only Bible readings) and the sacramentary (which contains only Mass prayers). Furthermore, the
lectionary was subdivided:

- ✔ The readings in weekdays Masses are more or less chronolog-
  ical and follow an alternating two year cycle (odd years being
  Year I and even years being Year II).

- ✔ The readings in Sunday Masses follow an independent three-
  year cycle (A, B, C). The Gospel of Matthew is read in Year A;
  Mark in Year B; and Luke in Year C. The Gospel of John is read
  periodically throughout all three years from time to time.

In response to the directives of the Second Vatican Council, the
Concillium for the Implementation of the Constitution on the
Sacred Liturgy allowed the various Catholic dioceses around
the world to develop their own lectionaries. The United States
Conference of Catholic Bishops (USCCB) developed the *Lectionary
for Mass* using passages from the *New American Bible.* They
selected and assigned the readings for Sundays, feasts, weekdays,
Masses of the saints, and other special occasions.

Book of the Gospels

The Book of the Gospels contains all four of the Gospels and is used by the celebrant when he reads or chants the Gospel during Mass. The use of the Book of the Gospels is optional because the readings are included in the lectionary for everyday use. However, the Book of the Gospels is the only other item carried in the opening processional at Mass along with the processional cross and candles.

When the deacon or lector reaches the altar, he bows in veneration and places the Gospel Book upon the altar, where it remains until the Alleluia, at which time the priest or deacon retrieves the book and walks with it to the ambo. The book is incensed before it is read and remains at the ambo through the duration of Mass.

When the bishop is celebrating Mass, the Book of the Gospels is brought to him after the reading is proclaimed, and he reverences (kisses) it. After that gesture, everyone may sit. If the celebrant is a priest, the deacon reverences the book (or the priest alone in the absence of a deacon).

Roman Pontifical

The Roman pontifical contains the text for special services, such as ordinations, confirmations, rites for dedicating churches, initiation rites, Episcopal services, and more. It is used by the bishop when he is celebrant for any of these services. In Latin, this text is referred to as the *Pontificale* or the *Pontificale Romanum.*

In addition to detailing the bishop's rites, the pontifical contains various historical pontifical manuscripts developed gradually throughout the Middle Ages. They became standardized in the Western Church as various popes issued normative versions that became known as *Roman pontificals.*

The pontifical includes both the texts that are used and the directions for performing each particular ritual, which are known as the rubrics for the liturgical celebration. But the pontifical does not include the rules or directions for the celebration of Mass or praying the Breviary.

Roman Ritual

Although texts for bishops were in common use by the early Middle Ages, priests didn't have a widely accepted text until the 17th century. Priests in the Middle Ages used many different local handbooks to guide their administration of various blessings and ceremonies until the publication of the Roman Ritual by Pope Paul V in 1614.

The *Rituale Romanum* (Roman Ritual) is now one of the official books of the Roman Rite. It contains all the blessings and services performed by the priest that are not contained in the Missal or Breviary. However, it remains the least uniform of all the liturgical books in the Western Church.

In keeping with a desire for uniformity that was growing in the Western Church after the Council of Trent, many books were issued by the Church. In 1586, Cardinal Santorio printed a handbook of different rites to be used by priests, and this book became the foundation of the Roman Ritual that was published by Pope Paul V in 1614.

Pope Paul V didn't abolish all other collections of blessings and sacred rituals, so the Roman Ritual was never meant to be the only text used by the Church on these occasions. As a result, many of the old local rituals from long ago have been preserved in churches around the world. Many countries have retained their own proper and legitimate traditions for marriages, visitations of the sick, and numerous special processions, blessings, and blessings that are not in the Roman Ritual.

The Roman Ritual itself is divided into ten sections, all but the first of which are then subdivided into chapters. Many of these blessings and practices remain in daily use in the Church. But many religious practices that are considered by some Catholics as *old fashioned* or *old-time* are also preserved in the Church through the Roman Ritual.

Today, the one volume Roman Ritual of the pre–Vatican II days has been replaced by separate books of the Roman Ritual for each sacrament, blessings, and exorcism.

Sacramentary (Missal)

The sacramentary, sometimes called the *Mass book,* is the collection of prayers that the celebrant uses for the celebration of the Liturgy of the Eucharist. Before the Second Vatican Council, a single book, the Roman Missal, had all the Bible readings and all the Mass prayers. After the Council, Pope Paul VI authorized the separation of the two into a lectionary of Scripture readings (used during the Liturgy of the Word) and a sacramentary for altar prayers (used in the Liturgy of the Eucharist).

With the revised English translation of November 27, 2011, the word *Missal* will again be used for the Mass prayers said by the priest and deacon at Mass, replacing the word *sacramentary.* The new Missal issued then will be for use by all English-speaking nations; however, each Episcopal Conference of Bishops will authorize a tailored edition that includes particular feasts for that country and incorporates specific dispensations and regulations unique to that locality.

Unlike the original pre–Vatican II Missal, the new Missal will not contain the Bible passages; they will continue to be in the lectionary, a separate book. Keeping the readings, responsorial psalms, and verses for the Gospel acclamation in the lectionary preserves the important distinction between the parts of Mass.

The Eucharistic prayer, contained in the sacramentary, is an expression of gratitude and a means of growth in holiness. It is the center and summit of the Mass. Following are the main aspects of the Eucharistic prayer:

- ✔ **Thanksgiving:** The priest praises and thanks the Father in the name of the entire people of God.

- ✔ **Acclamation:** The entire liturgical assembly sings or recites the *Sanctus,* or *Holy, holy,* which acclaims the greatness of God.

- ✔ **Epiclesis:** The Church (through the priest) calls on the power of God to ask that the gifts of bread and wine be changed into the Body and Blood of Jesus.

- ✔ **Institutional narrative and consecration:** Jesus's sacrifice is celebrated with the words that he used when taking the bread and wine at the Last Supper.

- ✔ **Anamnesis:** The Church keeps the memorial requested by Jesus by recalling his Passion, Death, and Resurrection.

- ✔ **Offering:** The Church offers the spotless victim to the Father in the Holy Spirit as the assembled faithful offer themselves through Christ the Mediator to an ever more complete union with the Father. The wheat bread and grape wine are offered as Jesus did at the Last Supper. Christ himself is also offered to the Father as a sacrifice to save the souls of the human race.

- ✔ **Intercessions:** Prayers are offered by the Church for all its members, both the living and the deceased, who are called to share in the salvation purchased by Christ's sacrifice.

- ✔ **Final doxology:** The assembly of the faithful says *amen* to the praise and gratitude offered by the Church to God.

Eastern Catholic Books

The Eastern Catholic Church has several liturgical families that are further delineated as separate autonomous Churches in union with Rome. Many of the words used to describe their books, vessels, and vestments have Greek names because the Eastern Church traces itself to the patriarchates of Antioch, Alexandria, and Constantinople that were located in the Eastern part of the Roman Empire.

Following are the Eastern books:

- **Apostolos (Epistle Book):** This book contains Bible readings from the Acts of the Apostles and the New Testament Epistles, arranged according to the liturgical calendar.

- **Archieratikon:** This is the bishop's liturgical service book, which is used when celebrating a Hierarchical Divine Liturgy (formal Divine Liturgy where several prelates and dignitaries are present as opposed to the typical parish liturgy with just the pastor and a deacon). The book contains pontifical editions of the Divine Liturgies of St. John Chrysostom and St. Basil the Great, as well as the Liturgy of the Presanctified Gifts and other Episcopal services, such as ordinations.

- **Euchologion:** Taken from the Greek word for *book of prayers,* the Euchologion is similar to the Roman sacramentary containing the Mass prayers of the priest, deacon, and bishop. The Great (Mega) Euchologion contains all the prayers for the priest to celebrate Divine Liturgy and the sacraments. The Small (Mikron) Euchologion has the blessings and other minor ceremonies.

- **Evangelion (Gospel Book):** Sometimes called the *Tetraevangelion* (Four Gospels), the Evangelion is the Book of the Gospels. It is arranged according to the liturgical calendar. Normally it's kept on the altar in a metal case decorated with icons of the evangelists.

- **Hieratikon:** The Hieratikon, or *Liturgikon,* is the book of the priest. It contains parts of the Mega Euchologion like prayers for Divine Liturgy and for Vespers and Orthros (also called *Matins* or the *Office of Readings*).

- **Octoechos:** Octoechos is the book of the eight tones, an eight-week cycle of liturgical chants used in sacred worship.

Chapter 12

Liturgical Vestments

· ·

In This Chapter

▶ Checking out some historical background

▶ Looking at the apparel worn by clergy

· ·

*T*he idea of wearing distinctive clothing for public ceremonies is not unique to Christianity and, in fact, can't even be attributed to Christianity. Most of the priests or officiates of ancient religions wore distinguishing robes, and Jewish priests wore special vestments when sacrificing bulls or other animals at the Temple in Jerusalem. Rabbis in synagogues wear special ceremonial dress when reading the Torah and proclaiming its contents.

This chapter describes the attire worn by Catholic priests and explains its meaning. Trust us, style and fashion sense have little to do with the robes and vestments that priests wear when presiding over a Mass.

The Origins of Liturgical Vestments

Catholic Christianity, with its roots in Judaism, borrowed some elements of *vesture,* or apparel, from Temple worship in Jerusalem. Other elements came from more pedestrian origins, such as Roman or Greek daily wear. Tunics and togas worn by average citizens became a pattern for Catholic ceremonial vestments worn by the clergy.

Most vestments worn in the Roman (Western) Church borrow their styles from the unique pattern of public dress characteristic of officials in the ancient Mediterranean world, especially those in imperial Rome. Likewise, the attire worn in the Byzantine Empire greatly influenced the vestments of Eastern Catholic clergy.

Fashions have changed much in the last 21 centuries, but Roman Catholic vestments have largely remained the same. There have been adaptations and even some innovations, but the style is generally same as it was in the early Church.

The chasuble, the sleeveless outer garment worn by priests, is a prime example of how vestments have changed and yet remained the same. In Roman times the chasuble was long, flowing, and conical in shape, but by the Gothic area it had been shortened, showing more of the sleeve of the underlying vestment. It changed again in the Baroque era, this time taking the shape of two flaps worn over the shoulder and tied at the waist.

What's Worn Today

The General Instruction of the Roman Missal 2002 explains the essential uses and requirements of Roman vestments: They are used to identify the sign of a particular office of the celebrant, such as bishop, priest, or deacon; they are to contribute to the dignity of the Mass; colors are to be employed throughout the liturgical year and for each Sacrament; and they are to be made of dignified materials and fabrics.

Why is so much emphasis and care placed on these items? Quite simply, they are symbols of the sacredness of the Holy Mass, which is instituted by the Lord Jesus Christ on the eve of his crucifixion at the Last Supper.

Shared vestments in both the East and the West

Pope John Paul the Great once described the Catholic Church as having two lungs, the East and West (also called Latin). Each has its own liturgical style, dress, and regulations. What binds the two is that they celebrate the same Mass in which Christ's sacrifice is made present.

A few vestments are shared by both traditions: the cassock, the biretta, and the zucchetto. The styles of each are different for each tradition, but the purpose and symbolism remain the same.

Cassock

The *cassock* is a floor-length black robe that is considered the ordinary street attire of clerics. In the West, two styles are acceptable: Roman, with 33 fastening buttons and a sash; and a semi-Jesuit model with fasteners and snaps in place of buttons. Latin Rite priests wear a black cassock with black buttons. Monsignors (Chaplains of His Holiness) wear a black cassock with purple trim and a purple sash or (for Prelates of Honor) a purple cassock. Bishops wear a black cassock with red trim and a purple sash, and cardinals wear a red cassock with red sash. The pope is the only person allowed to wear an all-white cassock, but in tropical climates, priests and bishops can wear white with black or purple buttons and trim, respectively.

Because of a strong anti-Catholic climate in the 19th century, priests in the United States wear a black clerical suit rather than the cassock when outside the church or rectory.

In the Eastern Church the inner cassock, *anteri,* is also black, but it has only a few buttons on the shoulder for fastening. Byzantine Catholics also have a secondary cassock, called a *ryasa* or *exorason,* worn over the inner one.

Biretta

The *biretta* is a square cap, usually with three peaks (ridges) on the top, that's worn by all clerics. A four-cornered biretta is worn by someone who has a doctoral degree, with green pom and trim for canon law; red for theology; and blue for philosophy. The biretta is worn in the Extraordinary form of Mass (sometimes called the Traditional Latin Mass, Pre-Vatican II Mass, or Tridentine Mass) by the clergy and removed at different times of the Mass. Celebrants and concelebrants in the Ordinary form (also called the Vatican II, Paul VI, or New Mass; the common Mass used in most parishes) normally do not wear the biretta during Mass, but visiting prelates (high-ranking clergy) and other clergy who are merely attending wear theirs. It can also be worn with a cassock as street attire, but that's usually only done in predominantly Catholic countries.

A celebrating bishop (or archbishop) or cardinal wears a *miter* (a different headdress) instead at Mass, both Ordinary and Extraordinary. The color depends on rank: A priest wears black, a bishop wears purple, and a cardinal wears red. *Kalymavchion* is the stovepipe Eastern Catholic version of the biretta, and its color denotes rank and office.

Zucchetto

A *zucchetto* is a small, round skullcap that is reserved normally for prelates. Because of its shape, the name is derived from the Italian word for gourd. Zucchettos are marked by color: Bishops wear purple, cardinals wear red, and the pope wears white. Bishops and cardinals wear them at Mass, except from the Sanctus until after Communion. Bishops, cardinals, and the pope wear them at Mass with a miter. Clerics (priests and deacons) can also wear a black biretta at Mass (especially in the Extraordinary form), and certain religious orders have retained the custom of donning them in corresponding color of their habits. Only prelates may wear the zucchetto under the biretta; lower clerics (priests and deacons) can wear birettas only at Mass. Eastern Catholic Clergy wear a *skoufos,* which is a soft cap worn much like the zucchetto is by the Latin Rite clergy.

Western Rite vestments

The vestments described in this section are worn by priests in the Western Roman Catholic Church.

Surplice

The *surplice* is a white garment with loose, wide sleeves that is worn over a cassock and typically made from lace, linen, wool, or cotton. It is used by the clergy in services or celebrations of sacraments outside of Mass, with a stole for the ordained. Clerics also wear a surplice with a stole at Holy Communion when attending Mass in choir dress (liturgical attire for clerics who are not con-celebrating). Spiritually the surplice represents the white garment that the baptized receives at Baptism.

Mozzetta and rochet

The surplice can be worn by those who are not ordained, such as acolytes and choristers, but it is not worn by prelates, such as bishops, cardinals, and popes. Prelates wear *rochets,* knee-length garments with narrow sleeves, for non-Eucharistic functions. A rochet is worn with a *mozzetta,* a short cape, draped over it. Like a surplice, a rochet is worn in conjunction with a stole. In recent times, the pope has reverted to an earlier custom of wearing a mozzetta of white ermine during Christmas and Eastertide and a velvet one with white ermine trim the rest of the time, with the stole draped over it.

Amice

The *amice* is a rectangular piece of white cloth that has two long ribbons attached from the upper corners of the material, usually with an embroidered cross positioned in the middle. It is always worn under the alb (see the next section) and over the street clothes of the priest (either a cassock or clerical shirt) and is tucked in under the neck. The ribbons are fastened around the waist. Its uses are both practical and spiritual. For practical purposes, the amice protects the vestments that are worn. Spiritually, it is called the *helmet of salvation,* which expresses the idea of putting aside street clothes and enveloping oneself in Christ. If the style of alb worn for Mass covers the Roman Collar, the amice isn't necessary, but some clergy wear it anyway for the symbolic value.

Alb

An *alb* takes its name from the Latin word for white, and it symbolizes purity. This long, flowing gown is worn over the cassock and amice. Albs are normally made from a combination of linen, wool, and now polyester, and sometimes have lace bottoms and cuffs. An alb can be worn loose over a cassock, or it can be tied at the top or made in square yoke shape, in which case an amice has to be worn underneath. The more contemporary style has a high collar and is fashioned for ease. An alb must always be worn underneath vestments (chasuble or dalmatic) for celebrants and concelebrants of Holy Mass. If a cleric is in choir, he then only wears the cassock and surplice.

The alb was an everyday garment for the Roman citizens, but for a priest it is a daily reminder that cleric is ordained to the priesthood of Jesus Christ.

Cincture

The *cincture* is a cord that girds the waist of the alb and is worn by priests and bishops to remind them of their commitment to chastity and purity. It often has tassels at the end and can be made in the liturgical color of the vestment worn. Priests and bishops tie the cincture into two loops in the front so that the stole may go through the loops to fasten it. Deacons and acolytes often wear cinctures, but theirs are fastened on the side. While some albs do not need cinctures, many clergy wear them anyway for the symbolic value.

Stole

The *stole* is a scarf-life garment that marks the ordination of the man wearing it. Whenever a cleric wears an alb, a stole must also be worn to distinguish rank and office. When it's worn over the left shoulder, drawn across the chest and back toward the lower right, it signifies the office of a deacon. In the Extraordinary form of the Roman Rite, priests wear the stole crisscrossed, and bishops wear stoles straight up and down over the neck. In the Ordinary form of the Roman Rite, both priests and bishops wear the stole in the same fashion, hanging straight down around the neck.

During the celebration of the Holy Mass, a stole is worn by deacons under a vestment called a dalmatic and by priests and bishops under a chasuble. It also can be worn over a cassock and surplice for devotions and administrations of some sacraments outside of Mass. Usually stoles are made to match the outer vestment of the clergy, but for non-Eucharistic celebrations they can also be worn in the same liturgical colors as chasubles and dalmatics. Stoles are also worn over choir dress, especially before receiving Holy Communion.

Dalmatic

Deacons sport an outer vestment at Mass known as a *dalmatic,* a long-sleeved tunic. It usually has a two bandings on either side of the panel front and back with two matching cross bandings. The name's origin is Dalmatia, a region of Croatia that lies opposite Italy on the Adriatic Sea. Secularly, it was a garb of rank and privilege. In AD 332, Pope St. Sylvester extended this garment to the order of deacons. It is made in the liturgical colors used at Mass and normally matches the main celebrant's chasuble. In the present Ordinary rite, a lighter version of the dalmatic is worn under a chasuble of a bishop. This signifies that the bishop has fullness of holy orders — deacon, priesthood, and episcopacy.

Tunic

A *tunic* is similar to a dalmatic and is worn in the Extraordinary form of the Mass by subdeacons. This vestment came in popular usage under Pope Gregory I in the seventh century. In the Ordinary form, this level was suppressed since 1972 when Pope Paul VI reformed the rites centering on the priesthood. When the Extraordinary form of the Mass is celebrated, priests often serve in the role of deacons and subdeacons and wear these vestments.

Maniple

No longer required in the Ordinary form of the Mass, the *maniple* is obligatory in the Extraordinary form. It's a band of cloth that is draped over the left arm of the celebrant and is often made of the same material and liturgical colors as the vestment being worn for Mass. It is only worn with either a chasuble, dalmatic, or tunic in a Solemn Mass.

Cope

A *cope* is a long cape fastened in front with clasps. Its origins are quite humble: Because churches were cold and unheated prior to the 20th century, copes provided warmth, and in processions that were led outside, copes provided a layer of protection from the elements. Made from beautiful and ornamental material, this vestment certainly adds solemnity to the celebration.

As a liturgical vestment it comes in the colors associated with the Mass. In the Extraordinary form of the Roman Rite, an archpriest wears a cope in Solemn High Masses. Also, the celebrant uses a cope in the Asperges Rite at the beginning of Mass. In the Ordinary form, the cope is used only in ceremonies or Eucharistic celebrations outside of Mass. In addition to bishops and priests, deacons may also wear this vestment.

A cope may be worn on the rare occasions when a Rite of Funerals is celebrated in place of a Mass of Christian Burial. During Solemn celebrations of the Liturgy of the Hours, especially evening prayer, the celebrant (either priest or deacon) normally wears a cope. It can either be worn over an alb or cassock and surplice and always with a corresponding matching stole.

Humeral veil

The *humeral veil* is a rectangular vestment that is fastened in the center with clasps, allowing the end to be draped. It's often made of the same material as the cope it's worn with, but the color is generally either white or gold, although in the Extraordinary form of the Mass the humeral veil can be the color of the liturgical season.

In Benediction of the Blessed Sacrament, the officiating clergy covers his hands with the humeral veil and lifts the monstrance containing the Real Presence of the Lord in the Host for blessing of the congregants, and in the Extraordinary form of a Solemn Mass a subdeacon uses a humeral veil in order to hold the paten. The inside of the veil is often made with pockets, making it easier for the celebrant to hold the object. This vestment came into wide use in the Medieval period, and after the Council of Trent in the 16th century it became a normative vestment.

Miter

A *miter* is a type of ceremonial headgear worn by abbots, bishops, cardinals, and popes during Mass and other vested religious functions. It is used in both Western and Eastern Churches, though the style and shape are quite different.

In the Roman Rite (the Western Church), the miter is a tall folding triangular cap consisting of two parts, front and back, forming a peak, with two pieces of matching material suspended from it in the back. Normally, it is made of either white or gold material; however, it can be also of the liturgical color of the day. Byzantine and other Eastern Catholic bishops wear miters that resemble crowns.

Papal tiara

In previous years, popes typically wore a three-tier crown, known as the papal tiara, instead of a miter. The three tiers corresponded with the pope's responsibilities: teach (prophetic), sanctify (priestly), and shepherd (kingly). Paul VI (1963–1978) was the last one to wear the crown, as John Paul I (1978) declined it and John Paul II (1978–2005) followed the example of his immediate predecessor. The papal tiara was never formally suppressed, and any pope is free to use this ancient symbol, though the pallium (see the following section) seems to be the current favorite symbol of papal authority.

Pallium

A narrow band made out of wool worn over the chasuble during Mass by archbishops, the *pallium* is common to both the East and West. In the East it is named *omophor* and is a much wider band than in the West. In the West a pallium takes the shape of a *Y* and contains three golden spikes and six black crosses. They are made of wool from sheep raised by sisters of the Convent of St. Agnes. On the feast of this saint, the lambs are blessed because their wool will be made into these special articles and presented by the pope. The palliums are given to the new archbishops each year and usually are bestowed on the Feast of SS. Peter and Paul, June 29. Since the pope is the Bishop of Rome, in addition to being supreme head of the Universal Church and patriarch of the West, he, too, wears a pallium.

Buskins

Ceremonial liturgical stockings, *buskins,* are worn by bishops in the Extraordinary Rite of the Mass by a prelate. They are worn over the pant leg and come in the liturgical colors of the season. Originally used to protect the cleric from drafts in the days of no central heating in churches, they now have a more ceremonial and festive meaning (in other words, they're used for only the most formal of occasions). They are worn only with special ecclesiastical slippers instead of the common shoe. Often the coat of arms of the prelate is embossed on both the buskin and slipper.

Episcopal gloves

In Solemn Mass of the Extraordinary Rite, prelates also wear the *Episcopal gloves.* Although they can be made in the liturgical colors, most often the gloves are white. They are worn from the start of Mass until the offertory with the Episcopal ring worn on the outside. The gloves are seen as a symbol of purity. The coat of arms of the prelate is often embossed on the glove.

Pectoral crosses

Pectoral crosses are worn by prelates of both rites. When the prelate is wearing a suit, the cross is extended on a gold or silver chain and tucked into a side shirt pocket. With a cassock, it usually hangs on the chain in the center of the chest, and with the rochet and mozzetta, choir dress, it is often worn on a special ornate rope. This same rope is worn under the chasuble and over the alb when the prelate is celebrating Mass. The pectoral cross reflects the dignity of the office of bishop or abbot.

Crozier

A pastoral staff known as a *crozier* is used by a prelate during liturgical ceremonies and at Mass. It is the symbol of the governing office of the bishop. The shape is likened to a shepherd's staff; just as a shepherd watches over his flock, so does the bishop, the chief shepherd of the diocese, watch over his people. In the East the crosier is made in a *T* shape and is called *paterissa,* but it keeps the same meaning as in the Western Church.

The crozier is made of many different materials, ranging from rarer woods to fine metals. Some are ornately decorated with jewels and statuary or even the bishop's coat of arms on the crook or curved part of the staff.

Vimp

A veil or shawl worn over the shoulders of a server is known as a *vimp*. Like a humeral veil, a vimp is a rectangular piece of material fastened in the center. They often have pockets on the inside, allowing the servants to hold onto the bishop's miter and crozier. Practically, a vimp preserves the integrity of the item being held so that it doesn't get worn or dirty.

If a server wears a vimp and holds the crozier for the bishop, the crook should be faced in. Holding it facing out is reserved only for the bishop, as a sign of his openness to guide his flock.

Gremial

The *gremial* is a square piece of cloth with two ribbons at the top that tied around the waist of a celebrant for Mass. In both the Ordinary and Extraordinary Rites of the Mass, this vestment is used by the celebrant of Confirmation and Holy Orders. The bishop is seated during the anointing, and the gremial is placed over his lap to protect his other vestments from being stained by any chrism oil that may leak onto him. It is also used by the celebrant on Holy Thursday at the washing of feet.

In the Extraordinary form of the Mass, prelates use the gremial when seated at the singing of the Kyrie, Gloria, and creed by the choir. This type of gremial is more ornate and usually made to match the vestment. In days of old before central heating in churches, it served to keep the bishop warm during the liturgical ceremony.

Liturgical colors in the West

The General Instruction of the Roman Missal in 2000 delineates the use of colors in the Ordinary Rite of the Mass in the West. The diverse colors in the liturgy demonstrate different religious meanings and mysteries of faith being celebrated. Vestments that are worn by the different ordained ministers and the accoutrement for the liturgy in the sanctuary correspond to the prescriptions of the day that can be found in a book known as the Ordo.

Many liturgical pieces change color for particular days. In addition to the vestments of the celebrant and deacons, the antependium of the altar — cloth draped over the altar, chalice veil, burse, and tabernacle veil — are usually coordinated to match the celebrant.

In the Ordinary form the chalice veil, burse, tabernacle veil, and antependium are optional. In the Extraordinary form they are mandatory, and the maniple, cope, humeral veil, and tunics are also used and should match the seasonal or festive color. On solemnities, the highest rank of feast in the church, and Sundays in which Vespers (evening prayer) is celebrated, the color of the anticipated day is normally changed, because liturgically the new day occurs after sundown (even though chronologically it doesn't happen until midnight).

Colors for the Ordinary form of the Roman Rite

For the Ordinary form, the Roman Rite uses the following colors:

- ✔ **White:** Used for festive seasons of Christmas and Easter; Holy Thursday; Our Lord's feast day; days of saints; and Feasts of the Blessed Virgin Mary, Angels, Conversion of St. Paul, Nativity of John the Baptist, John the Beloved Disciple, and the beatified. Exclusions include the Lord's Passion and days of martyrs. In addition, it is used for the Sacraments of Marriage, Baptism, First Holy Communion, Holy Orders, and Mass of Christian Burial in the United States of America. White is a symbol of joy, purity, and glory.

- ✔ **Red:** Used for Pentecost; Palm Sunday; Passion of the Lord; feasts of the holy cross, martyrs, Apostles, and evangelists (except for John the Beloved Disciple); and Confirmation. Red is a symbol of the burning charity of the martyrs and their generous sacrifice, tongues of fire of the Holy Spirit, and the blood shed by our Divine Lord.

- ✔ **Green:** Used in Ordinary Time. It is a symbol of hope in eternal life.

- ✔ **Violet or purple:** Used for seasons of Advent and Lent, Sacrament of Reconciliation, and Mass of Christian Burial. Purple is a symbol of penance and mortification.

- ✔ **Rose:** Used for Gaudete Sunday (the third Sunday in Advent) and Laetare Sunday (the fourth Sunday of Lent). It is a symbol that the Advent or Lent is half over and soon the Church will be celebrating the joyful season of Christmas or Easter.

- ✔ **Black:** Used for All Souls' Day, Masses for the Dead, and Mass of Christian Burial. Black is a symbol of mourning and signifies the sorrow of death.

- ✔ **Gold:** Can be used in place of white but is traditionally reserved for solemnities and very important feasts of saints. Often used in the season of Christmas. It is a symbol of richness and festivity.

Colors for the Extraordinary form of the Roman Rite

In the Extraordinary form, white, green, gold, and rose are used in the same ways as in the Ordinary form (see the preceding section). The following colors have different or additional uses:

- ✔ **Red:** Used for the blessing of palms and the procession on Palm Sunday (but not for Mass), Mass of the Holy Spirit, Pentecost, Confirmation, and feasts of the martyrs, Apostles, holy cross, and evangelists (except for John).

- ✔ **Purple:** Used for Ember days, Rogations days, three Sundays before Lent (Septuagesima, Sexagesima, and Quinquagesima), vigils of the Immaculate Conception, Epiphany, Assumption, and Pentecost. In addition, it is used for the seasons of Advent and Lent.

- ✔ **Black:** Used at all requiem Masses, All Souls' Day, and Good Friday (but not including Communion).

Eastern Rite vestments

Many of the vestments in the Eastern Catholic Church are similar to that of the West but with different names. However, distinct vesture peculiar to the Eastern Rite are also used. As with the Roman Rite, Eastern liturgical wear developed out of wear among members of Roman society, but over the years it was used less by ordinary people. Since the items fell out of use by society, the Church could preserve them with sacredness and special character.

- ✔ **Sticharion:** This floor-length, long-sleeved patterned garment is worn by all members of the clergy. Laity can also be dressed in it when they are performing liturgical functions, such as serving the Divine Liturgy. It is compared to the Western alb and is worn over the cassock. It is the oldest liturgical vestment. According to rank of the clergy, the sticharion may vary in weight and color.

- ✔ **Alb:** Like the Western Church's long flowing gown, the Eastern alb is usually white. However, priests and bishops can also wear red and light blue albs for feasts of Easter and the Blessed Mother. For a reader it's made of silk or similar fabric in the appropriate liturgical colors. Albs traditionally have inserts of darker fabric on the shoulders, sleeves, and bottom and are decorated with embroidery. The dark inserts symbolize the Blood shed by Christ during his Sacred Passion.

- ✔ **Orarion:** Deacons wear this long narrow strip of cloth over their left shoulder, extending to the ankle. It can also be worn by subdeacons. It's very similar to a deacon stole of the Western Rite, which is also worn across the shoulder.

- **Epitrachelion:** Priests and deacons use this stole, draped around the neck with two adjacent sides buttoned together, as a symbol of their priesthood.

- **Epimanikia:** These ornate cuffs are worn on the sleeves and tied. The deacon wears them beneath the alb, and priests and bishops wear them above.

- **Zone:** This cloth belt is worn by priests and bishops with a stole and a phelonion (see the following).

- **Phelonion:** This vestment for priests is a large, conical, sleeveless garment worn over all the other vestments. The front is cut away so it exposes the ornate matching stole and alb.

- **Sakkos:** Instead of wearing a phelonion, bishops wear this tunic. It reaches below the knees with wide sleeves and ornate trim and is buttoned at the sides.

- **Epigonation or palitsa:** This vestment is a stiff diamond-shaped cloth draped on the right side and suspended by one corner with strap over the left shoulder. It is reserved for bishops or priests who have been given a special recognition, much like scarlet color denotes monsignors in the West.

- **Omophorion:** A wide cloth band draped around the shoulders, this distinctive vestment is worn by bishops.

Liturgical colors in the East

The Eastern Church, which is made up of more than 13 rites, does not have a universal codified system for colors used in vestments. Generally, though, it keeps to the following liturgical norms:

- **Gold:** Like the color green in the Roman Rite, used in Ordinary Time

- **Light blue:** Feasts of the Blessed Virgin Mary

- **Purple or red:** Saturdays and Sundays during Lent

- **Red:** Holy Thursday; feasts of the cross, John the Baptist, and martyrs; Nativity Fasts; and Apostles' Fasts

- **Green:** Palm Sunday, Pentecost, and feasts of monastic saints

- **Black:** Weekdays during Lent and Holy Week, except Holy Thursday

- **White:** Easter, Christmas, feasts of the Lord, and funerals

Chapter 13

Liturgical Vessels, Altar Linens, and Artifacts

*I*n order for the Sacred Liturgy to operate effectively, it needs certain vessels, furnishings, and equipment in addition to vestments. The Church has always taught that we worship God not only with our minds but with also all our senses. Both the Eastern and Western Rites arrange a feast for the senses: music for the ears; vestments, architecture, vessels, furnishings, and art for the eyes; the reception of the Holy Eucharist for taste; incense and candles for smell; and holy water for the touch.

While the celebration of Mass can take place virtually anywhere — in homes, hospital rooms, or military camps, for instance — for the purposes of our discussion here, we refer to Masses that take place in a building consecrated to the Lord, a church.

In this chapter, we explain the significance of the various items you typically see in a Catholic Church. The Western or Latin Rite churches and Eastern Rite churches have some minor differences, but the two rites share quite a bit in common.

Common Items for Both East and West

Although the Eastern and Westerns Rites have many differences, the churches have some consistent features.

Altar

The *altar* is the primary piece of furniture in the church. It is a table that represents Christ, and at the beginning and end of Mass the priest kisses the altar as a sign of reverence for the Lord.

The altar is the furniture at which the Holy Sacrifice of the Mass is offered. Although the Bloody Sacrifice of Christ on the altar of the cross took place once and on Good Friday, it's renewed on the altars of the churches. Therefore, the Mass is not a new or different sacrifice, but rather the same sacrifice of Christ, just in an unbloody manner. Just as the cross was the pulpit for Christ in his office as Prophet (teacher), and throne for Christ in his office as King (leader), the cross was finally the altar for Christ in his office as priest (sanctifier).

The same Jesus who willingly gave up his life on the cross at Calvary on Good Friday is the same Jesus who renews that same sacrifice on the altar at every Holy Mass and Divine Liturgy.

The altar has taken many shapes through the years. In the Extraordinary form of the Roman Rite, the altar often contains a high back drop, *reredos,* made of either wood or marble, which holds the tabernacle and sometimes intricately carved statues of saints or angels. The altar should contain six candles and an altar cross on a ledge just above the mensa (flat, horizontal surface of the altar) where the Holy Mass takes place. The altar has to contain an altar stone that holds the relics of saints and martyrs. The shape of the altar is long and rectangular but not very deep. The relics and shape of the altar harkened back to the days in which Mass was celebrated on martyrs' tombs.

In some churches, especially in the Eastern Rite, a *baldachin* is built over the altar. Baldachins are canopies made of brocade fabric or solid materials, and historically they were used over royal thrones and beds to denote a special place. That meaning transferred to the Catholic Church, as well, and a four-post baldachin over the altar represents the specialness of the altar as the place of the Eucharistic Sacrifice. The most notable example of a baldachin was designed by Bernini and is over the pontifical altar at St. Peter's Basilica.

Tabernacle

The word *tabernacle* has Latin roots and means *a dwelling place.* In the Old Testament Moses was instructed by God to build a tabernacle to house the Ark of the Covenant.

In the Catholic Church, the tabernacle is where priests keep the Blessed Sacrament. After the consecration of the Mass, the consecrated hosts — the Holy Eucharist — that are left are placed in the tabernacle for safekeeping to be later removed and brought as Holy Communion to sick members of the congregation. The leftover consecrated hosts are not only for Holy Communion to the sick, but also just to be there in the tabernacle for adoration of God by the faithful. Often, Catholics spend time in quiet prayer outside of Mass but physically near the tabernacle knowing that it contains the Body and Blood, Soul and Divinity of Christ.

Tabernacles can take many shapes and can be placed on the old high altars with veils or be an *ambry* (a chest or cupboard) built into the wall. Near the tabernacle is a lamp, which is constantly lit to symbolize that the Real Presence of Jesus abides in the Sacrament and is reserved in the tabernacle.

Normally, the Holy Eucharist remains in the tabernacle in the sanctuary. On Holy Thursday it is removed and placed on an altar of Reservation and is not returned to the sanctuary until Easter.

Candles

Candles are used at Mass to signify Christ as the Light of the World. Candles were used to light the church in the days before electric lighting, but today they are used to spiritually note the Light of Christ. In the Ordinary Rite of the Mass, at least two candles are used. In the Extraordinary Rite, two candles are used for Low Mass without a bishop, four are used for Missa Cantata and Low Mass with a bishop, and six candles are used for High Mass. A seventh candle is used in the presence of a bishop.

Candles in the Extraordinary Rite are made of at least 51 percent or more beeswax to symbolize the pure flesh of Jesus. In the Ordinary Rite, candles can be made from oil, usually burning with a wick in a white canister made to look like a beeswax candle.

In the Ordinary Rite of the Mass, servers often carry processional candles and flank the crucifer (the server who carries the cross mounted on a pole, carried in procession at the beginning and end of Mass).

Candles used in special Masses

In addition to regular altar candles, the church also uses a *paschal* candle. *Paschal* comes from Latin and means *Easter* in English. The candle is the largest one in the church. It's blessed by the new fire at the Easter Vigil and burns every Mass for the 50 days of

Easter. It is also burned for celebrations of Baptism, Confirmation, and Mass of Christian Burial. It symbolizes Christ, the Light of the World, and it also reminds the faithful of his Resurrection from the dead when he conquered the forces of darkness once and for all.

Smaller tapers are given to the congregation at the Easter Vigil. The Mass is in total darkness until the paschal candle is blessed, and from that one candle, all the people's candles are lit, lighting the entire church merely by candlelight.

Additionally, in churches that the bishop has consecrated with chrism oil, special candles are permanently placed and lit on special occasions, such as the anniversary of the parish, the blessing of the building, the principal feast of the parish, Christmas, and Easter Liturgy.

Candles used outside of Mass

Votive candles are usually found in front of images of the saints in the church. Members of the congregation who want to pray for a special reason make a small offering to compensate for the cost of a candle and then light one, letting it burn itself out (usually after one or seven days, depending on the size). The candles have nothing magical about them, and the mere lighting of them has no supernatural effect. They are meant to remind the faithful who come to the church that someone in the parish is praying for a special intention. Members of the church, the Mystical Body of Christ, are encouraged to unite their prayers with those who have lit a candle. Even though they may not know the requests represented by the candles, they can join in the petition before God in solidarity with their neighbors. Seeing lit votive candles urges individuals to meditate on the needs of others as well as their own spiritual ones.

In churches with statues and saints, devotees often light a candle to symbolize the prayer of intercession of the particular saint.

The sanctuary lamp is a candle, usually made of beeswax, that burns before the tabernacle containing the Blessed Sacrament. It can either be hung from the ceiling or placed in a stand. The candle of the sanctuary lamp should never burn out, because it signifies the Real Presence of Jesus in the Holy Eucharist (the consecrated wafers of bread that Catholics believe become the Body of Christ). A Catholic always knows that the Lord is present in the tabernacle when he sees the sanctuary lamp burning brightly.

Candelabras

Candelabras are branched candlesticks that hold many candles. They're primarily used in the church in the celebration of the Benediction or blessing of the people with the Real Presence of the Lord in the Eucharist. Normally, at least two candles are lit for exposition or Benediction. However, an older custom uses candelabras that contain seven candles on each. They look like the Jewish menorah, but the number has no significance. Candelabras for exposition can hold three, five, or seven candles. Normally, two are placed on either side of the monstrance.

The *Tenebrae tree* is a very large candelabra that contains 15 places for candles. Tenebrae service is often sung during Holy Week and consists of the Book of Lamentations in the Old Testament.

Vessels, Artifacts, and Linens in the Latin Rite

Some artifacts and vessels are common in each church, but a number of items are specific to the church of either rite.

Chalice

The *chalice* is the sacred vessel containing the wine and drop of water used at Mass. Catholics believe that after the consecration in which the sacred words of Institution are said, the wine turns into the substance of the Precious Blood of Christ. It is the noblest of church vessels, and many legends center on the chalice our Divine Lord used at the Last Supper, also called the Holy Grail.

As with many other vessels of the church, the chalice has taken many styles and shapes over the 21 centuries. The General Instruction of the Roman Missal in 2000 reiterates a centuries-old custom on what elements can be used to make a chalice: The chalice should be made from precious metal with the inside gilded in gold or silver, and it should be made of a nonabsorbent material so the Precious Blood doesn't leak through. Some modern liturgists have been tempted to employ nonprecious material in the cup, such as cut crystal, hand-blown glass, alabaster, or rare woods. While incorporating these materials is acceptable, the inside of the cup must be gilded with either silver or gold to secure the Precious Blood from leaking through.

Ciborium

One of the earliest styles of the tabernacle, one that is often still used in Eastern Catholic churches, is type of vessel that looks like a dove. In the Western Church the dove took the form of a *ciborium* — a covered chalice-like vessel that contains the Blessed Sacrament for distribution. At Mass the unconsecrated hosts that will be distributed to the congregants are placed in the ciborium. After Holy Communion is distributed, the remains are gathered into one ciborium and placed in the tabernacle.

Paten

The *paten* is the second-most illustrious vessel used in Mass (after the chalice). Patens made before the Second Vatican Council, and some still made today, are small disks designed to contain the main celebrant's host. Most patens used in the Ordinary form of the Roman Rite are dish-like and can contain not only the main celebrant's host, but also enough for the congregation. Regardless of the shape, the General Instruction of the Roman Mass 2000 retains the same requirements for the substance that can be used in its composition: The area that will hold the consecrated host, the Sacred Body of the Lord, must be gilded.

Monstrance

The *monstrance* or *ostensorium* is a sacred vessel used in exposition, procession, and Benediction of the Most Blessed Sacrament. It stands on a base and rises to height of 2 feet, fanning out in a magnificent sunburst of rays made out of precious metal. The sole purpose is to show the *monstrare,* the Latin word for *consecrated host.* Smaller monstrances that contain relics are called *reliquaries.* The consecrated host is only in the monstrance when it is placed on the altar for public adoration and subsequent Benediction. Otherwise, the monstrance stays in a closet or cabinet or safe and the hosts remain in the tabernacle.

Candlesticks

Candlesticks simply hold the candles that are used for Mass. In the Ordinary form of the Roman Rite, at least two candles must be used, usually placed on either side of the altar. The candlesticks can be either floor-length and freestanding or placed atop the mensa (top, flat part) of the altar. They are usually made of brass and hold either beeswax candles or oil canisters.

Normally in Requiem Masses, the paschal candle and candlestick are used, but in Requiem Masses in the Extraordinary Rite of the Roman liturgy, six candlesticks are place around the bier of the coffin, known as the *catafalque,* instead of the paschal candlestick.

Thurible

Incense is burned at different points of the Mass, exposition and Benediction, Solemn celebration of the Liturgy of the Hours, or at Mass of Christian burial. The item used for burning is known as a *thurible,* or *censer.* Accompanying the censer is the incense boat that contains the aromatic resins to be burned. Thuribles were originally used in Jewish Temple services at the altar of incense. Spiritually, the burning of incense symbolizes prayers going to heaven, reflective of Psalm 140. It symbolizes adoration and worship of God. Practically, burning incense can help purify the air.

Thuribles can either be freestanding or carried at the end of chain by a person called a *thurifer* during the liturgy. In the Byzantine Rite the thurible often has little bells on the chains of the censer. During the celebration of Mass in the Roman Rite and exposition and Benediction of the Blessed Sacrament, the thurifer carries the thurible, which contains burning charcoal. Incense is placed on the burning charcoal and then taken by the celebrant to be used for the incensation. In the Solemn celebration of the Liturgy of the Hours, the handheld thurible is still used; however, recently the stationary style of thurible that's located near the altar has also been permitted. When singing the Benedictus (at Morning Prayer) or the Magnificat (at Evening Prayer), incense is placed in the urn containing burning charcoals.

Bells

Bells are used in the liturgy along with chanting, singing, and the use of other musical instruments. The *Sanctus bells* are held by the servers and used specifically at the Consecration of the Mass. In the Ordinary form of the Roman Rite, they're used four times at the Mass: at the epiclesis, or when the priest invokes the Holy Spirit to bless the Eucharistic bread and wine; at the elevation of the host after the consecration; at the elevation of the Precious Blood after the consecration; and at the reception of Holy Communion by the priest. In the Extraordinary form of the Roman Rite, the Sanctus bells are also rung at the "Holy, Holy . . . ," or Sanctus, which is where they derived their name.

Other bells are also used to prepare the people for the celebration of Mass. The sacristy bell is sometimes rung before Mass to signal people to stand and greet the main celebrant. Bells in the church's tower are used to call people to Mass and are sometimes used in place of the altar bell at the consecration of Mass. They are also used at the Mass of Christian Burial after the closing prayer, and they're used more plentifully at the end of a wedding ceremony.

Bells can be rung at end of the angelus or at the recitation of the Regina Caeli during the Easter Season.

Bells are not used in the liturgy between the singing of the Gloria on Holy Thursday and the singing of the Gloria at the Easter Vigil Mass.

Missal stand

A *missal stand* is, quite simply, a stand to hold the missal. It's not always used in Mass in the Ordinary Rite but is a requirement in the Extraordinary form of the Roman Rite. The Roman Missal is placed on the stand so the celebrant of the liturgy can better see it. In the past, the stand has taken the form of a pillow made from beautiful brocades, but it also can be composed of wood, brass, or silver.

Lavabo bowl

The *lavabo bowl* takes its name from the section of the liturgy in which the celebrant washes his hands before the consecration at the offertory. *Lavabo* is a Latin word denoting *washing*. It is also used in the Divine Liturgy of the Eastern Rite after the vesting of the priest before he approaches the altar. In addition to the ordinary use at the Mass, the lavabo bowl is used by the bishop after administering the Sacrament of Confirmation or Holy Orders when using chrism oil. A type of lavabo bowl is used on Holy Thursday when the celebrant in honor of our Divine Lord's initiation at the Last Supper washes the feet of 12 men from the parish who represent the 12 apostles.

The lavabo bowl developed out of a device usually found in the sacristy (the room where sacred items are kept) also known as the lavabo. Before vesting, the celebrant customarily washes his hands and prays a special prayer. The washing of the hands at the offertory is known as the *lavabo proper*.

Cruets

Cruets are small vessels that contain wine and water required for Mass. They may come in all types of materials, such as crystal, silver, blown glass, and other metals. The styles range from the most simple glass to the most ornate Baroque with filigree. In normal parish situations, cruets are typically glass or crystal so they can be easily stored in a refrigerator. The custom of using a large flagon (giant cruet) to consecrate wine and then dispersing it in a chalice is no longer allowed, so either chalices are already filled with wine or it is done at the altar. The water cruet is then used to put a drop of water into each chalice. (The water symbolizes the sharing of divinity the human race enjoys because Christ has a full human nature and a full divine nature in his one divine personhood. As true God and true Man, Christ unites humanity and divinity and thus the one drop of water represents humanity uniting with divinity.) The water cruet is used again at the end of Mass to purify the chalices.

Special cruets without handles are also used in storing the sacred oils blessed at the Chrism Mass. They are often placed in an *ambry,* a cabinet that is placed in a wall near the sanctuary. Newer ambries often have glass fronts and are lit within so the oils are exposed to the congregation.

Crosier

A staff used by bishops and cardinals is called a *crosier.* It is the symbol of the pastoral office of the bishop and is used when the bishop is vested for Mass or celebration of other sacraments, such as Confirmation outside of Mass. The pope does not use a crosier, because his jurisdiction is universal.

During the liturgy, the crosier is held during procession and recession, when listening to the Gospel, during a homily, when accepting vows, during professions of faith, and when blessing someone. The celebrant carries the crosier in his right hand with the crook facing open. It is styled in many different ways from ornate and gothic to contemporary or wooden, and may have the coat of arms of the bishop painted in the crook. Along with the pectoral cross and ring, the crosier designates the office of bishop.

Processional cross

The *processional cross* is generally a crucifix carried in processions by a server known as the *crucifer.* In the order of procession at a Solemn Mass, the crucifer comes between the thurifer and the acolytes holding lit processional candles. In the Ordinary Rite of the Roman Mass, the candles and processional cross often remain in the sanctuary and even serve as the candle for Mass and the cross for the people to reflect upon.

Crosses can be made from a wide variety of materials, from wood to brass, and be gilded in silver or gold. Some have painted representations of the crucifix on them, such as the famous crucifix of San Damiano. Others are made like traditional crucifixes. High Liturgy Protestant churches often incorporate such crosses in their processions along with a crucifix-type processional cross.

Latin Rite altar linens

The following linens are used on the altar during the Latin Mass.

- ✔ The **pall** is a stiff square of material that can be made in the liturgical colors of the season: white, red, green, and purple. It's optional in the Ordinary Rite and yet has the practical function of keeping foreign material or insects from flying into the Precious Blood. Some palls are ornately embroidered or have hand-painted images of the Lord, the Blessed Virgin, saints, or other appropriate Christian symbols. They are placed on top of the chalice and underneath the chalice veil and burse.

- ✔ A **purificator** is a piece of absorbent fabric draped from the chalice to wipe the cup after someone receives the Precious Blood and used for cleaning the chalice after Communion. The cloth is rectangular, folded twice the long way and, creased in the middle into the shape of an *M* so that it drapes nicely over the chalice. Second, over the purificator and chalice is the paten with celebrant host, and third, the pall over the paten.

- ✔ The **chalice veil** usually is made of the same material and color of the vestments worn for Mass and normally has an embroidered cross on the front. It is draped over the chalice after the purificator has been draped over the cup, followed by the paten with unconsecrated host and then with a pall placed on top of all that.

- ✔ The **burse,** a sort of envelope that houses the corporal, is placed on top of the chalice veil. The burse is made of the same material as the pall.

- ✔ The **corporal** is a white, square piece of linen that is folded twice horizontally and twice vertically with an embroidered cross in the middle. It's always made of linen because this is the material believed to be used in the burial of Christ. In the Extraordinary form of the Mass, the host of the priest is taken off the paten and placed directly on the corporal along with the chalice and ciboria. In the Ordinary form of the Mass the host rests on the paten and the chalice and ciboria are next to it. In Masses in which several vessels are used at the consecration, more than one corporal is used. The corporal never remains on the altar after Communion; rather it's placed in the burse and later stored in the sacristy, or if dirty, washed in the sacrarium and then laundered with the other liturgical linens.

Eastern Rite Vessels, Artifacts, and Linens

The following items are used in the Byzantine Rite exclusively.

- ✔ In the center of Byzantine churches is the **tetrapod,** a table on which an icon of the Christ, Blessed Virgin, or saint being celebrated is placed. It may have candles and be richly adorned with a beautiful cloth. When worshippers come into the church, they go to the tetrapod and make the sign of the cross three times and then kiss the icon.

- ✔ The **iconostasis** (icon screen) is located between the nave and the sanctuary, because in Eastern Catholic thought, the sanctuary represents the holy place, heaven, and the nave represents the created world. It is a symbol of joining the created with the Creator. The *Royal Doors* located on the iconostasis are opened and closed during the Divine Liturgy to represent the relationship of God with his people. The *Deacon door* is located on the side and suggests the constant communication of God with his people.

- ✔ The **aspersorium,** or holy water bucket, is the vessel used to contain water that will be blessed for the Asperges rite of the Mass. During this rite, which takes the place of the Penitential Rite in the Ordinary form of the Mass, the people are blessed with holy water to remind them of their Baptism. The holy water bucket is also used at other times, such as at the grave for burial or for the blessing of sacramental or secular items. In the Extraordinary form of the Mass, the Asperges rite takes place before Mass commences. The **aspergillum** is the metal cylindrical device with small holes in the end that the priest uses to dip into the holy water in the aspersorium and sprinkle the people.

- ✔ The **diskos** is much like the paten in the Roman Rite in that it contains the sacramental bread that will become the Body of Christ. Unlike the paten, however, the diskos sits on a pedestal, and after the Communion it can only be touched by an ordained clergyman.

- ✔ The **zeon cup** contains boiling water used in the Divine Liturgy and represents the water that flowed from Christ's side on the cross on Good Friday.

- ✔ The **exapteriga** is a fan made with a representation of a six-winged seraphim, the highest rank of angels, mounted on a pole for hand carrying.

✔ The altar is covered with an arrangement of altar linens. A white linen called the **katasarkion** is placed first. An embroidered cloth called the **endyton** is placed on top of that. Finally, the **eileton** (silk cloth) is placed on top of those two. Inside the eileton is the **antimension,** which is similar to the Roman corporal and altar stone combined. Whereas in the Latin Rite relics of the martyrs are embedded in stone and inserted inside the altar on top of which Mass is celebrated, in the Eastern Rite, relics are sewed inside the antimension cloth.

✔ **Dikirion** and **trikirion** are liturgical candlesticks used by a bishop when he celebrates the Divine Liturgy. The former has two candles to symbolize the two natures of Christ (human and divine) while the latter has three candles representing the three Persons of the Divine and Holy Trinity (God the Father, God the Son, and God the Holy Spirit).

✔ An **analogion** is a lectern where the Book of Gospels or an icon is placed for public veneration.

✔ The **asterisk** is a cross-shaped object which is placed on the *diskos* during the *Proskomedia* (Office of Oblation performed by priest before Divine Liturgy).

✔ **Prosphora** is leavened bread used in the Divine Liturgy. One part of it, called the *amnon,* is cut during the proskomedia to be consecrated during the Divine Liturgy. The rest is cut up for the *antidoron* (blessed but not consecrated bread) given after the Divine Liturgy.

Chapter 14

Architecture, Art, and Music

• •

In This Chapter

▶ Looking at churches, cathedrals, and other buildings of worship

▶ Seeing how architectural styles have evolved

▶ Performing music in services

▶ Displaying art to enhance worship

• •

*M*any aspects of the Catholic Church have remained the same over its 21-century history, but much has changed, as well. The type and architecture of church buildings have been adapted through the years to accommodate changes in liturgy or to avoid expensive construction, and the art and music have changed according to the type of worship experience used in the Church at different times.

Some building styles, such as the ostentatious Baroque style, are just too expensive to try to reproduce nowadays. Other styles, such as neoclassical and neo-Gothic, have been reinvented as new, *(neo)* versions of their early ancestors to better accommodate the changes in worship, because the architecture of churches is more than just a matter of style or taste. In the Catholic Church, worship environment sets an important tone for the worship itself, and therefore the building styles must be right. Here's what Pope Benedict XVI had to say about the Gothic style:

> A merit of the Gothic cathedrals was the fact that, in their construction and decoration, the Christian and civil community participated in a different but coordinated way; the poor and the powerful, the illiterate and the learned participated, because in this common house all believers were instructed in the faith. Gothic sculpture made of cathedrals a "Bible of stone," representing the episodes of the Gospel and illustrating the contents of the Liturgical Year, from Christmas to the Lord's glorification.

This chapter helps you understand how churches and other buildings of worship are designed and laid out. We also discuss how architectural styles, art, and music play a part in the buildings and in the Catholic Church itself.

Meeting in Sacred Spaces: Church Buildings

We live and work in the world around us, but at the same time we need a quiet, reserved space for worship. That's not to say the world outside worship is bad or sinful; in fact, Genesis tells us that that the world is good. But as people who are made up of both the material and the spiritual, we need worldly or secular space and a sacred space.

The church building is so important because it's the sacred space dedicated to the worship of God. It is where his written word (the Bible or Sacred Scripture) is read aloud, where hymns are sung, and where ritual worship of God is given with reverence and devotion.

Regardless of its shape, style, or size, the following fundamental elements are needed in each Catholic church:

- **Sanctuary:** Area in front of church where the altar and Tabernacle reside and where the clergy perform their liturgical ministry

- **Nave:** Main body of church where congregation stands up or sits on pews (benches to sit on with built in kneelers)

- **Narthex:** Outer vestibule of church where the casket is brought for funerals and where people get their weekly bulletin as they leave Mass

- **Baptistery:** Can be a separate room or an area in church reserved for the celebration of Baptism

- **Sacristy:** Room off of sacristy where clergy vest and where the items needed for Mass are kept (wine, hosts, candles, linens, etc)

- **Confessional:** Booth or room where faithful go to confess their sins to a priest and receive absolution

- **Choir:** Area in balcony at rear of church near organ or some other location where members of the choir can sing during the Mass and also where they can rehearse beforehand

As the Church as a body was developing, so was the church as a building. Some elements have been expanded, moved, or even abolished through the years. The location of the choir changed several times throughout the history of the Church; at one time the choir was actually located between the sanctuary and the rest of the congregation. Here are some other examples of design changes through the centuries:

✔ Side aisles have come and gone through the years. In some early churches the aisles had heavy columns that would obstruct the view for many parishioners, which led to a more open nave in churches built in the 20th century.

✔ Some older churches were built with several side chapels with altars for private Mass celebrations. It wasn't uncommon for more than one priest to be celebrating Mass at the same time at different altars in the church. Many of the older churches still have these side altars, but they are use mostly as shrines for saints.

✔ In the early church, many large churches such as cathedrals and basilicas located the baptistery in a separate building. By the mid-20th century, parish churches had separate areas within the building set aside for Baptisms. Before the Second Vatican Council in the 1960s, Baptisms were for the baby and godparents only, so they didn't need much room. After the Council, however, Baptisms could be celebrated at Mass and more people attended the actual sacrament, and holding Baptisms in the small area became increasingly difficult. The baptismal font was relocated to different areas within the church.

The sections that follow describe the form and function of many different types of church buildings.

Parish churches

The *parish church* is the most common and most frequent church building in the *diocese,* the territorial division headed by a bishop appointed by the pope. A diocese contains a cathedral (mother church) and several parishes. A parish church is headed by a priest who is appointed by the bishop and serves as the bishop's representative. The parish church exists on the local level in communities.

The church is the religious center of the parish; it is where the sacraments are celebrated in the lives of ordinary parishioners on a daily basis. In addition to a church building, a parish may have included a rectory, or priest's residence, as well as the offices of the parish, a parochial school to educate the parish children, and a convent to house the religious teachers who teach in the school. However, in the 21st century, many parishes do not have either convents of sisters or parish schools.

Chapels, shrines, and oratories

Chapels, shrines, and oratories are special places of worship and adoration that may be a part of a parish but also can exist independently from a parish. For example, a parochial convent for sisters may have a chapel located within where the sisters pray the Liturgy of the Hours and private devotions. It is not a public place of worship but rather a private place designed for the sisters. A chapel can also be independent and more of a public place for worship. For example, most Catholic hospitals, colleges, and universities have chapels in which Mass is celebrated. Usually these chapels are for people connected to the institutions, but they can be open the general public.

Chapels can also subsist within a larger church structure. For example, in St. Peter's Basilica in Rome, a special chapel exists for the Reservation of the Blessed Sacrament. In this chapel the faithful can come and worship the Lord in the Holy Eucharist in a quiet area of the basilica without the distractions of visitors and tourists who wander around. Many large cathedrals or historical churches have these types of chapels. In addition, a chapel can exist for the housing of relics of a particular saint or martyr. They often become pilgrim destinations in which Catholics visit with the intention of intercession of the saint.

Oratories are similar to chapels. They're designated by ecclesiastical authority for Mass and devotions and are for public, semi-public or private use.

A *shrine* is a designated devotional place, usually for reasons of historical event or specific association. For example, the apparitions of Our Lady in Lourdes, France; Fatima, Portugal; and Guadalupe, Mexico are designated shrines to which the faithful make pilgrimages. Shrines that are dedicated to apparitions, like that of the Blessed Virgin Mary, are often duplicated around the world. For instance, the oldest Shrine of Our Lady of Lourdes, France, was duplicated in Emmitsburg, Maryland, in 1858.

A shrine can also be a burial place of a saint or where a saint lived or died, or it can be dedicated to a particular saint even if the location has no historical importance. For example, the Shrine of St. Anne in Quebec, Canada, was built out of pure devotion to that particular saint.

Cathedrals

A cathedral is the chief church of a diocese, home to the bishop's throne, the *cathedra* (hence the name *cathedral*). Despite their significance within the diocese, cathedrals also serve as parish churches in which parish families worship.

Some cathedrals have or had monasteries attached to them, particularly in Europe. In England, cathedrals that were part of monasteries are called *minster* churches; in Germany, they're called *munster* churches. Cathedrals and monasteries are not connected in the United States.

Like many parish churches, cathedrals come in various sizes and styles but all have the same basic elements inside: choir, sanctuary, and nave. The bishop's throne is located in the sanctuary along with the altar and pulpit, but is a fixed item that can't be moved.

Basilicas

A *basilica* is another distinctive church within a diocese. The canonical status of basilicas has two major divisions: major and minor. Only four basilicas are major, and they all stand within a few miles of each other.

St. Peter's Basilica

The most significant and widely known basilica is the *Basilica of St. Peter* in Vatican City State. The cathedral is the mother church of the diocese, but St. Peter's Basilica is the mother church of the Universal Church. This basilica is on the site of the first-century Christian cemetery where it is believed that St. Peter, the first Bishop of Rome and the first pope, was martyred and buried. This area is known as Vatican Hill, and St. Peter's Basilica is often simply called the Vatican.

The first basilica built over the tomb of St. Peter was built by Emperor Constantine in the traditional Roman basilica style. A palace to serve as the pope's quarters was built near the church. A wall was later built around this area to block barbarian pillagers and invaders. A long wall that houses a causeway to the Tiber River and terminates in a structure known as Castle of St. Angelo served as an escape route for the pope when the area fell under attack.

Basilica of St. John Lateran

St. John Lateran, the oldest of the four major basilicas, is considered the Cathedral of the Archdiocese of Rome. The pope is the Bishop of Rome, and St. John Lateran is where his cathedra (throne) is located. It has been considered the headquarters of the Roman Catholic Church for centuries, and the papal palace and private chapel were originally part of its compounds.

The palace has since been demolished, but the chapel survives and exists across the street from the basilica. The holy stairs that led to the Praetorium (palace of the Roman governor) of Pontius Pilate in Jerusalem are housed in the chapel, giving the chapel its name, *Scala Sancta.*

The land where the basilica stands originally belonged to the Lateran family. Constantine became the owner of this property and donated it to the church in AD 313. The basilica was dedicated to its patrons, St. John the Baptist and St. John the Evangelist, in the tenth century and was formally named the Basilica of St. John the Baptist and St. John the Evangelist in the Lateran.

Basilica of St. Mary Major

St. Mary Major, the third major basilica, is believed to be the first dedicated to the Virgin Mary after the Ecumenical Council of Ephesus, which defined Mary as the Mother of God. It is built on Esquiline Hill, one of the Seven Hills of Rome. Construction of the basilica began under the reign of Pope Liberius in the fourth century.

According to legend, a wealthy Roman family wanted to honor the Blessed Virgin and prayed to her for help in accomplishing this dream. The city of Rome is typically very hot in the summer, so when it snowed on Esquiline Hill on August 5, the family took that as the sign they needed and built the basilica there. The full title of the basilica is St. Mary Major of the Snow.

One of the most striking relics in the basilica, the holy relic of the crib of Our Lord, resides beneath the baldachin of the main altar. The church also bears a ceiling made with the first gold brought back from the New World and donated to the pope by the king and queen of Spain.

Basilica of St. Paul, Outside the Walls

The fourth and final major basilica is *St. Paul, Outside the Walls,* so named because it was built outside the ancient Roman city walls. The basilica was founded by Constantine in the fourth century and, because it did not have the benefit of city walls to protect it, was pillaged in the ninth century. After the pillaging the pope fortified the basilica with walled courtyards.

Some of the most magnificent mosaics in the world are located inside the apse of the sanctuary, and in one of the side chapels is a miraculous crucifix, in which our Lord came to life in a vision from the cross to St. Bridget. Along the top of the colonnades are medallions of all the popes. Local legend has it that when the last medallion is painted, it will be the end of the world.

Minor basilicas

The next group of basilicas is the canonical minor basilica, those that are smaller and far more numerous. The pope holds the sole authority of naming a church a minor basilica, and certain items must be present in a qualifying church:

- ✔ A papal umbrella that acts as a baldachin, usually decorated with the keys of St. Peter

- ✔ A bell, which is carried in procession on state occasions

- ✔ The cappa magna (exceptionally long and elaborate cape of silk), worn by the canon (priests attached to a cathedral or basilica for honorary purposes and duties) of the basilica when assisting at the Liturgy of the Hours

Over 1,500 minor basilicas exist in the world. In Baltimore, Maryland, the first cathedral built in the United States was designated by Pope John Paul II as the Basilica and National Shrine of the Blessed Virgin Mary.

Four minor basilicas in the world are considered *pontifical minor basilicas,* the highest rank:

- ✔ The Pontifical Basilica of Our Lady of the Rosary, in Pompeii, Italy

- ✔ The Pontifical Basilica of St. Nicholas, in Bari, Italy

- ✔ The Pontifical Basilica of St. Anthony, in Padua, Italy

- ✔ The Pontifical Basilica of the Holy House, in Loreto, Italy

Second division in the minor basilicas are the *papal basilicas,* including the Papal Basilica of St. Francis, Assisi, Italy, and the Papal Basilica of St. Lawrence outside of the Walls, Rome, Italy. The third class is *patriarchal,* denoting that it's attached to an archbishop who has the title of patriarch. The final class is *general,* and countless cathedrals, shrines, and oratories throughout the world have this distinction.

Architectural Styles

Just as buildings changed to meet liturgical needs, so did the styles of architecture. The Church is over 21 centuries old, and much development and variation in design and styles of the buildings have taken place. Sometimes these changing styles worked well with the liturgy, and sometimes they didn't.

Whatever the style may be, churches are places where the faithful meet God: in the Mass, the Sacraments, prayer life, and devotions of the liturgical calendar. The buildings need to be dignified and edifying places that promote worship and prayer instead of inhibiting it. When a design is good it becomes a timeless classic, and with a few modifications it can easily be used in any century.

Roman basilica

One of the earliest styles of churches is based on the *Roman basilica,* which was a public building often found in the forum in Roman cities. Many people turned to Christianity after the Edict of Milan made it became a "respectable" religion, and many wealthy patrons (including Emperor Constantine) donated property and buildings to the Church. These early buildings were oblong and quite large.

Early Roman basilicas contained many features still used today:

- **Sanctuary:** Area in the front of the church where the altar and tabernacle reside and where the clergy perform their liturgical duties

- **Ambo:** The pulpit for the proclamation of the word

- **Apse:** The semicircular roof located in the sanctuary where the altar, bishop's throne, and seats of the clergy are located

- **Side apse:** Where the side altars are located

- **Nave:** The body of the church extending from the sanctuary to the main entrance

- **Aisles:** Interior divisions of the church running parallel with the nave and separated by rows of pillars

- **Choir:** The area for the singers usually located in the front of the nave

- **Court:** The enclosed space wholly or partly surrounded by walls of a building

- **Cloisters:** Covered arcades along the walls of the church or its courts designed for meditation by the monks or nuns

- **Narthex:** The long narrow portico or porch that is in the front of the church

Byzantine

The Roman Empire was not just in Rome, but also in the East, centered in Constantinople (now Istanbul, Turkey). The style of architecture used in that part of the world was *Byzantine.* Although the style originated in the East, it's reflected in church structures that were still under the Byzantine Empire in the West, such as in Venice, Ravenna, and parts of Sicily in Italy. The style is a mixture of classical Greek and Roman coupled with a distinctive Eastern or Middle Eastern Oriental features.

The Byzantine churches differed from Roman basilicas in their vaulted ceilings, domes, and half domes richly adorned in mosaics depicting Christian art. Roman Basilicas also had art, but it was typically *frescoes,* paintings in wet plaster. Some churches in the West mixed styles and had elements of Byzantium and Roman architecture.

Romanesque

Changes and adaptations made within the Byzantine churches gradually developed in the West into the *Romanesque* style of architecture.

This style came in vogue in the early 10th century and lasted until the 12th century when it was supplanted by the Gothic style. Some of the finest examples of Romanesque style can be founded in Italy, France, England, and Spain. It maintained rounded Roman arches, massive, thick walls, and heavy decorations.

Romanesque ornamentation is not subtle, and includes geometric patterns and grotesques of animals or humans. It also incorporated *blind arcading,* brick or stone walls outlined with arches. The doors of Romanesque churches were heavily decorated and emphasized the transition from the secular world on the outside to the spiritual world within.

The footprint of the medieval, Romanesque cathedral is cruciform — that is, it looks like a cross from above. Usually, a Romanesque church has a central nave and two side apses on either side of it. The central nave is separated by a series of columns, and the roof of the aisle and the outer walls help support the upper walls of the vault of the nave, which have an area of windows known as the clerestory. The narthex is the entrance of the church, and the choir is usually located near the sanctuary, sometimes at the transept (the short horizontal bar of the cruciform).

Gothic

By the beginning of the 13th century, the *Gothic* style replaced Romanesque. Its chief difference was the development of the pointed arch that allowed a vast range of new architectural possibilities.

Gothic buildings are taller and have larger windows than preceding structures. French and English Gothic are two great examples of the architectural style, although variations are found in Spain, Portugal, and Italy.

- ✔ French Gothic is typified by great west doors with three pointed rows surrounding each door and topped off by a magnificent rose window. It is normally flanked by two soaring towers with spires. The rib vaults inside are revealed on the outside by flying buttresses.

- ✔ English style is more perpendicular and horizontal than vertical. The ceilings are usually ribbed quite ornately with intersecting arches. The tower is usually located in the center of the transept, but sometimes two towers were built at the west end. On smaller churches, a single tower may be used through which people enter the church. Where two towers are used, the central window is not a circular rose but a very large arched window.

Elaborate stone carvings on Gothic churches create a sense of lightness and delicateness as opposed to the massive feeling of the Romanesque church. Columns and capitals (the structural elements at the tops of columns) often have foliage predominantly carved into them, usually in clusters. Capitals are small, emphasizing the vertical aspect of the Gothic style.

The pointed arch is the quintessential element of Gothic architecture. They're visually lighter, though structurally stronger because the blocks at the top of the arch press inward rather than downward. Fancy lattice and decorative carvings are incorporated into the arches. Moldings of windows and doors also employed the high and pointed arch.

Gothic door sashes and arches above them use the pointed arches, richly decorated by fine moldings and reliefs. The doors themselves may even be elaborately carved. The windows of the Gothic church — plentiful and large, containing stained-glass depictions of Christ, Mary, the saints, and scenes from the Bible — are another hallmark of the style.

The plan of the Gothic church followed the Latin cross, like the earlier Romanesque style. The nave was intersected by the transept to form the cross. Beyond the transept lies the choir and sanctuary. The nave is taller than the side aisle, allowing a series of windows on the top known as the clerestory windows. Directly behind the main altar of the sanctuary, a special chapel was dedicated to the Blessed Virgin Mary.

Renaissance

By the end of the 15th century a new mode came into fashion, the *Renaissance*. This style affected not only architecture but also art, food, poetry, politics, economics, and the sciences. One of the chief characteristics of the Renaissance was a rediscovery of the classics of ancient Greece and Rome.

Classically inspired Renaissance churches incorporate strong horizontal lines, pointed front pediments, flat ceilings, and symmetrically positioned windows. Columns of arcades with their simple curve and Corinthian columns add to the balance of the building. Nothing is out of proportion or overly ostentatious, but rather a unique architectural harmony exists.

The designs were based on designs of buildings from ancient Rome and evoked the glory of the Empire. However, innovations and adaptations were made in this period to the basic classical style. For instance, Renaissance columns are based on a classical style but decorated with roses, leaves, and other naturalistic concepts.

The construction of domes, which had fallen out of style, experienced a rebirth in the Renaissance churches. St. Peter's Basilica, in Vatican City, and the Duomo in Florence are among the two most famous examples. Windows in this period took their basic form from ancient Rome and were usually rectangular with pediments, cornices, classical columns, and pilasters.

The inside plan of a Renaissance church also followed ancient Roman architecture, with long naves columned on the side to allow aisles, and a sanctuary at the top with a rounded apse. A dome was at the transept, instead of an imposing tower as in English Gothic style. The ceiling of the Sistine Chapel at St. Peter's Basilica is an example of the frescoes that adorned these churches. Other ceilings were made of wood and gilded in gold, with fruit or leaves as decoration.

One of the most important architects of this period whose influence has far reaching effects is Andrea Palladio, founder of the Palladian motif, which was the inspiration for Georgian style in England and the Colonial style in America. Christopher Wren's St. Paul's Cathedral of London, England, is a perfect example of Palladian Renaissance architecture in England.

Baroque

By the 17th century the Renaissance style was being replaced or adapted into the more flamboyant *Baroque*. This style was characterized by grand elaboration of detail and space. Architects took the classical motifs and kicked it up a notch in order to create a sense of drama. In the Church's history, this was the Counter-Reformation Period. Protestant revolt in Northern Europe resulted in a type of iconoclasm or stripping of the churches of any ornamentation. Counter-Reformation preached reform but also the glories of Catholicism, and therefore the churches became even more adorned and splendid.

Some of the chief characteristics of this period included monumental pilasters, curved pediments, and curved floor plans. With the use of rounded shapes, Baroque churches exploited the form with intersecting ovals and circles. The Church of St. Agnes in the Piazza Navona, Rome, is a chief example.

The roofs of Baroque churches carried a style similar to the Renaissance but with more ornamentation. Windows and doors received the decoration of rounded or pointed pediments and sculpture. The famous Church of the Gesu, Rome, is a style that has been copied in many Baroque churches.

The Baroque fashion spread throughout Europe, even in the Protestant countries in the north. However, the style in these areas was limited to palaces and other public places. In Catholic southern and central Europe, particularly Italy, Bavaria, and Austria, many churches being built in this era were constructed in the Baroque design. The Kingdom of the Two Sicilies centered in Naples developed its own distinctive Baroque style.

Some of the greatest architects of the period are Bernini, who designed the colonnade at St. Peter Square, Vatican City, and Borromini, who designed the quintessential oval Baroque Church, San Carlo alle Quatro Fontana, Rome. Many examples of Baroque architecture can be found in the countries that were part of the Spanish Empire in the New World. The Cathedral in Mexico City is the prime example.

Neoclassical

The 18th and 19th centuries gave rise to many revivals. One of the most splendid examples was *neoclassical* architecture, which started as a reaction to the heavily ornate Baroque style. Its style is very similar to Renaissance and classical Greek and Roman.

Andrea Palladio and the Palladian manner heavily influenced this period, often referred to as *romantic classicism*. The trend displayed in architecture in this time was the desire to return to the purity of clean lines of Ancient Grecian buildings, which is why neoclassical architecture is also often called *Greek revival*.

In the United States, many white clapboard churches were built in the Greek revival style. It gave rise to the Federalist style in the United States. Many of our national buildings, such as the Capitol in Washington, D.C., are built in the neoclassical style and architectural motif. Benjamin Latrobe, who designed the United States' Capitol, also designed the United States' first Catholic cathedral, the Basilica of the Blessed Virgin Mary in Baltimore, Maryland, in this neoclassical style.

19th- and 20th-century revivals

In addition to the revival of neoclassicism, both Romanesque and Gothic styles had a resurgence in the 19th century. The Romanesque revival began in the 1830s and lasted into the 20th century, and it was used for secular buildings, from universities to warehouses in the city, as well as for churches. With the use of steel, windows became larger, and so many of the famous department stores of the late 19th century and early 20th centuries were built in the Romanesque style, but with windows. In church architecture, the Shrine Basilica of St. Anne in Quebec is a perfect example of Romanesque revival.

Gothic revival, also referred to as Victorian Gothic or neo-Gothic, became very prevalent in church architecture of the 19th and early 20th centuries. The major difference between the original style and the revival was construction. The latter centuries employed steel for building frames, which made flying buttresses obsolete, and therefore neo-Gothic churches were constructed without them. In the United States, Gothic revival was a favorite style among many immigrants, who wanted to establish churches like the ones in their native lands.

Modern

The 20th century saw the rise to modern art and architecture. Art deco, which took its design from machines, came into vogue in the 1920s. The Chrysler building with its automobile ornamentation of the era is a prime example in secular buildings. However, some suburban Catholic churches also incorporated art deco with traditional architecture and so you have a variation of the design. The Cathedral of Mary Our Queen in Baltimore, Maryland, was built in the 1950s, and its style can be described as art deco meets Gothic revival.

Architecture in the second half of the 20th century was dominated by modernism, with its chief characteristic being a minimalist approach to art and design. Some important monastic chapels, such as Delbarton in Morristown, New Jersey, and St. John Abbey in Collegeville, Minnesota, have incorporated modern design with the simplicity of life. The Cathedral of Archdiocese of Los Angeles is also an example of modernism.

Postmodern

The late 20th and early 21st centuries comprise the period known as postmodernism. In this period many of the designs take inspiration from the styles of the past but reconfigure them for the present. One of the most famous examples of postmodern ecclesiastical architecture, the new chapel at Ave Maria University, Florida, combines modern, art deco, and neo-Gothic.

Many new churches are also being built in the traditional styles of Romanesque, Gothic, Renaissance, and neoclassical. Architects continue to reinvent creatively without being reduced to simply copying existing buildings. One of the most beautiful examples of postmodern classical style is the chapel at St. Thomas Aquinas College in California.

Music in Worship

Music is essential in liturgical art and worship. Christian music can be divided into Gregorian (plain chant), polyphonic (multiple voice levels), English chant (Anglicanism), Baroque concerto Masses, folk music, and hymnal music. In the Church, the king of instruments for over five 500 years has been the pipe organ. However, and especially in Baroque Masses, orchestral ensembles (strings, winds, and brass) have also been employed. Music, like art and architecture, should always complement the Liturgy and not detract from it.

Looking at the early use of music

Christian music has its roots in Judaism. Before it was destroyed in the first century, the Temple of Jerusalem was the center of Jewish worship. Along with Temple ceremonies, music, choir, and instruments accompanied the worship. After the destruction of the Temple, the tradition of music in the synagogues continued. Today, Jewish synagogue cantors continue to bring the Psalms of King David and other literary poems and prayers to life through chant.

Church music is one of the most revered and major components of the Church's heritage. The singing of hymns is in fact a prayer of the Church that cannot be separated from the liturgical celebration. In past centuries, the Church has taught that singing, especially at Mass and the Liturgy of the Hours, should be performed to the best of the choir or congregation's ability. When performed or prayed in this fashioned it expresses a deep meaning of faith that is beautiful and expresses the singers' thoughts and feelings being raised to God.

Christianity was banned for most of the first four centuries AD. Overt displays of music in the "small house" churches and chapels was likely very limited. Even in times of relative peace, music was still restrained, but it did exist. In Ephesians 5:19, St. Paul reminds the early Christians about songs of praise with these words: " . . . addressing one another in psalms and hymns and spiritual songs, singing and making melody to the Lord with all your heart."

Chanting: Pope Gregory's legacy

A significant development in liturgical music can be attributed to Pope Gregory the Great, who was a great liturgical reformer who reigned from 590 to 604. This pope sat on the Throne of St. Peter many centuries after the Edict of Milan, which allowed Christians to worship in public.

After the Edict, larger churches had to be built in the fourth century to accommodate the many converts to Catholicism. The liturgies became more elaborate right along with the grander buildings, and more music was used. In the sixth and seventh centuries, more hymns were written to reflect theological truths of Christ, Mary, and the Church.

By this time, the threat of martyrdom was decreasing, and many people wanted to witness to the Faith in a radical way. This desire lead to the birth of monastic life, which requires many hours to be spent in communal prayer, not only the Holy Sacrifice of the Mass, but also recitation of the Liturgy of the Hours.

These services established a need for music, and Pope Gregory the Great, who started his religious career as a monk, championed a new style of singing known as *Gregorian chant,* which was a perfect fit.

Gregorian chant is a form of plainchant or monophonic chant that almost anyone can learn and do. It has simple melodies and rhythm that are easily learned and when done in choir have a soothing and comforting melody.

In addition, parts of the Mass are still sung in Gregorian chant They include Kyrie (Lord have mercy), Gloria (Glory to God in the Highest), Credo (Creed), Sanctus and Sanctus (Holy, Holy), and the Agnus Dei (Lamb of God).

Reforming music in the Counter-Reformation

Many political and religious changes occurred at the end of the 15th century, most notably the deep schism in the church that gave rise to the Protestant Revolt. Also at this time the Church convened the Council of Trent to address some of the abuses in the Church, reiterate Catholic doctrine, and reform the liturgy and Sacraments. This meeting gave rise to the Counter-Reformation period in which many new religious communities were established to disseminate Catholic information.

According to the liturgical reforms, sacred music could not resemble secular music and it could not obscure liturgical texts. But within these restrictions, many new innovations were being added, including *polyphonic chant.* Giovanni Pierluigi da Palestrina was one of the greatest composers of this style of chant.

Polyphony is a more elaborate and sophisticated evolution of plain chant (alias Gregorian chant). Polyphonic chant employs two or more voices whereas plain chant uses only one. Besides the monks and nuns who would chant their Office (Breviary or Liturgy of the Hours), many churches and cathedrals formed choirs to chant parts of the Mass, especially for feasts and holy days.

The Church of England was being established at this time, and so was a variation of polyphonic chant known simply as *Anglican chant.* Today if you attend Evensong, or the Eucharistic Liturgy, the choir traditionally sings in this chant mode. Although it resembles its Roman Catholic counterpart, it is a distinctive style. With the Anglo form of the Roman Rite, this chant is used in liturgies.

As Counter-Reformation church architecture changed in the 17th and 18th century, so did liturgical music, giving rise to the Baroque Masses. Hayden, Scarlatti, Vivaldi, Bach, and Mozart all wrote magnificent Mass settings that at first seem to be more for concerts than a Mass. The Baroque Masses included orchestras and usually were performed for special occasions, such as Christmas, Easter, or for special events such as Coronation Mass.

Using music in the modern Church

By the 20th century excessiveness of the Baroque Masses prompted reform. Pope Pius X wrote in his directive of 1903 that Church music should be of the highest excellence, preserve purity of form, exclude any profane influence, and because the Church is universal, possess collective qualities. By the Second Vatican Council of the 1960s, many reforms were established.

Hymns sung in church originated from the Psalms and developed into the music we know today. Many were composed to convey a theological teaching of Christ or the Virgin Mary. Since the time of the Protestant Reformation, hymns have been translated and sung in the local language (the vernacular). In the early 20th century, hymns in the vernacular were sung at Low Masses of the Extraordinary Rite, but today, Latin or the vernacular are common in hymns in the Ordinary Rite. The proper places for hymns are the procession, offertory, Communion, and recession.

When the Second Vatican Council (1962–1965) decided to reform the liturgy, it took place during the time of cultural revolution when popular music took a dramatic turn toward innovative, unconventional, nontraditional, and sometimes bizarre lyrics and melodies. Simultaneously, fold songs (by artists such as Peter, Paul, and Mary) became popular, and tunes like "Kumbaya" as well as music by Simon and Garfunkel and the Beatles crept into Catholic liturgies.

Despite changes in Church music in the 20th century, Gregorian and polyphonic chant are still preferable options and can easily be adapted to the Ordinary form of the Roman Rite.

Art in Churches

Church art is considered the most uplifting effort of humanity. It aims at communicating the divine beauty and directing the faithful to praise and thank God.

Pagans like the ancient Greeks and Romans worshiped statues, images, and amulets. They made gods out of material things and worshiped these idols, which was repugnant to the Hebrew monotheistic religion (the belief that there is but one God). Ancient Jewish tradition does not employ the use of images, lest they be misused as idols, which is firmly forbidden by the First Commandment: "Thou shall not have not strange gods and thou shall not adore them."

Catholic Christianity, on the other hand, has no problems using religious symbols and even depictions of the Almighty, because the Church firmly believes in the Incarnation, which is to say that God the Son had a human nature and was both human and divine. Therefore worship should also include the material and the divine. The images, statues, paintings, mosaics, icons, frescoes, and so on were never objects of worship (as in paganism) but merely tools to remind believers that God created the physical as well as the spiritual world. Jesus is considered both God and Man, and therefore, representing the Divine in art is merely a way to enhance the faith.

The earliest examples of Christian art can be found in catacombs, where Christians drew or painted Christian symbols. One of the finest and oldest examples of this art can be found in the Catacomb of Priscilla on the Via Salaris, Rome, Italy.

Frescoes

Frescoes date from the second century AD in catacombs. The historic image of Christ, the Good Shepherd, is painted in one of the catacomb chapels' apse. Frescoes are painted on specially applied wet plaster. It is a technique found in many churches, basilicas, and cathedrals from throughout the centuries. In the 15th century, Leonardo da Vinci and Michelangelo both used fresco technique when the former painted *The Last Supper* in Milan and the latter painted the Sistine Chapel in St. Peter's Basilica.

Iconography

Also around the second century, *iconography* was growing in popularity in Rome and in the East. This art form is most commonly associated with the East. Icons are flat paintings of God, saints, angels, or scenes from the Bible. They are painted on wood, and the background is usually in gold leaf. St. Luke the Evangelist is believed to have painted the first image of the Blessed Virgin Mary, and he did so in an icon form.

The eighth and ninth centuries saw a great controversy called *iconoclasm*. It was a heresy that harkened a horribly literal interpretation of the First Commandment (forbidding idolatry or the worship of idols). As a result of the movement, many precious icons were lost and destroyed in Eastern Christian Churches. Eventually the pope condemned iconoclasm as a heresy in AD 731, but it wasn't until years later at the Second Council of Nicea that an official articulation guided the veneration of sacred images such as icons. In AD 842 the empress of the Byzantine Empire restored venerations of icons, which lead to the Feast of Triumph over Iconoclasm.

Paintings

In addition to frescoes and iconography, other paintings play an important role in church art. The Florentine school of painters in the 14th and 15th centuries took the first major step forward from the flat artwork of iconography. Depth and drama were added to the figures in order to convey motion and emotion, though like iconography, the paintings were done on wood instead of canvas or plaster. Giotto of the 14th century and Fra Angelico of the 15th century typify the style of the Florentine school.

Painting took a dramatic turn in the 16th century at the dawn of the Renaissance. Artists such as Raphael, Michelangelo, and Leonardo da Vinci used different kinds of color and shading to create almost lifelike sacred images. Cardinals, popes, and bishops were generous patrons, and their support made it possible for such works of art to adorn many of the churches throughout Europe.

In the Romantic period of the 19th and early 20th centuries, artists often made works that were heavily ornate and at times went overboard. Ornamentation was reproduced and copied by artists into apses, walls, and narthexes of churches. These ostentatious displays really didn't reflect the proper dignity that should be used in church art, and it led to an overreaction called *modernism.* A form of minimalism, modernism treats less as better and divests a church of any art.

This antiseptic and sterile response denied the elegant beauty of art and environment. Catholicism firmly teaches the doctrine of the *Incarnation,* that God became Man in Jesus Christ. The Savior is both human and divine. Hence, the material world and the spiritual world need to be used in worship. Today, in the postmodern era, art is used well once again. Thanks to modern technology, many great pieces of art by the old masters can be reproduced on canvas to be displayed in churches.

Mosaics

Art employs many different mediums to achieve its effectiveness. *Mosaics* are small pieces of glass or marble that when put together, like a puzzle, create a scene. Ancient Greeks and Romans used mosaics to adorn their villas, important buildings, and marketplaces. Christian basilicas built in the fourth century often used frescoes and mosaics to decorate the spaces. Ravenna, Italy, is an important town on the Adriatic coast that has a large collection of mosaics throughout the town.

Byzantine churches are often adorned with golden mosaics. This type of art was used all the way through the late Gothic period in the West. Prime examples are the Cathedral of St. Mark in Venice and St. Paul outside the Wall in Rome. The 20th century had a revival of the use of mosaics. The Cathedral Basilica of St. Louis of Archdiocese of St. Louis; St. John on the Mountain, Jersey City, New Jersey; and the Basilica of the Immaculate Conception, Washington, D.C., have some of the largest collections of mosaics in the world.

Statues

What icons are to the Eastern Catholic Church, statues are to the Roman Catholic Church. Statuary in churches was never a problem in Rome as they were in the Eastern Empire. The Iconoclasm heresy never took root in the West as it did in the East. Additionally, marble quarries, stone masons, and sculptors punctuated the Italian Peninsula for centuries, and they remain viable trades to this day. In fact, statuary from antiquity was the inspiration of the Renaissance artists such as Michelangelo. Who is not inspired by the magnificent David in Florence, Pieta at St. Peter's Basilica, or Moses in Rome?

The practice of carving statues in wood dates from the Romanesque period and reached its pinnacle in the Baroque period. To this day, in northeastern Italy, southwestern Austria, and parts of Bavaria, Germany, are some of the finest wood carvers of statuary on earth. This skill has been handed down from generation to generation. Many postmodern churches that are rediscovering classical architecture are once again adorning them with these beautiful wood carvings.

Stained glass

Stained-glass windows are another means of not only adorning churches but also telling a message. Glass blowing has been around for many centuries, but it really took off in the medieval era. Due to new technology in construction of churches, vast wall space could be converted to windows. Stained-glass windows usually depict God, Jesus, Mary, the saints, scenes from the Bible, or Christian life. The glass is held together by lead ribbing that forms the image. The largest stained-glass window is in the Cathedral of Milan, Italy.

During the Renaissance, Baroque, and neoclassical periods, stained-glass windows fell out of favor. However, with the Romanesque and Gothic revivals, this craft had a resurgence. Many of the beautiful immigrant churches built in the United States in the late 19th and early 20th centuries contain fine examples of stained glass.

Stained glass became the peasant's catechism. As only the nobility and clergy were literate, the poor had to rely on the pictures depicted in the stained glass windows to learn the Christian religion from Bible stories to dogmatic truths.

Part IV

The Part of Tens

The 5th Wave   By Rich Tennant

"I always take St. Genesius and St. Rodney
with me on stage. Genesius is the patron saint
of comedians, and Rodney is the saint of
crushing humiliation in case Genesius
isn't working."

In this part . . .

*L*ike all *For Dummies* books, we end the chapters with
top ten lists. Here, we present ten famous sites of
miracles where Mass is celebrated, and we give you comments on the Mass from ten saints and beatified persons.

Chapter 15

Ten Special Places of Eucharistic Miracles

● ●

In This Chapter

▶ Discovering the Real Presence of Christ through miracles

▶ Exploring sites where miracles involving the host have happened

● ●

*I*n this chapter, we look at ten miraculous locations where the consecrated host (the flat wafer of bread used at Catholic Mass) manifested the normally hidden qualities of the Holy Eucharist. In each of these ten places, weak or absent faith in the Real Presence (the Catholic doctrine that the bread and wine are changed by the priest at Mass to become the Body and Blood of Jesus) was bolstered by a divine miracle affirming the supernatural change.

For centuries, Eucharistic miracles have occurred to dispel doubts about Christ's presence in the Most Blessed Sacrament. These miracles reaffirm the Church's teaching on the Doctrine of Transubstantiation, which states that Christ is really and truly present in the Eucharist — his Body, Blood, Soul, and Divinity. Catholics take literally Jesus' statement when he said, "Take, eat: this is my body. Drink of it, all of you; for this is my blood of the covenant, which is poured out for many for the forgiveness of sins" (Matthew 26:26–28).

These miracles, though approved by the Catholic Church, are truly a matter of private devotion. In other words, Catholics are under no obligation to believe in them or give them merit but rather are free to make up their own minds according to their devotional state.

Throughout the history of the Church, more than 140 documented miracles of the Eucharist have occurred. Through these miracles, the Lord makes his Sacred Presence present in a very tangible way. Of the 140 miracles, we have chosen 10 for this chapter that represent different areas, times, and people of the Universal Church.

Lanciano, Italy, 750

In a little church now known as St. Francis in Lanciano, Italy, a monk doubted Jesus's Real Presence in the Eucharist. During Mass, after the two-fold consecration, the host was changed into live flesh and the wine was changed into live blood, which congealed into five pellets. The flesh and pellets can still be observed today. That miracle of AD 750 was just the beginning; the flesh and blood should have deteriorated, but 1250 years later, they are still intact. Not only was the monk's faith renewed, but for subsequent generations this miracle has been a source of inspiration for many faithful.

Soon after the miracle, many thousands of pilgrims started to flock to Lanciano. Over the centuries its popularity increased, and it was chosen as the site of the First Eucharistic Congress in Abruzzi, Italy, in 1921.

The flesh and blood were tested in 1574, and researchers discovered that although the five pellets of coagulated blood are of different size and shapes, they all weigh the same. Several more tests of the flesh and blood have been done since 1574, but none more conclusive than the scientific investigations of 1970 and 1981: Professor Odoardo Linoli, a professor of anatomy and pathological history and chemistry, and Professor Ruggero Bertelli of the University of Siena determined that the flesh is real human flesh and the blood is real human blood. The flesh was found to consist of the muscular tissue of the heart, and both the flesh and blood have the same blood-type, AB, as that present in the Holy Shroud of Turin, which is believed to be the cloth that Jesus's crucified body was wrapped in.

Santarem, Portugal, Early 1200s

A 13th-century woman with an unfaithful husband is the center of this Eucharistic miracle. Santarem, the site of this miracle, isn't far from Fatima, where the Blessed Virgin appeared to three children in the early 20th century.

As the story goes, the woman in Santarem met with a witch who promised to cure her husband's infidelity at the cost of a consecrated host from the church. The woman, unhappy in her marriage, consented to the sacrilege.

The woman accepted the host at Mass but removed it from her mouth and wrapped it in a cloth. Before she was able to leave, however, the host started to bleed. It bled so much that concerned parishioners thought she had cut her hand and tried to help her.

When she reached home, she threw the bloody host in a trunk in bedroom. A bright light emanated from the chest, however, and soon she confessed her actions to her husband. They both knelt in adoration until the early morning. The couple summoned the parish priest, who transported the sacred host in a wax container back to the church. Word of the miracle began to spread, and pilgrims started coming to see the host.

A second miracle occurred after some time: The wax that had been used to transport the host was found broken into pieces in the tabernacle, revealing a crystal pyx (a special round container used to keep consecrated hosts in order to bring Holy Communion to the sick and dying). The pyx is believed to have been a message from the Lord, telling the priest that the miracle needed to be viewed and venerated so that the faithful are inspired to devotion.

Recent tests on the relic have revealed that the congealed blood at the bottom of the receptacle is at times the color of fresh blood and at other times appears to be dried. Though it is 750 years old and has gone through many handlings, you can still visit this shrine, housed today in the parish church of St. Stephen in Santarem.

Bolsena-Orvieto, Italy, 1263

In 1263, a German priest, Peter of Prague, stopped in the little Umbrian town of Bolsena en route to Rome. He was having doubts in his belief in the Real Presence of Christ in the Eucharist. While celebrating the Holy Sacrifice of the Mass in this town, drops of blood seeped from the host and landed on the corporal, one of the altar linens. The priest was shaken and initially tried to hide the blood, but then stopped the Mass and went to the neighboring town of Orvieto where Pope Urban IV was visiting.

The Pope listened to the priest's account and absolved him, and then sent a special envoy to investigate. At the end of the inquiry, the blood-stained corporal was brought to Orvieto for the Pope to venerate. It was solemnly placed in a reliquary located in the cathedral.

The Pope commissioned a Mass in honor of the miracle. St. Bonaventure, a Franciscan, and St. Thomas Aquinas, a Dominican, worked to compose prayers and a preface for Mass, hymns, and devotional prayers. (The story goes that after St. Bonaventure read St. Thomas' composition, he was moved to withdraw from the competition, citing the superiority of Aquinas's work.)

A year after the miracle, Pope Urban IV established the feast of Corpus Christi (Body of Christ) and introduced the new Mass composed by St. Thomas. Today, Corpus Christi is known as the Feast of the Body and Blood of Christ, but all the prayers and songs remain the same as they did in 1264.

In the church of St. Christiana, Bolsena, where the miracle occurred, four marble stones that contained the spilled Blood of Christ were exhumed. Three were placed in altars, and one in a reliquary. Every year on the feast of the miracle, the marble relic is carried in procession. Pope Paul VI raised the status of this church to a minor basilica.

Siena, Italy, 1330

Siena is a beautiful Tuscan city that was once a rival to prosperous Florence. Two saints, Bernadine and Catherine, came from Siena; Bernadine was a Franciscan friar who had great devotion to the Holy Name of Jesus and created the famous symbol of the Lord, the word *HIS* enclosed in a sun with rays. Catherine belonged to the Dominican order of nuns and is most famous for convincing the pope in a letter to move the papacy from Avignon, France, where it had been located, back to Rome where it belonged.

Siena is also home to miracles. In 1330, a priest was summoned to distribute Communion to a sick person in the country. Rather than using a pyx (a special container holding consecrated hosts to be brought to the sick), however, the priest placed the hosts in the pages of his prayer book. When he opened it to distribute Holy Communion, he noticed that the host had practically melted and had left the pages bloody.

The priest went to Confession and left the bloody pages with his confessor. A page was gifted to Cascia, Italy, the hometown of the confessor, and can be viewed in the crypt church of the Basilica of St. Rita.

The relic was placed under investigation in 1962, at which time it was discovered that when magnified, the blood on the host looks redder than to the naked eye. If viewed through a weaker lens, there appears to be a shadow of a sad man.

Blanot, France, 1331

A miracle occurred on Easter Sunday in 1331 in the French village of Blanot. Father Hugues de la Baume celebrated the first Mass in the parish. The priest didn't realize that toward the end of the distribution, a part of the host fell and landed on a special cloth used to cover the altar rail. An altar server told the priest what had happened and that he needed to return to the altar rail to retrieve the Sacred Particle.

Rather than finding the remnant of the host, however, the priest found a blood-stained spot. At the conclusion of Mass, the celebrant took the cloth into the sacristy, placed the stained area in a water-filled basin, and tried to scrub it clean. Instead of brightening, the spot became darker and larger. The water in the basin also became bloody.

The priest then cut the area of the blood-stained cloth into the shape of a host, lifted it up before the people, and placed it into the tabernacle. Fifteen days later the relic was authenticated by ecclesiastical authorities. Finally, Pope John XXII proclaimed the authenticity of the miracle and relic. Subsequently, every year on Easter Monday the relic is solemnly exposed in the church. In addition, the remaining hosts that were consecrated at that Easter Mass were never subsequently distributed. Many centuries later they were found to be perfectly intact and undecayed.

Amsterdam, Holland, 1345

A local parish priest was called to give the Holy Eucharist to a dying parishioner in 14th century Amsterdam. The man was so ill, however, that after receiving Holy Communion, he brought it back up. The nursemaid cleaned up after the man and put the host into the fire. The next morning she discovered that the host was lying in perfect state among the ambers of the fire.

The nursemaid immediately called the priest, who placed the host in a vessel for transporting Holy Communion to the sick, known as a pyx. When he returned to the church and opened the pyx in order to place the host in the tabernacle, he discovered that it was empty. The host had miraculously returned to the house of the sick parishioner.

A small chapel was built on this site, and pilgrims soon began coming to venerate the miraculous host. In 1452, a fire burned much of the city, including the small chapel, but again, the miraculous host remained unharmed. A new chapel was built and an organization of consecrated women took care of it. Pilgrims came daily until the Protestant Revolt of the 17th century that closed many Catholic churches, convents, and chapels. The relic continued to be cared for and prayed over in secret. When an era of tolerance was established, public veneration commenced.

Disputes between Protestants and Catholics in 1908 again led to the closing and destruction of the little chapel. The host was stolen but not forgotten; when a new chapel was built later it included windows and paintings depicting the miracle.

Seefeld, Austria, 1384

In 1384, during a special Mass on Holy Thursday — the Mass of the Lord's Supper — a pompous knight approached the altar with his sword drawn and demanded to receive the large priest host in place of the smaller congregant host. The very moment he was about to receive Communion, the pavement began to tremble and broke apart. The knight grabbed the altar so he would not fall, and the priest immediately took back the host out of the man's mouth. The trembling stopped, and live blood began to flow from the host.

The knight repented and confessed his sins. He died two years later and asked to be buried near the entrance of the church where this miracle occurred. He donated a silver monstrance to enshrine the miraculous host.

Soon pilgrims came in devotion, and by 1423 a larger church was built to accommodate devotees. A separate chapel of the Holy Blood was built in which the miraculous host is now enshrined. In 1984, the parish church celebrated its 600th anniversary, and it continues to be a popular pilgrim destination where the faithful can renew their belief and devotion to the Lord in the Most Blessed Sacrament.

Ludbreg, Croatia, 1411

A parish priest was overcome with doubts about the Real Presence of Jesus as he was consecrating the wine into the Precious Blood. In a truly miraculous occurrence, the wine turned into physical blood. The priest, shaken, didn't know what to do and buried the chalice in a wall near the altar. He kept his secret until he was on his deathbed, at which time he wanted to make things right and so confessed.

The wall was soon removed, and the chalice was found. In 1513, Pope Leo X declared it a miraculous appearance of the Precious Blood in the church. Since 1721, the relic has been kept in a monstrance commissioned by Countess Eleonora Batthyany-Strattman, who gave it as a gift to the church in Ludbreg.

Throughout the centuries, people have testified to miraculous cures and recoveries while praying in the relic's presence. In the 18th century, as a terrific plague was sweeping through northern Croatia, people prayed to God for protection and pledged to build a chapel. The plague was averted, but it took more than 200 years for the chapel to be built, finally coming to reality in 1994.

Ettiswil, Switzerland, 1447

The Blessed Sacrament was stolen from the parish church in Ettiswil, Switzerland, in 1447. It was later found by Margaret Schulmeister when the pigs she was tending wouldn't go near the area where the Blessed Sacrament was discarded.

After close investigation, the police arrested another young lady, Anna Vogtli, who eventually confessed to the crime. She told police that as she was carrying it, the host became unbearably heavy, and that's when she threw it into the nearby field.

The hosts had divided into seven sections, six of which formed a flower similar to a rose, and a great light surrounded the area. When the local priest tried to retrieve the seventh group of hosts, it wouldn't move. The priest saw this as sign from God to build a chapel to mark the spot where the Holy Eucharist was discarded. The other six sections were transported back to the village church. The chapel and altar in the field were dedicated a year and half after the event, and the relic of the Holy Eucharist can still be viewed today in the tiny village of Ettiswil, Switzerland.

Alcala, Spain, 1597

During the 16th century, Spain was infiltrated from time to time with Moorish thieves who roamed the countryside, pillaging villages. One such group targeted churches, searching for golden vessels and chalices. They stole items from three churches, including items for Holy Communion, but on one occasion one of the thieves had a guilty conscience and returned the host in a heavy paper wrapping.

Normally, the returned hosts would have been consumed by the priest after having them returned by the thief. A previous incident, however, took place nearby where someone stole hosts only to poison them before giving them back. Fearing this scenario, the priest decided to place them in a special silver container and allow them to decompose naturally and then dispose of what remained.

Ten years later, the segregated hosts were found intact and as fresh as new ones. In other words, there was no mold and no decay whatsoever. A study found that not only did they not deteriorate, they were fresh and not stale. The priest's superior, in an attempt to test the authenticity, decided to place the hosts in the humid, damp basement. In a box he properly labeled the hosts that were believed to be a miracle along with hosts that were new and not consecrated. In a few months, they discovered that the unconsecrated hosts spoiled but the miraculous hosts remained fresh and white. This preservation was the proof that was needed.

A chapel off the main church in Alcala was the dedicated place for the miracle. The relic was moved from the parish church into the main church and was venerated there until the Spanish Civil War of 1936. The priests knew that leftists were desecrating churches and killing nuns and priests, so in an attempt to preserve the host, a group of priests hid it. However, they were killed, and the hiding place remains unknown.

Chapter 16

Ten Saintly Commentaries on the Holy Sacrifice of the Mass

• •

In This Chapter

▶ Seeing how devotion to the Eucharist influenced saints' lives

▶ Taking guidance and inspiration from the saints' writings

• •

*I*n this chapter, we examine ten holy men and women of the Catholic faith who were enormously influenced by the Mass or had a profound insight on the Holy Eucharist. The stories of their lives and actions show how they internalized and personalized the official theology and doctrine through spirituality and piety.

St. Ignatius of Antioch

Ignatius (AD 35–108) is considered one of the Apostolic Fathers of the Church. He was a student of St. John the Apostle and Evangelist (the Beloved Disciple) and was also the third Patriarch of Antioch, after St. Evodius and St. Peter himself. Before being martyred for the Christian faith, Ignatius wrote several pastoral letters to encourage his fold.

Ignatius writes of the Holy Mass in his Letter to the Smyrnaeans:

> *Take note of those who hold heterodox opinions on the grace of Jesus Christ which has come to us, and see how contrary their opinions are to the mind of God. . . . They abstain from the Eucharist and from prayer because they do not confess that the Eucharist is the flesh of our Savior Jesus Christ, flesh which suffered for our sins and which that Father, in his goodness, raised up again. They who deny the gift of God are perishing in their disputes.*

St. Justin Martyr

Justin (AD 100–165) was born to a pagan family in Flavia Neapolis (Palestine) and was baptized a Christian in AD 135. He is one of the most ancient apologists (defenders) of the faith; after studying a variety of other faiths, it was only in Christianity that he found true peace.

Here is a selection from Justin's *First Apology in Defense of the Christians.* He clearly and accurately describes the Masses being celebrated as it was being done from day one.

> *The apostles, in their recollections, which are called gospels, handed down to us what Jesus commanded them to do. They tell us that he took bread, gave thanks and said: Do this in memory of me. This is my body. In the same way he took the cup, he gave thanks and said: This is my blood. The Lord gave this command to them alone. Ever since then we have constantly reminded one another of these things. The rich among us help the poor and we are always united. For all that we receive we praise the Creator of the universe through his Son Jesus Christ and through the Holy Spirit.*

> *On Sunday we have a common assembly of all our members, whether they live in the city or the outlying districts. The recollections of the apostles or the writings of the prophets are read, as long as there is time. When the reader has finished, the president of the assembly speaks to us; he urges everyone to imitate the examples of virtue we have heard in the readings. Then we all stand up together and pray.*

> *On the conclusion of our prayer, bread and wine and water are brought forward. The president offers prayers and gives thanks to the best of his ability, and the people give assent by saying, "Amen." The Eucharist is distributed, everyone present communicates, and the deacons take it to those who are absent.*

St. Ambrose

Aurelius Ambrosius (AD 339–397) is more famously known by his Anglo name, Ambrose, than his original Latin Roman one. He is also best known for being the Bishop of Milan who baptized St. Augustine of Hippo. Ambrose is considered a Doctor of the Church, someone revered for profound wisdom in his writings defending or explaining the faith.

Ambrose speaks of the doctrine of Real Presence, that the bread and wine truly become the Body and Blood of Christ at every Mass and that this spiritual food for the soul is as necessary as physical food is for the body.

> *The Lord Jesus himself declares: This is my body. Before the blessing contained in these words a different thing is named; after the consecration a body is indicated. He himself speaks of his blood. Before the consecration something else is spoken of; after the consecration blood is designated. And you say: "Amen," that is: "It is true." What the mouth utters, let the mind within acknowledge; what the word says, let the heart ratify.*

> *So the Church, in response to grace so great, exhorts her children, exhorts her neighbors, to hasten to these mysteries: Neighbors, she says, come and eat; brethren, drink and be filled. In another passage the Holy Spirit has made clear to you what you are to eat, what you are to drink. Taste, the prophet says, and see that the Lord is good; blessed is the man who puts his trust in him. Christ is in that sacrament, for it is the body of Christ. It is therefore not bodily food but spiritual. Thus the Apostle too says, speaking of its symbol: Our fathers ate spiritual food and drank spiritual drink. For the body of God is spiritual; the body of Christ is that of a divine spirit, for Christ is a spirit. We read: The spirit before our face is Christ the Lord. And in the letter of Saint Peter we have this: Christ died for you. Finally, it is this food that gives strength to our hearts, this drink which gives joy to the heart of man, as the prophet has written.*

St. Cyril of Jerusalem

A Bishop of Jerusalem and Doctor of the Church, most of Cyril's (AD 313–386) early personal history remains a mystery. But what is known is that in his time as bishop and in his ministry to the people under his spiritual care, he was very devoted to the Holy Eucharist and to the Sacred Liturgy. In one of his writings, he reminds his flock that the words of Christ in the Gospel can be trusted completely.

> *On the night he was betrayed our Lord Jesus Christ took bread, and when he had given thanks, he broke it and gave it to his disciples and said: "Take, eat: this is my body." He took the cup, gave thanks and said: "Take, drink: this is my blood." Since Christ himself has declared the bread to be his body, who can have any further doubt? Since he himself has said quite categorically, This is my blood, who would dare to question it and say that it is not his blood?*

> *Therefore, it is with complete assurance that we receive the bread and wine as the body and blood of Christ. His body is given to us under the symbol of bread, and his blood is given to us under the symbol of wine, in order to make us by receiving them*

one body and blood with him. Having his body and blood in our members, we become bearers of Christ and sharers, as Saint Peter says, in the divine nature.

Do not, then, regard the Eucharistic elements as ordinary bread and wine: they are in fact the body and blood of the Lord, as he himself has declared. Whatever your senses may tell you, be strong in faith.

You have been taught and you are firmly convinced that what looks and tastes like bread and wine is not bread and wine but the body and the blood of Christ. You know also how David referred to this long ago when he sang: Bread gives strength to man's heart and makes his face shine with the oil of gladness. Strengthen your heart, then, by receiving this bread as spiritual bread, and bring joy to the face of your soul.

St. Hilary of Poitiers

Hilary (AD 300–368) was the son of wealthy pagan Romans. He became Christian with his wife and daughter after studying the Old and New Testament books of the Bible. He later became Bishop of Poitiers, France, and was a staunch defender of the Church's teaching on the divinity of Christ. He fully opposed the heretical ideas of Arianism, which maintained that Jesus only had a similar but not same substance as God the Father. The incarnation (God becoming man) is also an integral part of the doctrine of the Real Presence, which teaches that the bread and wine become the Body and Blood of Christ at the Holy Mass.

Here is a section from St. Hilary's treatise on the Trinity, which is used by the Liturgy of the Hours in the Office of Readings for Wednesday of the fourth week of Easter. The saint explains how and why the faithful eat the flesh of Christ in Holy Communion at Mass.

We believe that the Word became flesh and that we receive his flesh in the Lord's Supper. How then can we fail to believe that he really dwells within us? When he became man, he actually clothed himself in our flesh, uniting it to himself for ever. In the sacrament of his body he actually gives us his own flesh, which he has united to his divinity. This is why we are all one, because the Father is in Christ, and Christ is in us. He is in us through his flesh and we are in him. With him we form a unity which is in God.

Christ himself bore witness to the reality of this unity when he said: He who eats my flesh and drinks my blood lives in me and I in him. No one will be in Christ unless Christ himself has been in him; Christ will take to himself only the flesh of those who have received his flesh. He had already explained the mystery of this perfect unity when he said: As the living Father sent me and I draw life from the Father, so he who eats my flesh will draw life from me. We draw life from his flesh just as he draws life from the Father. Such comparisons aid our understanding, since we can grasp a point more easily when we have an analogy. And the point is that Christ is the wellspring of our life. Since we who are in the flesh have Christ dwelling in us through his flesh, we shall draw life from him in the same way as he draws life from the Father.

St. Gaudentius of Brescia

Gaudentius (AD ?–410) was Bishop of Brescia, Italy, and a friend of St. John Chrysostom. Twenty-one of his writings survive today. Here is an excerpt from his discourse on the Sacrifice of the Mass and the Real Presence in the Holy Eucharist.

The heavenly sacrifice, instituted by Christ, is the most gracious legacy of his new covenant. On the night he was delivered up to be crucified he left us this gift as a pledge of his abiding presence.

This sacrifice is our sustenance on life's journey; by it we are nourished and supported along the road of life until we depart from this world and make our way to the Lord. For this reason he addressed these words to us: Unless you eat my flesh and drink my blood, you will not have life in you.

It was the Lord's will that his gifts should remain with us, and that we who have been redeemed by his precious blood should constantly be sanctified according to the pattern of his own passion. And so he commanded those faithful disciples of his whom he made the first priests of his Church to enact these mysteries of eternal life continuously. All priests throughout the churches of the world must celebrate these mysteries until Christ comes again from heaven. Therefore let us all, priests and people alike, be faithful to this everlasting memorial of our redemption. Daily it is before our eyes as a representation of the passion of Christ. We hold it in our hands, we receive it in our mouths, and we accept it in our hearts.

St. Augustine

Augustine (AD 354–430) was the wayward son of a woman (St. Monica) who prayed for 30 years for his conversion. He lived a decadent youth, immersed in self-indulgence, and then overreacted to the other extreme of severe asceticism and heresy (dualism and Manicheanism). Finally, he, his illegitimate son, and his own father were baptized Christians at the hands of St. Ambrose, Bishop of Milan.

After living the next phase of his life in monasticism, Augustine was made Bishop of Hippo in North Africa. He wrote and preached extensively, and his comments on the Mass defend the doctrine of the Real Presence. The following three excerpts are taken from some of his sermons on the Holy Eucharist and the Mass.

> *That Bread which you see on the altar, having been sanctified by the word of God is the body of Christ. That chalice, or rather, what is in that chalice, having been sanctified by the word of God, is the blood of Christ. Through that bread and wine the Lord Christ willed to commend His body and blood, which He poured out for us unto the forgiveness of sins.*

> *The Lord Jesus wanted those whose eyes were held lest they should recognize him, to recognize Him in the breaking of the bread. The faithful know what I am saying. They know Christ in the breaking of the bread. For not all bread, but only that which receives the blessing of Christ, becomes Christ's body.*

> *What you see is the bread and the chalice; that is what your own eyes report to you. But what your faith obliges you to accept is that the bread is the Body of Christ and the Chalice of wine is the Blood of Christ.*

St. Fulgentius of Ruspe

Fulgentius (AD 465–527) was the Bishop of Ruspe, North Africa. Although he began his adult life as a civil servant for the Roman Empire, after reading the writings of St. Augustine of Hippo, he decided to become a monk. He later became a bishop and excelled in spiritually shepherding his people by prayer, preaching, and example.

This excerpt is from a book addressed to Monimus, a philosopher. St. Fulgentius explains that the Holy Eucharist is the source of unity and love.

> *When we offer the sacrifice the words of our Savior are fulfilled just as the blessed Apostle Paul reported them: On the same night he was betrayed the Lord Jesus took some bread, and thanked God for it and broke it, and said: "This is my body, which is for you: do this as a memorial of me." In the same way he took the cup after supper, and said, "This cup is the new covenant in my blood. Whenever you drink it, do this as a memorial of me." Until the Lord comes, therefore, every time you eat this bread and drink this cup, you are proclaiming his death.*

So the sacrifice is offered to proclaim the death of the Lord and to be a commemoration of him who laid down his life for us. He himself has said: A man can have no greater love than to lay down his life for his friends. So, since Christ died for us, out of love, it follows that when we offer the sacrifice in commemoration of his death, we are asking for love to be given us by the coming of the Holy Spirit. We beg and we pray that just as through love Christ deigned to be crucified for us, so we may receive the grace of the Holy Spirit; and that by that grace the world should be a dead thing in our eyes and we should be dead to the world, crucified and dead. We pray that we should imitate the death of our Lord. Christ, when he died, died, once for all, to sin, so his life now is life with God. We pray, therefore, that in imitating the death of our Lord we should walk in newness of life, dead to sin and living for God.

St. Thomas Aquinas

Thomas (1225–1274) was the son of a wealthy merchant who wanted his son to become a Benedictine monk and eventually go up the ecclesiastical food chain to become abbot (head of a men's monastery) in order to bring honor, prestige, and power to the family. Thomas, however, chose to enter a new religious community, the Order of Preachers (also known as the Dominicans), founded by St. Dominic de Guzman.

Thomas was renowned for his theological and philosophical wisdom and genius. His most beloved works are the prayers he composed for the Feast of Corpus Christi. Following is one of his prayers.

Sing, my tongue, the Savior's glory, of His flesh the mystery sing; of the Blood, all price exceeding, shed by our immortal King, destined, for the world's redemption,from a noble womb to spring.

Of a pure and spotless Virgin born for us on earth below, He, as Man, with man conversing, stayed, the seeds of truth to sow; then He closed in solemn order wondrously His life of woe.

On the night of that Last Supper, seated with His chosen band, He the Pascal victim eating, first fulfills the Law's command; then as Food to His Apostles gives Himself with His own hand.

Word-made-Flesh, the bread of natureby His word to Flesh He turns;wine into His Blood He changes;what though sense no change discerns? Only be the heart in earnest, faith her lesson quickly learns.

Down in adoration falling,
Lo! the sacred Host we hail;
Lo! o'er ancient forms departing,
newer rites of grace prevail;
faith for all defects supplying,
where the feeble senses fail.

To the everlasting Father,
and the Son who reigns on high,
with the Holy Ghost proceeding
forth from Each eternally,
be salvation, honor, blessing,
might and endless majesty. Amen.

St. Elizabeth Ann Seton

Born Elizabeth Bayley in New York City, St. Elizabeth Seton (1774–1821) was the daughter of devout Episcopalian parents and the granddaughter of an Episcopal priest. She married at the age of 19 and had five children. The Setons experienced financial hardships when her husband's family business went bankrupt and he later contracted tuberculosis. After his death, Elizabeth lived with the Felicchi family, devout Catholics with a chapel at their home. This family's devotion inspired Elizabeth to convert to Roman Catholicism.

After realizing that the Real Presence (the Body and Blood of Christ) is truly in the Holy Eucharist when the priest consecrates the bread and wine, Elizabeth Seton longed to be able to make that intimate union with the Lord. On the day of her First Communion as a Catholic, on March 25, 1805, St. Elizabeth knew she was in union with her Lord and Savior, and she declared:

> At last God is mine and I am His! Now let all go its round —
> I have received Him!

She established a religious community of women, the Sisters of Charity in Emmitsburg, Maryland. St. Elizabeth wanted her sisters and her students to fully appreciate that they should prepare themselves to be worthy vessels (receptacles) of the Real Presence when they are about to receive Holy Communion. She instructed her Sisters of Charity:

> The heart preparing to receive the Holy Eucharist should be like a crystal vase.

Just as you would place a beautiful and valuable rose in an elegant and worthy vase, so, too, should the communicant be disposed to receive Christ.

Index

Latin (language)
translations, 11, 17–18
Latin Mass. *See* Extraordinary Mass
Latin Rite. *See* Roman Rite
layperson/laypeople. *See* liturgical
ministers, non-ordained
lectionary/lectionary cycle, 32,
195–196
lector/reader, 19–20, 56, 60, 67–69
Leo III (Pope, 795-816), 81, 114
Leo XIII (Pope, 1878-1903), 183
lex orandi, lex credendi ("law of
prayer is law of belief"), 1, 144
Litany of the Saints, 49
liturgical books, Eastern Church, 200
liturgical books, Western Church
Book of the Gospels, 197
lectionary, 195–196
Missal (Sacramentary), 198–199
Roman Pontificale, 197
Roman Ritual, 197–198
liturgical colors
about clergy rank, 202–204
about the meaning, 209–210, 212
altar linens, 222
black, 210, 211, 212
green, 46, 210, 211, 212
purple/violet, 33, 210, 211, 212
red, 46, 210, 211, 212
rose, 39, 210
white/gold, 43, 44, 45, 210, 212
liturgical east, 18–19
liturgical hours, 133–136
liturgical ministers, non-ordained
acolytes/servers, 54–55, 57–58, 59
extraordinary ministers,11, 55
lectors/readers, 56, 60
master of ceremonies, 57, 58–59
music director/organist/choir,
56–57
psalmist/cantor, 56
role in the Mass, 19–20
sacristan, 59
ushers, 58
weddings, 118
women, 58

liturgical ministers, ordained
about, 51–52
bishop of the diocese, 52
deacons/subdeacons, 53–54, 55, 60
Extraordinary Mass, 84
priests, 53
liturgical music
about use in worship, 238–239
Counter-Reformation, 240
Gregorian chant, 239
music director/organist/choir,
56–57
Vatican II reforms, 240–241
weddings, 118
liturgical space. *See* church buildings
liturgical vessels and artifacts, 138,
141, 217–221, 223
liturgical vestments
about the origins, 201–202
Byzantine Divine Liturgy, 149–150
Eastern Rites, 211–212
East-West shared tradition, 202–203
symbolism of color, 209–211, 212
Western Rite, 204–209
liturgical year/calendar
about the cycles, 31–32
Advent, 32–35
Christmas, 35–38
Easter, 45–46
Holy Week, 41–45
Lent, 38–41
Ordinary Time, 46–48
veneration of the Saints, 49–50
veneration of Virgin Mary, 48–49
liturgy, defined, 11, 133
Liturgy of Catechumens, Byzantine
introductory rite, 158
Litany of Peace, 159–160
Litany for Departed, 160, 165–166
First/Second Antiphon, 160–161
Hymn of the Incarnation, 161–162
troparions and kontakions, 162–163
Trisagion/Gospel/Sermon, 163–164
Litany of Supplication, 165
Liturgy of Preparation, Byzantine
about the parts, 145–146
Kairon, 146–149